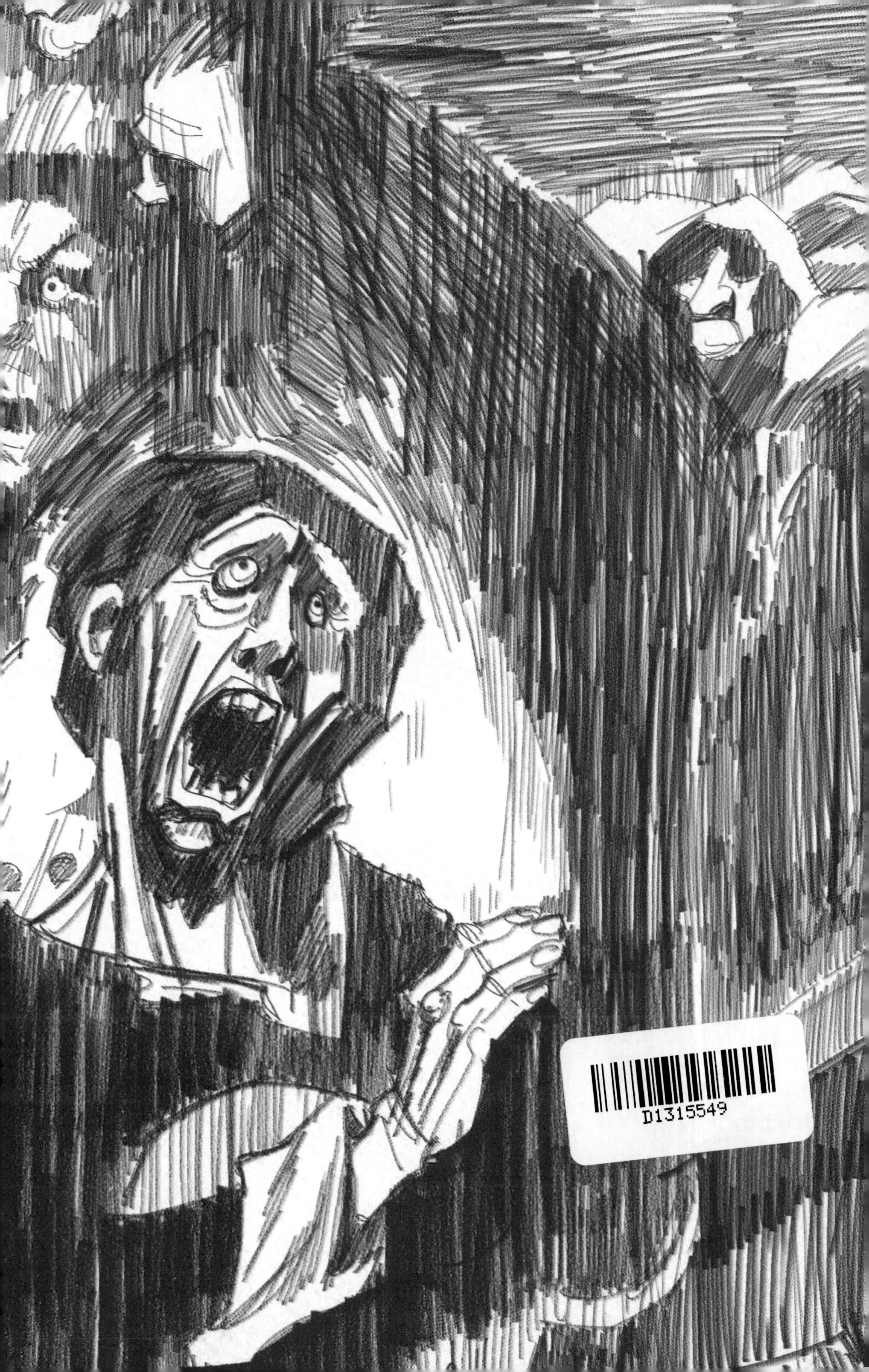

# GOYA

## the terrible sublime

# GOYA: The Terrible Sublime

Pegasus Books, Ltd.
148 West 37th Street, 13th Floor
New York, NY 10018

copyright © 2019, El Torres & Fran Galán
First Pegasus Books edition March 2019
First Published in Spain by Dibbuks. www.dibbuks.com

Editors: Ricardo Esteban Plaza and Marion Duc
Design: El Torres

ISBN: 978-1-64313-016-3

10  9  8  7  6  5  4  3  2  1

Printed in the United States of America
Distributed by W. W. Norton & Company, Inc.
www.pegasusbooks.com

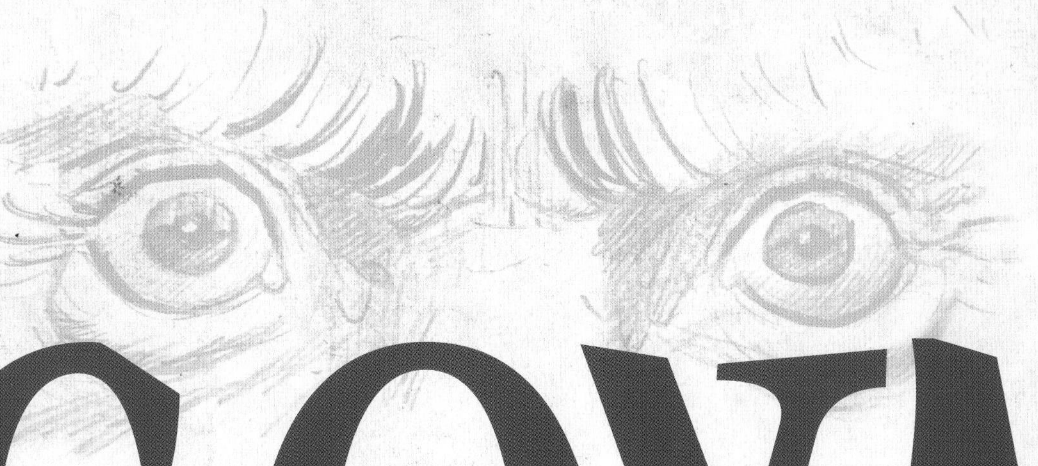

# GOYA

## *the terrible sublime*

*written by* **EL TORRES** *art by* **FRAN GALÁN**

PEGASUS BOOKS
NEW YORK LONDON

# Prologue

**G**oya has returned to comics.

It is about time. It is justice served. Because, you see, not only did Francisco de Goya y Lucientes, one of the great deaf artists of the nineteenth century (the other, of course, being Beethoven), blow up painting as we knew it, break with canon, create new styles, and dive headfirst into styles assimilated by all who followed, but his famous series of six oils set the stage for what would become the comic strip: storytelling through a series of successive images. I refer to Brother Pedro de Valdivia and the Bandit Maragato, which, as a popular anecdotal event of the time (resistance and victory of a friar over a bandit who attacks him—go ahead and laugh at Batman) serves as a prelude to what others would call sequential art. How these six fun vignettes, which in any other's hands may have been mere sketches, would position Goya as the patron saint of the seventh art in Spain and namesake of Sapin's Cinemagraphic Academy's prize, is somewhat hard to grasp. Unless, of course, we frame them in the context of the typically lackadaisical efforts of our graphic novels and novelists.

Goya is a big, Spanish romantic. In his life—disorderly, chaotic, driven and ambitious—we find portraiture and social criticism, the horrors of war, examination of traditions, flirtation with sex and death, horror at the passing of the years, gods and satyrs, and abominable creatures that can only stalk the mind of someone who seeks illumination through the paintbrush.

That is the subject of this admirable book (sorry, but I hesitate to call it a "graphic novel") that El Torres and Fran Galán offer to dazzle the reader. It is fiction, yes, but it is also history. Goya's life has been the subject of Planet Awards, movies, and television series, in Spain and beyond. His relationship with the independent duchess of Alba, his hapless marriage, his illness and constant confrontation with reality that perhaps drove him dangerously close to insanity, his drive as a rationalist, and the superstitions from which no one can free themselves, form the basis of the this narrative.

Here we have a piece that is, on occasion, a horror comic threatening to plunge fully into the depths of terror. We have also a historical comic in which the author, who has studied the history, wastes no time feeding us history lessons, tasking the curious reader with researching the secondary characters that appear so brilliantly in these vignettes (an easy click away, these days).

El Torres once again stakes his claim as a solid author, possessing a magnificent sense of drama and an almost supernatural ease with colloquial dialogue—respectful enough of how people may have spoken at the time, yet tastefully modern. For his part, Fran Galán, in his clear, bright style, places himself at history's orders and offers a range of nuanced expressions in the characters, portraying perfectly their moods swings, freely crossing the line between reality and the surreal—spectacular when he needs to be, and intimate when called for. Discovering, as the book advances, how Goya's gaze (the authors' and the readers' point of view as well) observes, almost at a glance, what would become his paintings, amplifies the enormous value of this book. I would would go so far as to say it is a first for a Spanish graphic novel.

Upon reading this book, I am left with an admiration for the wisdom in the choice of setting—the reflection, perhaps shared by the artists, of how monsters of reason are necessary to create art.

Because creation is, beyond all else, an act of self-exorcism. And this is where El Torres and Fran Galán, with the figure of great Goya as their vehicle, offer a beautiful parable on the act of creation, the search for inner peace, that moment when the artists puts down the brush (or the pen) and sighs happily . . . for that brief moment before another imagined creature returns to gnaw at the depths of their mind.

Reason's dreams produce monsters, but the terrible is sublime.

*Rafael Marín,*
writer of *Fantastic Four* vol. 3 (2000 and 2001), and *The Inhumans*, novelist, translator, and scholar

# First Act

## A curse

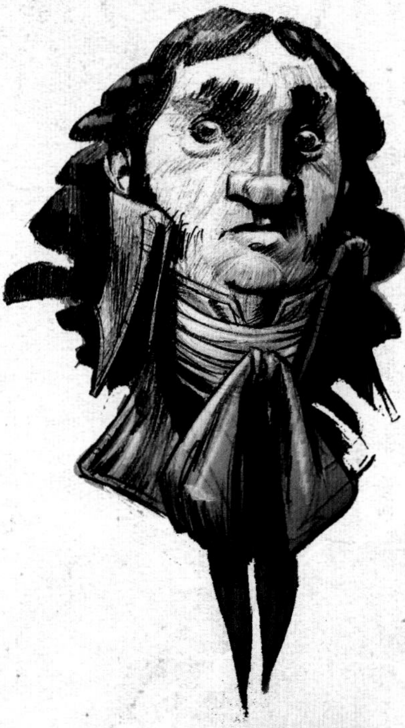

Cádiz, 1793

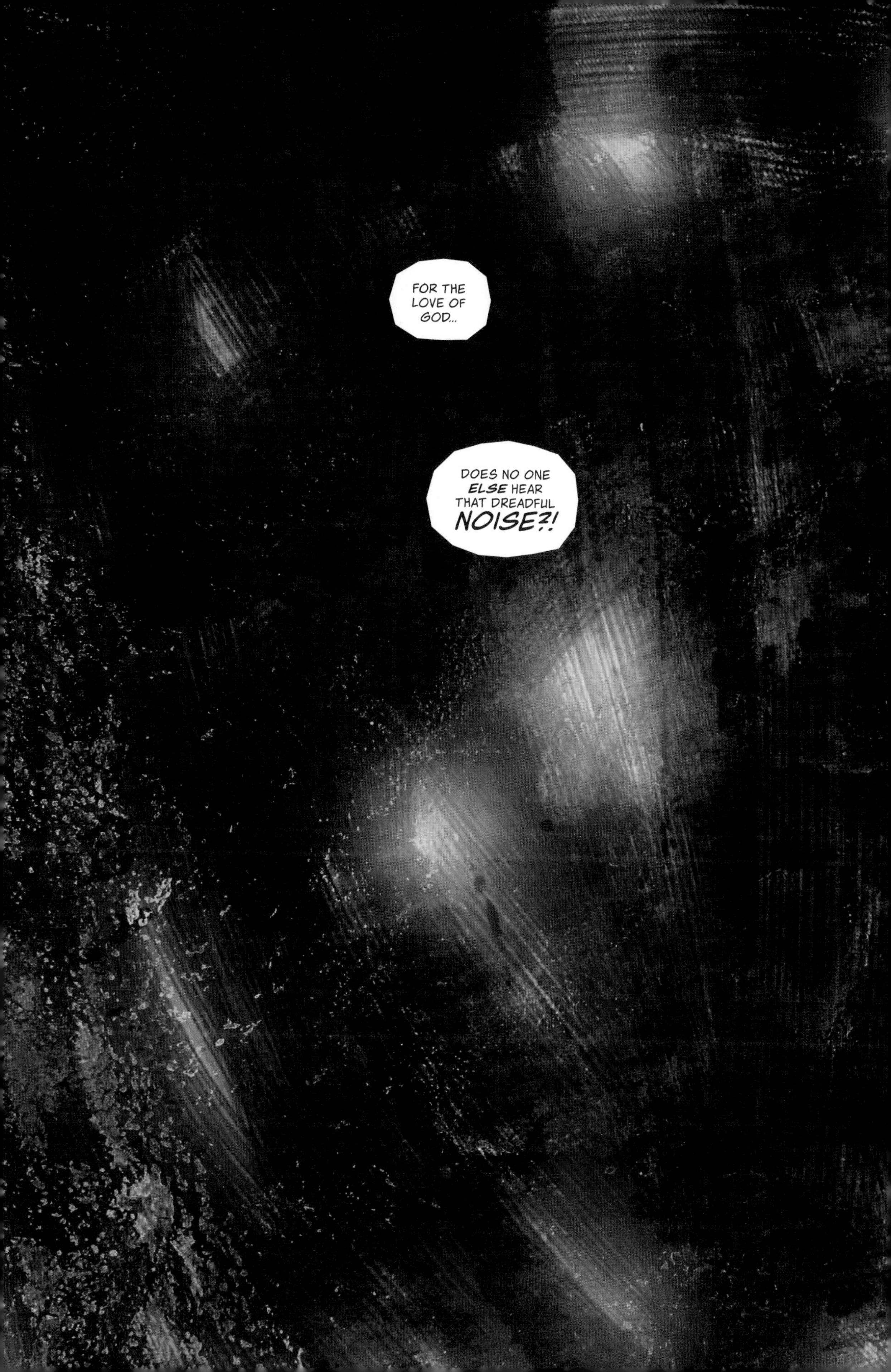
FOR THE LOVE OF GOD...
DOES NO ONE *ELSE* HEAR THAT DREADFUL *NOISE?!*

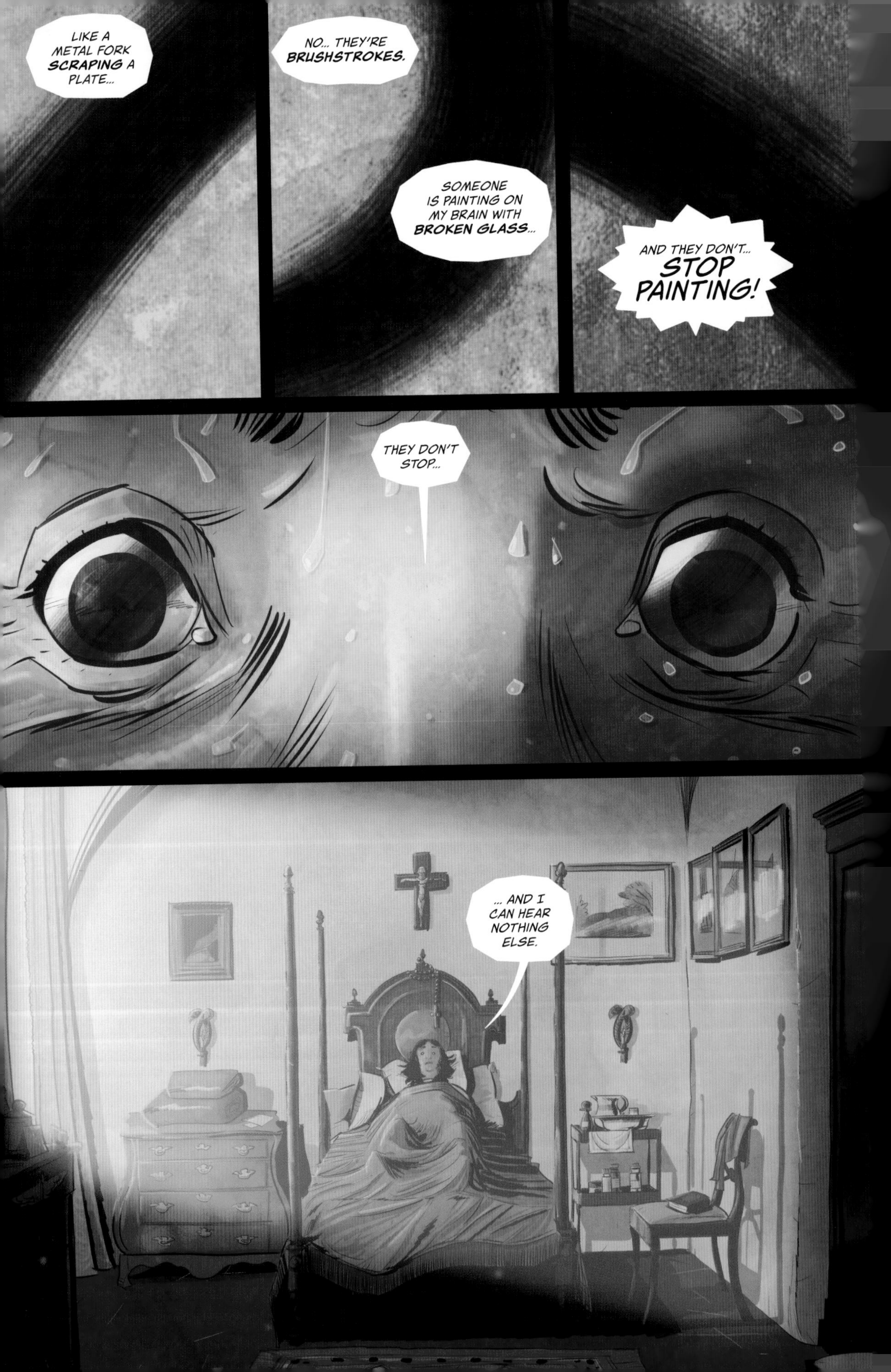
LIKE A METAL FORK SCRAPING A PLATE...
NO... THEY'RE BRUSHSTROKES.
SOMEONE IS PAINTING ON MY BRAIN WITH BROKEN GLASS...
AND THEY DON'T... STOP PAINTING!
THEY DON'T STOP...
... AND I CAN HEAR NOTHING ELSE.

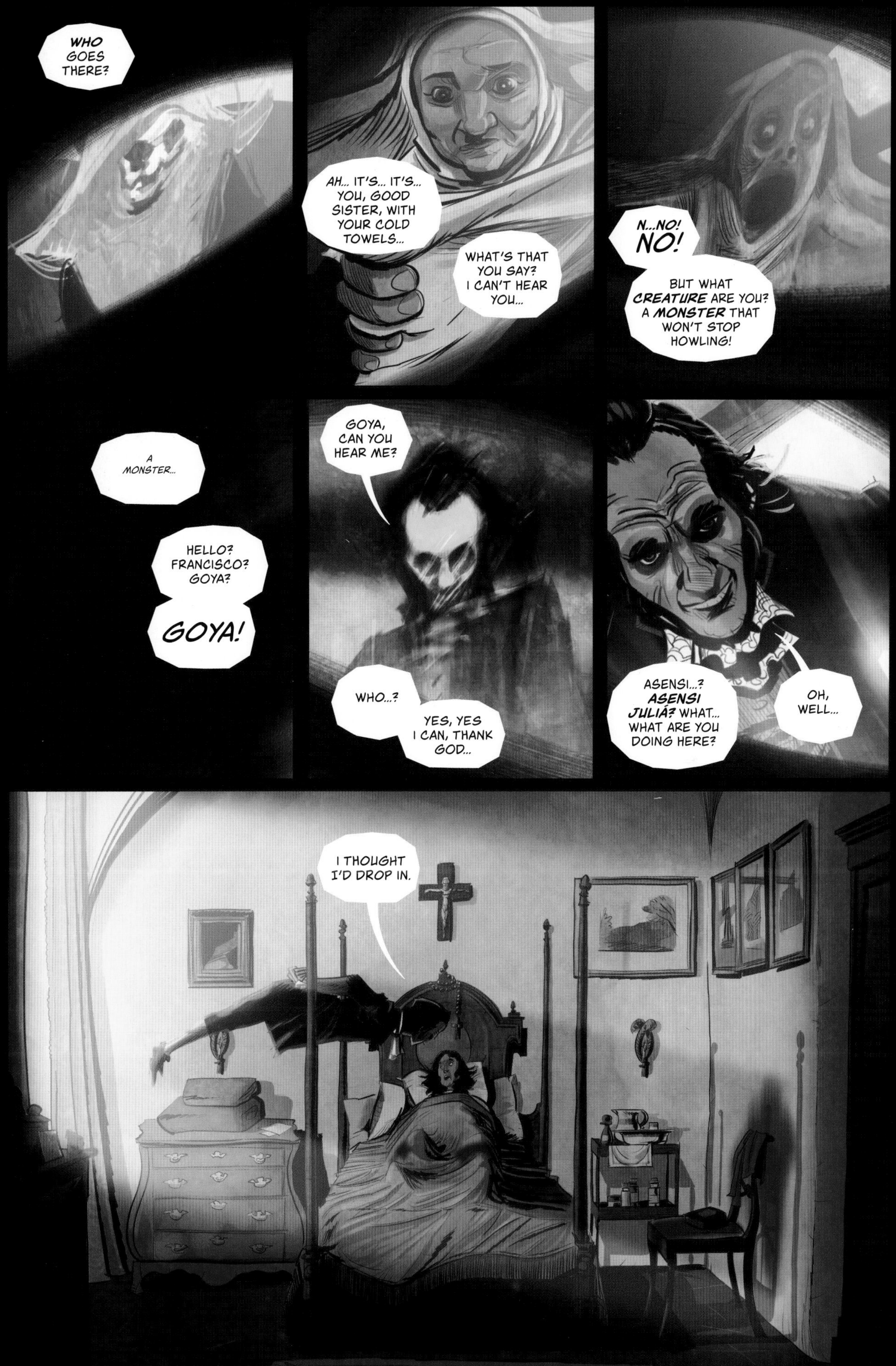
WHO GOES THERE?
AH... IT'S... IT'S... YOU, GOOD SISTER, WITH YOUR COLD TOWELS...
WHAT'S THAT YOU SAY? I CAN'T HEAR YOU...
N...NO! NO!
BUT WHAT CREATURE ARE YOU? A MONSTER THAT WON'T STOP HOWLING!
A MONSTER...
HELLO? FRANCISCO? GOYA?
GOYA!
GOYA, CAN YOU HEAR ME?
WHO...?
YES, YES I CAN, THANK GOD...
ASENSI...? ASENSI JULIÁ? WHAT... WHAT ARE YOU DOING HERE?
OH, WELL...
I THOUGHT I'D DROP IN.

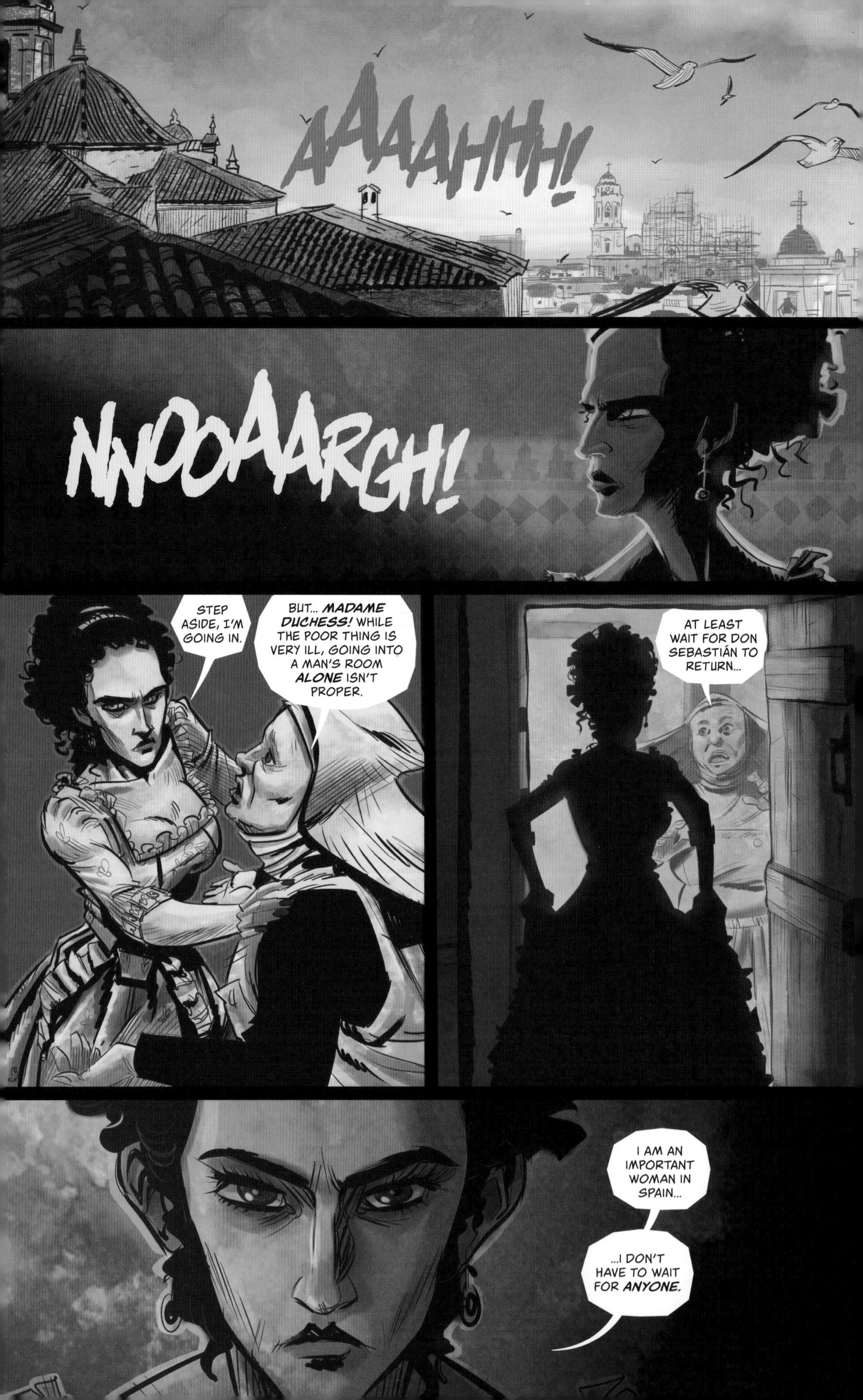
AAAAHHH!
NNOOAARGH!
STEP ASIDE, I'M GOING IN.
BUT... MADAME DUCHESS! WHILE THE POOR THING IS VERY ILL, GOING INTO A MAN'S ROOM ALONE ISN'T PROPER.
AT LEAST WAIT FOR DON SEBASTIÁN TO RETURN...
I AM AN IMPORTANT WOMAN IN SPAIN...
...I DON'T HAVE TO WAIT FOR ANYONE.

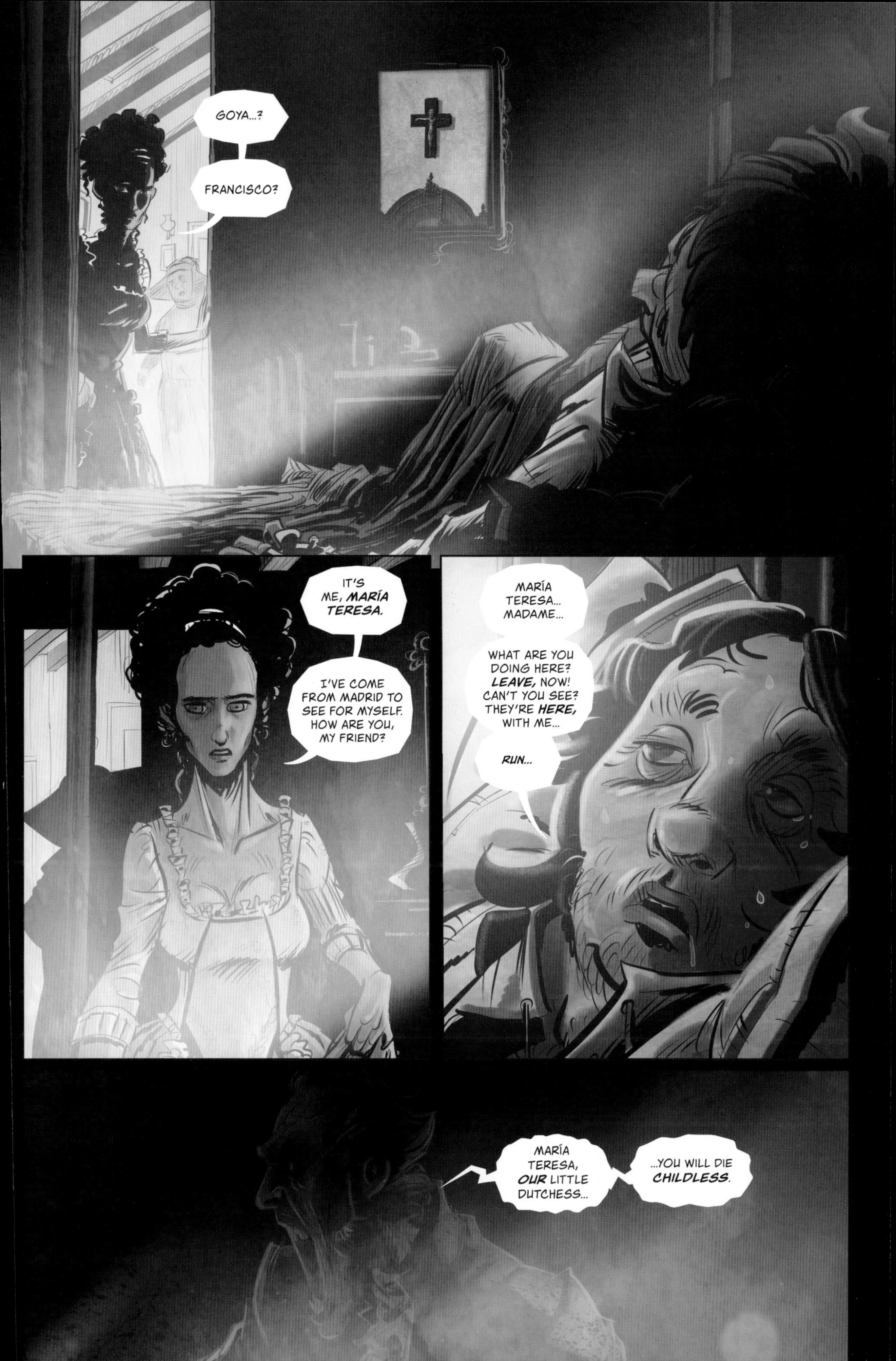
GOYA...?
FRANCISCO?
IT'S ME, MARÍA TERESA.
I'VE COME FROM MADRID TO SEE FOR MYSELF. HOW ARE YOU, MY FRIEND?
MARÍA TERESA... MADAME...
WHAT ARE YOU DOING HERE? LEAVE, NOW! CAN'T YOU SEE? THEY'RE HERE, WITH ME...
RUN...
MARÍA TERESA, OUR LITTLE DUTCHESS...
...YOU WILL DIE CHILDLESS.

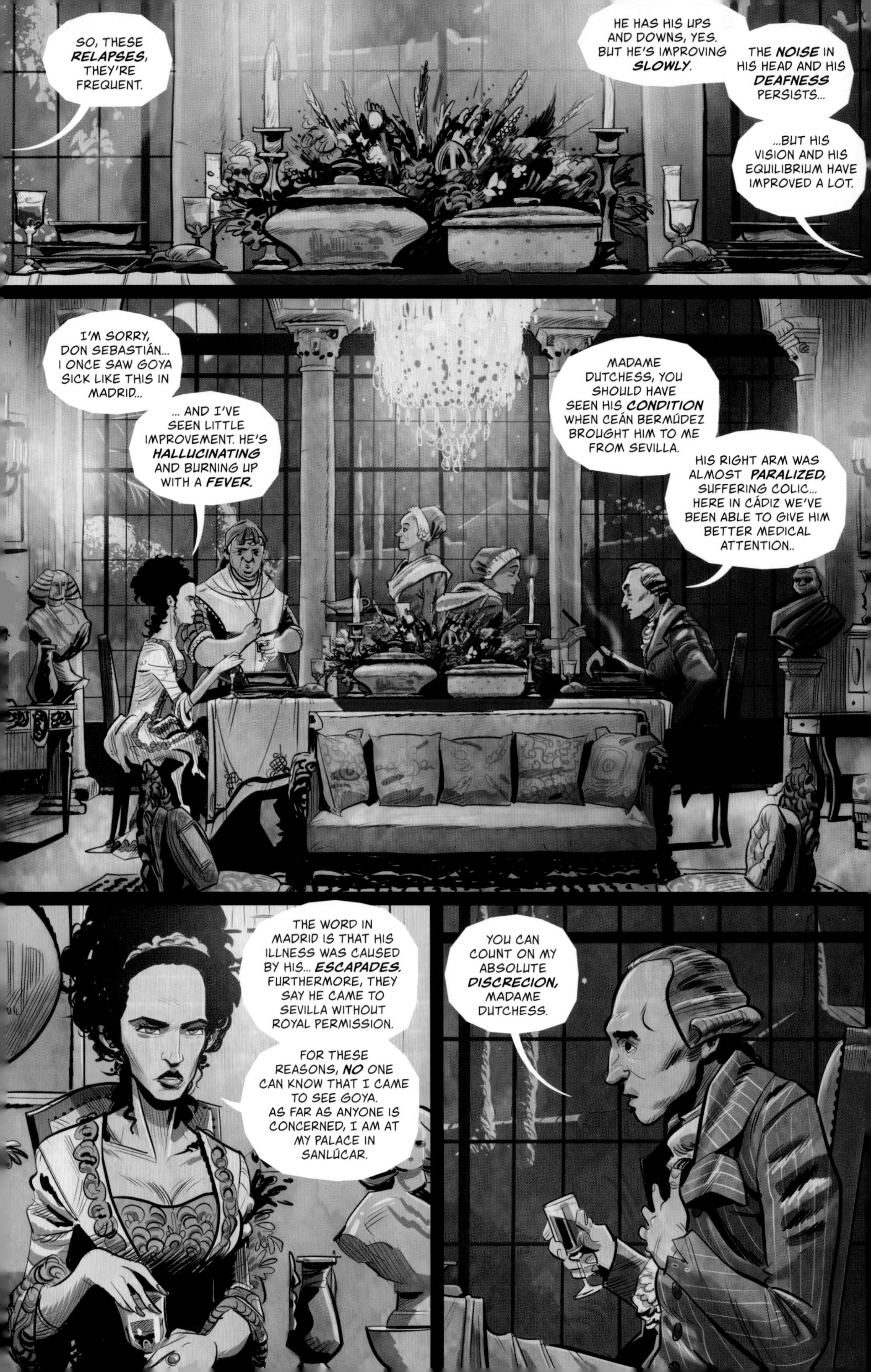

SO, THESE RELAPSES, THEY'RE FREQUENT.
HE HAS HIS UPS AND DOWNS, YES. BUT HE'S IMPROVING SLOWLY.
THE NOISE IN HIS HEAD AND HIS DEAFNESS PERSISTS...
...BUT HIS VISION AND HIS EQUILIBRIUM HAVE IMPROVED A LOT.
I'M SORRY, DON SEBASTIÁN... I ONCE SAW GOYA SICK LIKE THIS IN MADRID...
... AND I'VE SEEN LITTLE IMPROVEMENT. HE'S HALLUCINATING AND BURNING UP WITH A FEVER.
MADAME DUTCHESS, YOU SHOULD HAVE SEEN HIS CONDITION WHEN CEÁN BERMÚDEZ BROUGHT HIM TO ME FROM SEVILLA.
HIS RIGHT ARM WAS ALMOST PARALIZED, SUFFERING COLIC... HERE IN CÁDIZ WE'VE BEEN ABLE TO GIVE HIM BETTER MEDICAL ATTENTION..
THE WORD IN MADRID IS THAT HIS ILLNESS WAS CAUSED BY HIS... ESCAPADES. FURTHERMORE, THEY SAY HE CAME TO SEVILLA WITHOUT ROYAL PERMISSION.
FOR THESE REASONS, NO ONE CAN KNOW THAT I CAME TO SEE GOYA. AS FAR AS ANYONE IS CONCERNED, I AM AT MY PALACE IN SANLÚCAR.
YOU CAN COUNT ON MY ABSOLUTE DISCRECION, MADAME DUTCHESS.

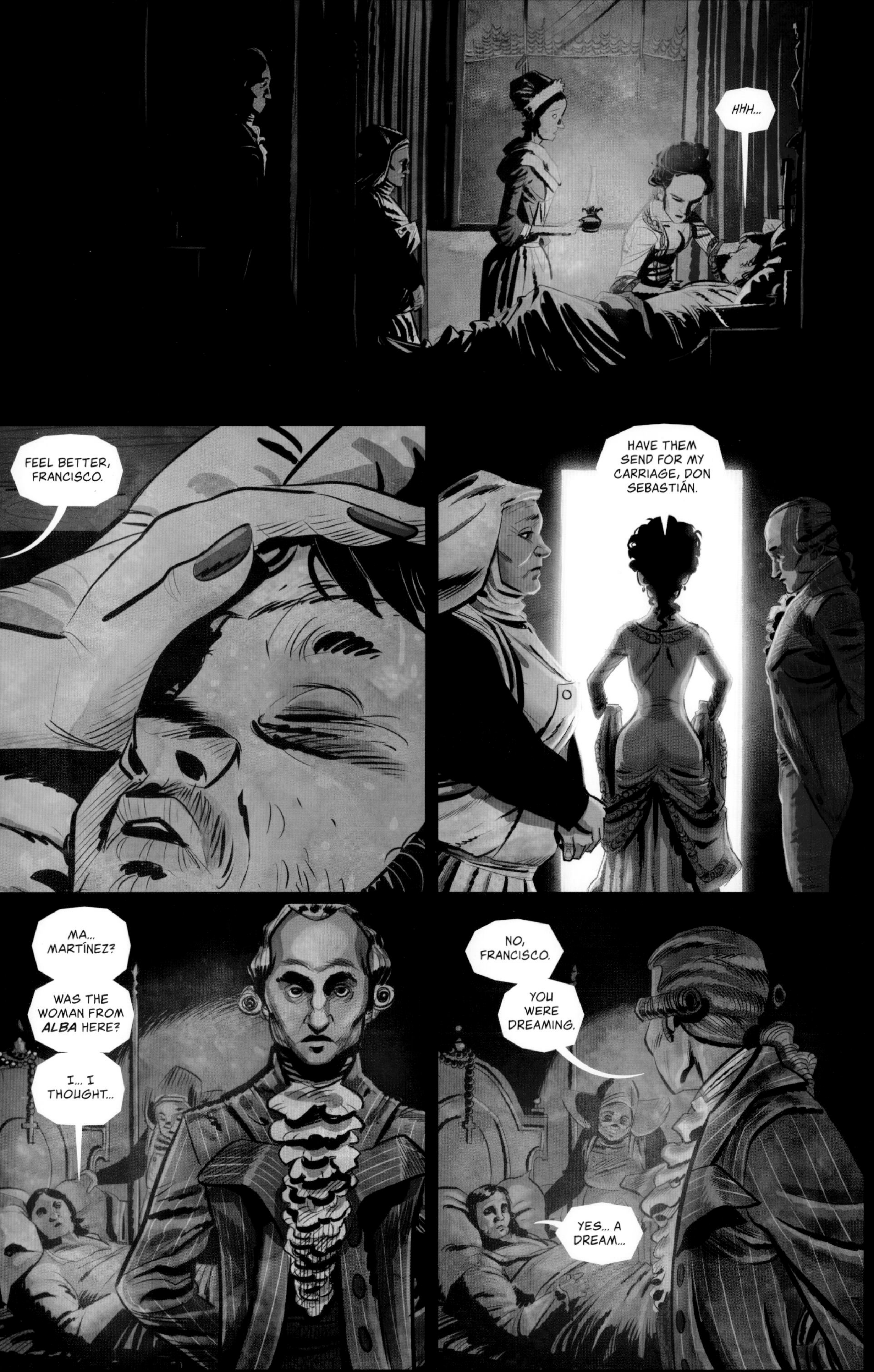
HHH...
FEEL BETTER, FRANCISCO.
HAVE THEM SEND FOR MY CARRIAGE, DON SEBASTIÁN.
MA... MARTÍNEZ?
WAS THE WOMAN FROM ***ALBA*** HERE?
I... I THOUGHT...
NO, FRANCISCO.
YOU WERE DREAMING.
YES... A DREAM...

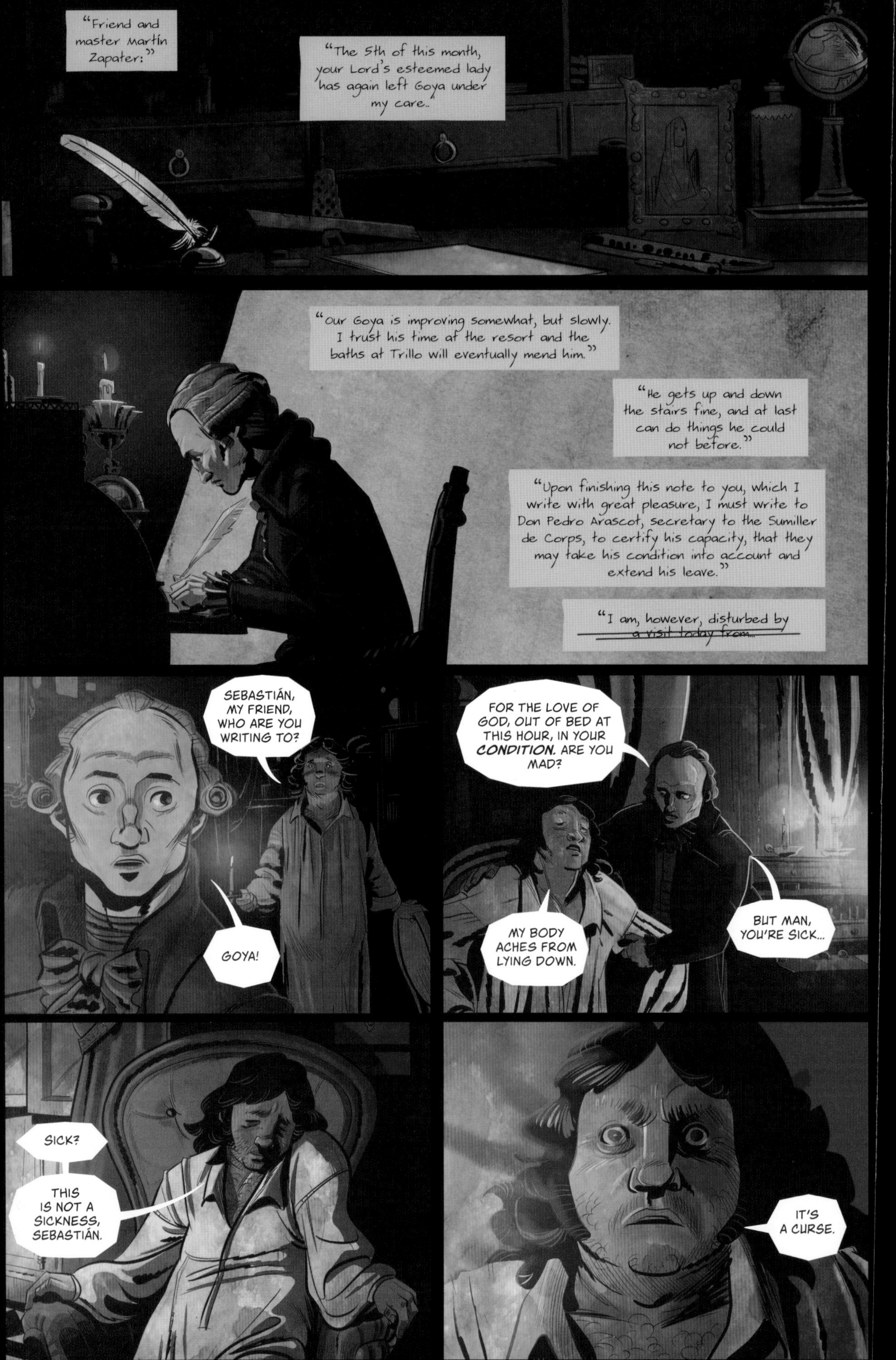
"Friend and master Martín Zapater:"
"The 5th of this month, your Lord's esteemed lady has again left Goya under my care.."
"Our Goya is improving somewhat, but slowly. I trust his time at the resort and the baths at Trillo will eventually mend him."
"He gets up and down the stairs fine, and at last can do things he could not before."
"Upon finishing this note to you, which I write with great pleasure, I must write to Don Pedro Arascot, secretary to the Sumiller de Corps, to certify his capacity, that they may take his condition into account and extend his leave."
"I am, however, disturbed by ~~a visit today from...~~
SEBASTIÁN, MY FRIEND, WHO ARE YOU WRITING TO?
GOYA!
FOR THE LOVE OF GOD, OUT OF BED AT THIS HOUR, IN YOUR **CONDITION.** ARE YOU MAD?
MY BODY ACHES FROM LYING DOWN.
BUT MAN, YOU'RE SICK...
SICK?
THIS IS NOT A SICKNESS, SEBASTIÁN.
IT'S A CURSE.

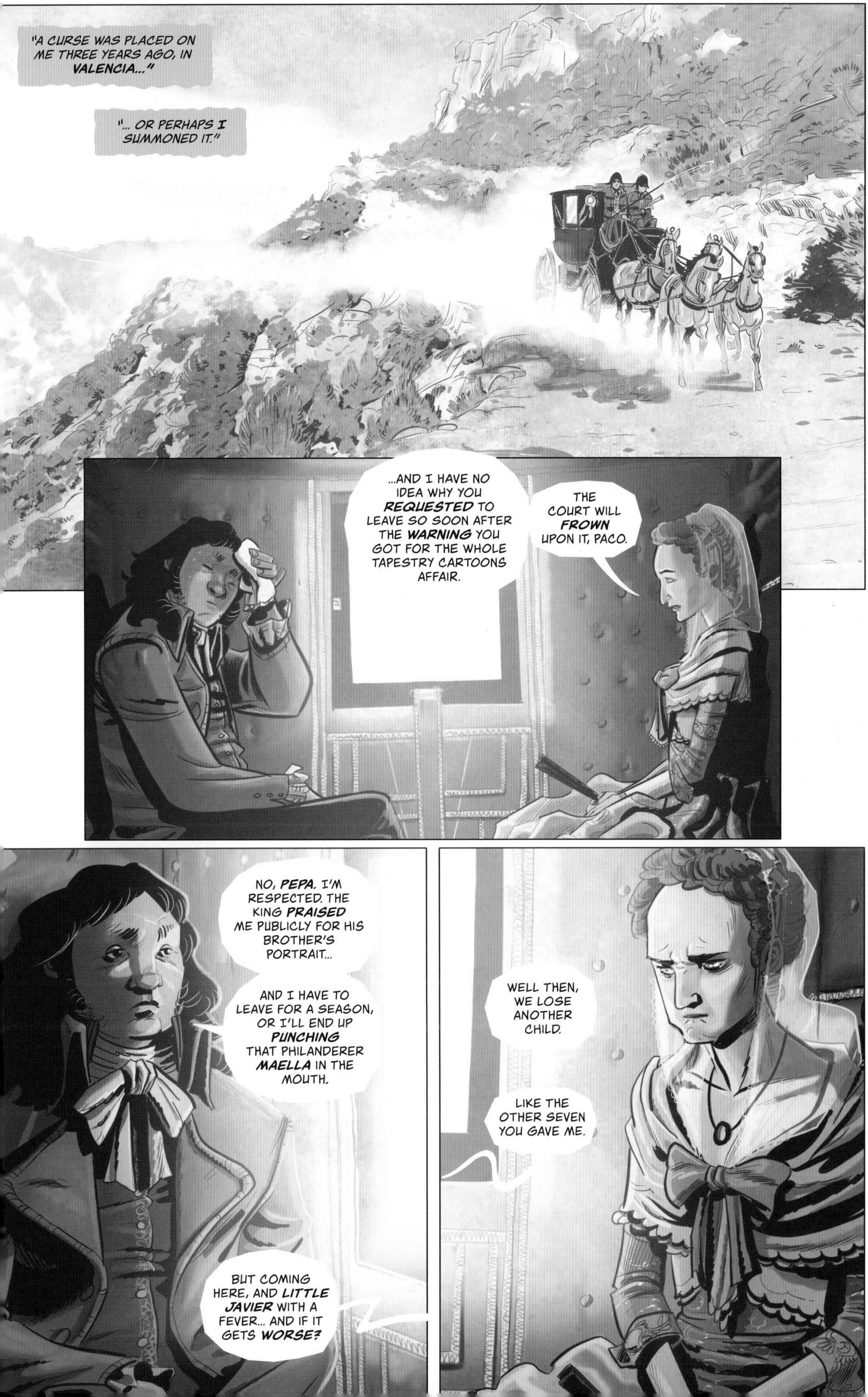
"A CURSE WAS PLACED ON ME THREE YEARS AGO, IN VALENCIA..."
"... OR PERHAPS I SUMMONED IT."
...AND I HAVE NO IDEA WHY YOU REQUESTED TO LEAVE SO SOON AFTER THE WARNING YOU GOT FOR THE WHOLE TAPESTRY CARTOONS AFFAIR.
THE COURT WILL FROWN UPON IT, PACO.
NO, PEPA. I'M RESPECTED. THE KING PRAISED ME PUBLICLY FOR HIS BROTHER'S PORTRAIT...
AND I HAVE TO LEAVE FOR A SEASON, OR I'LL END UP PUNCHING THAT PHILANDERER MAELLA IN THE MOUTH.
BUT COMING HERE, AND LITTLE JAVIER WITH A FEVER... AND IF IT GETS WORSE?
WELL THEN, WE LOSE ANOTHER CHILD.
LIKE THE OTHER SEVEN YOU GAVE ME.

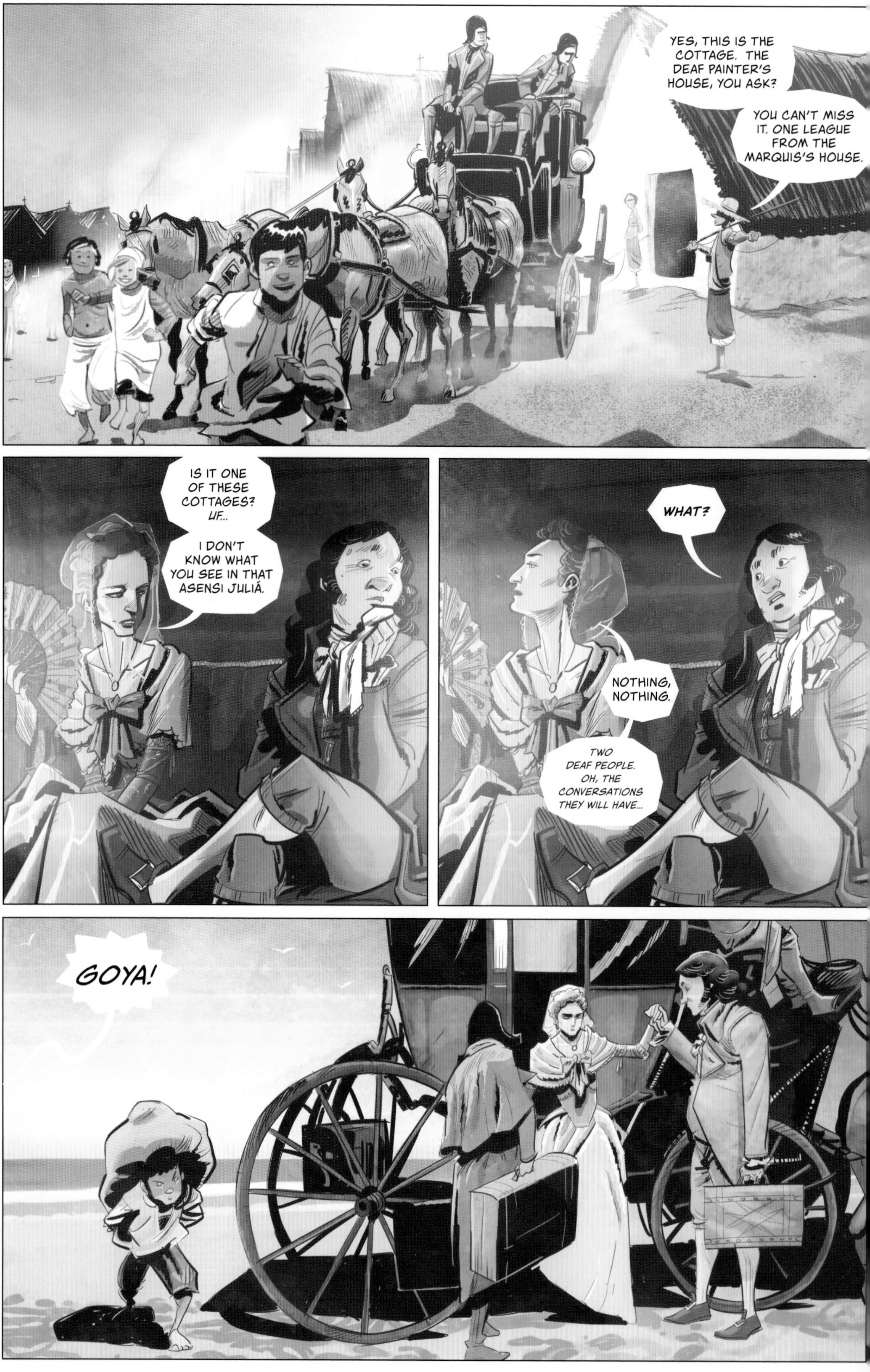
YES, THIS IS THE COTTAGE. THE DEAF PAINTER'S HOUSE, YOU ASK?
YOU CAN'T MISS IT. ONE LEAGUE FROM THE MARQUIS'S HOUSE.
IS IT ONE OF THESE COTTAGES? UF...
I DON'T KNOW WHAT YOU SEE IN THAT ASENSI JULIÁ.
WHAT?
NOTHING, NOTHING.
TWO DEAF PEOPLE. OH, THE CONVERSATIONS THEY WILL HAVE...
GOYA!

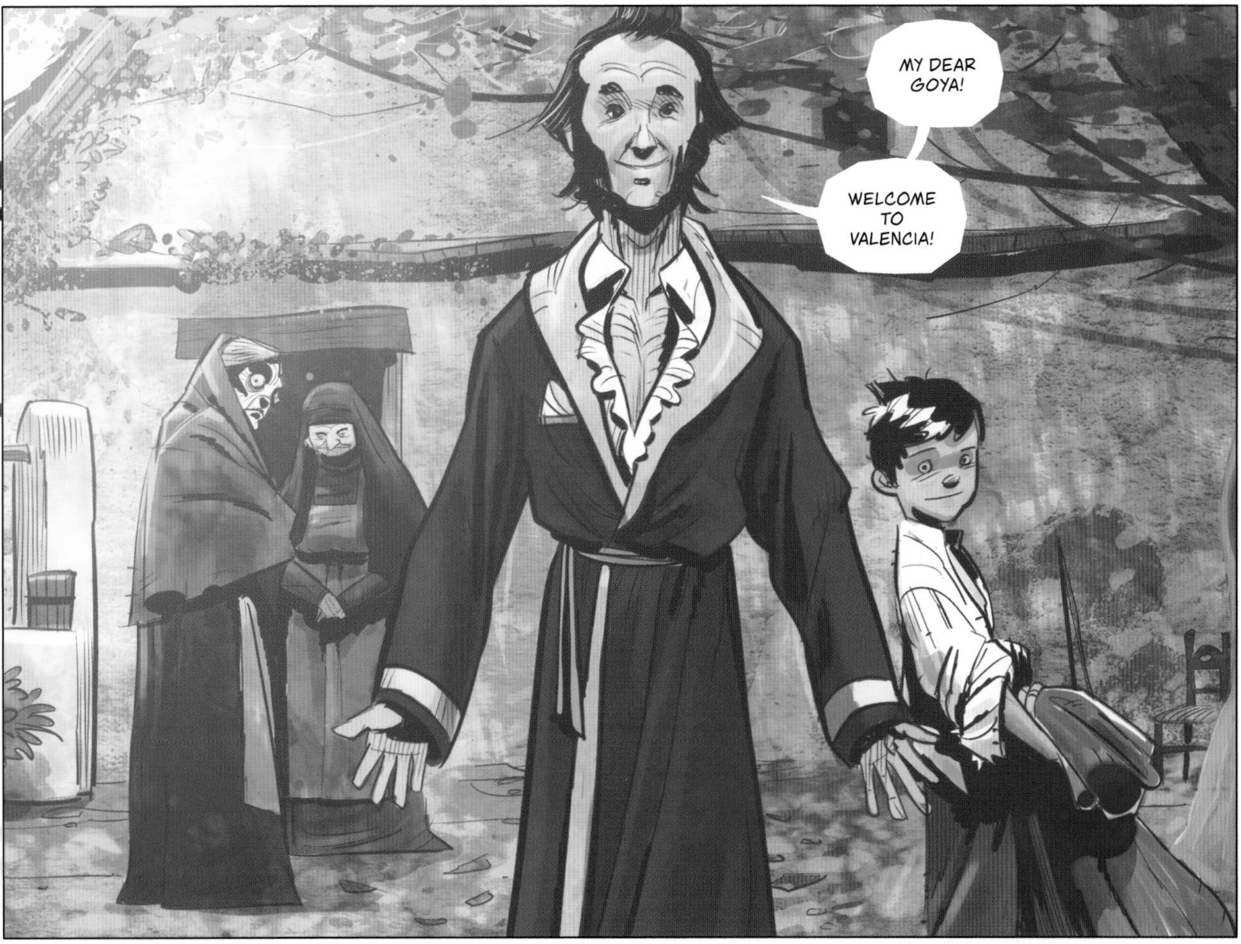
MY DEAR GOYA!
WELCOME TO VALENCIA!

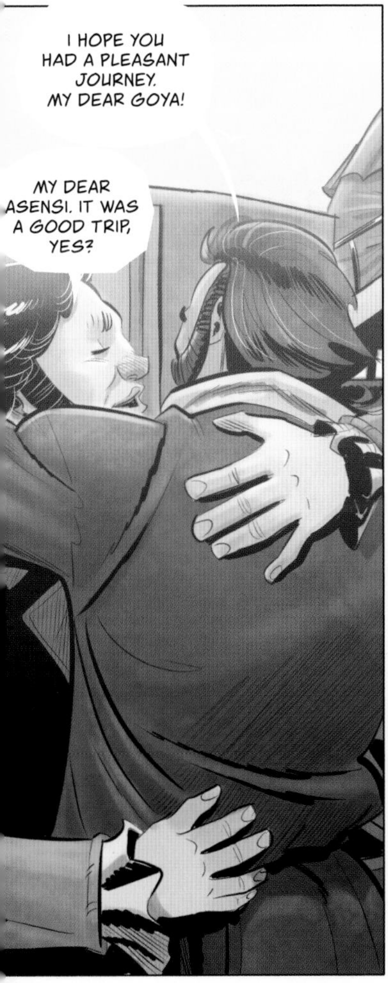
I HOPE YOU HAD A PLEASANT JOURNEY. MY DEAR GOYA!
MY DEAR ASENSI. IT WAS A GOOD TRIP, YES?

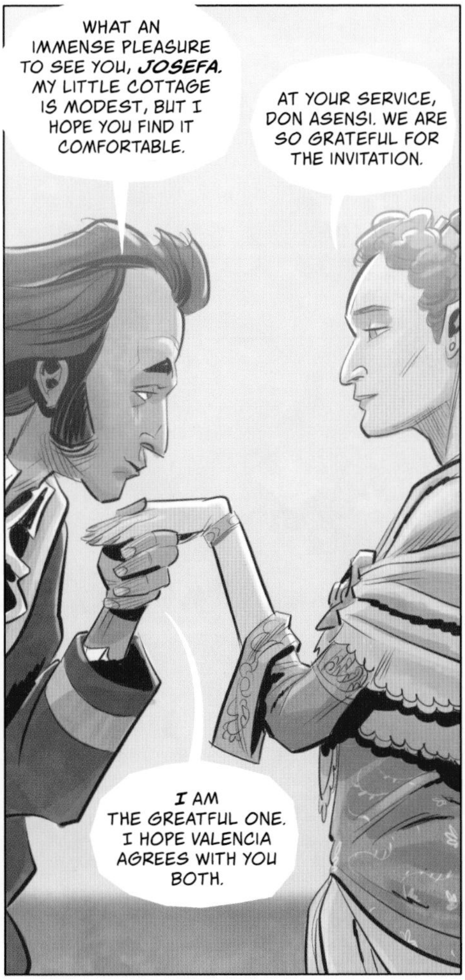
WHAT AN IMMENSE PLEASURE TO SEE YOU, ***JOSEFA.*** MY LITTLE COTTAGE IS MODEST, BUT I HOPE YOU FIND IT COMFORTABLE.
AT YOUR SERVICE, DON ASENSI. WE ARE SO GRATEFUL FOR THE INVITATION.
***I*** AM THE GREATFUL ONE. I HOPE VALENCIA AGREES WITH YOU BOTH.

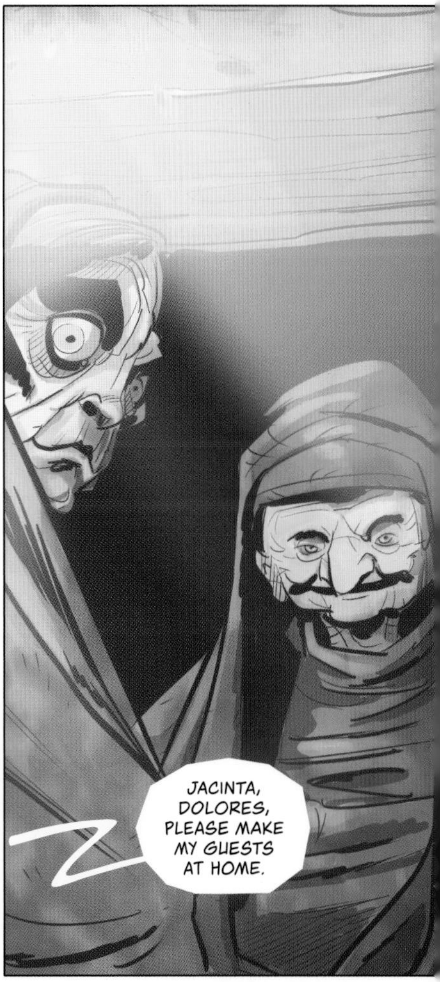
JACINTA, DOLORES, PLEASE MAKE MY GUESTS AT HOME.

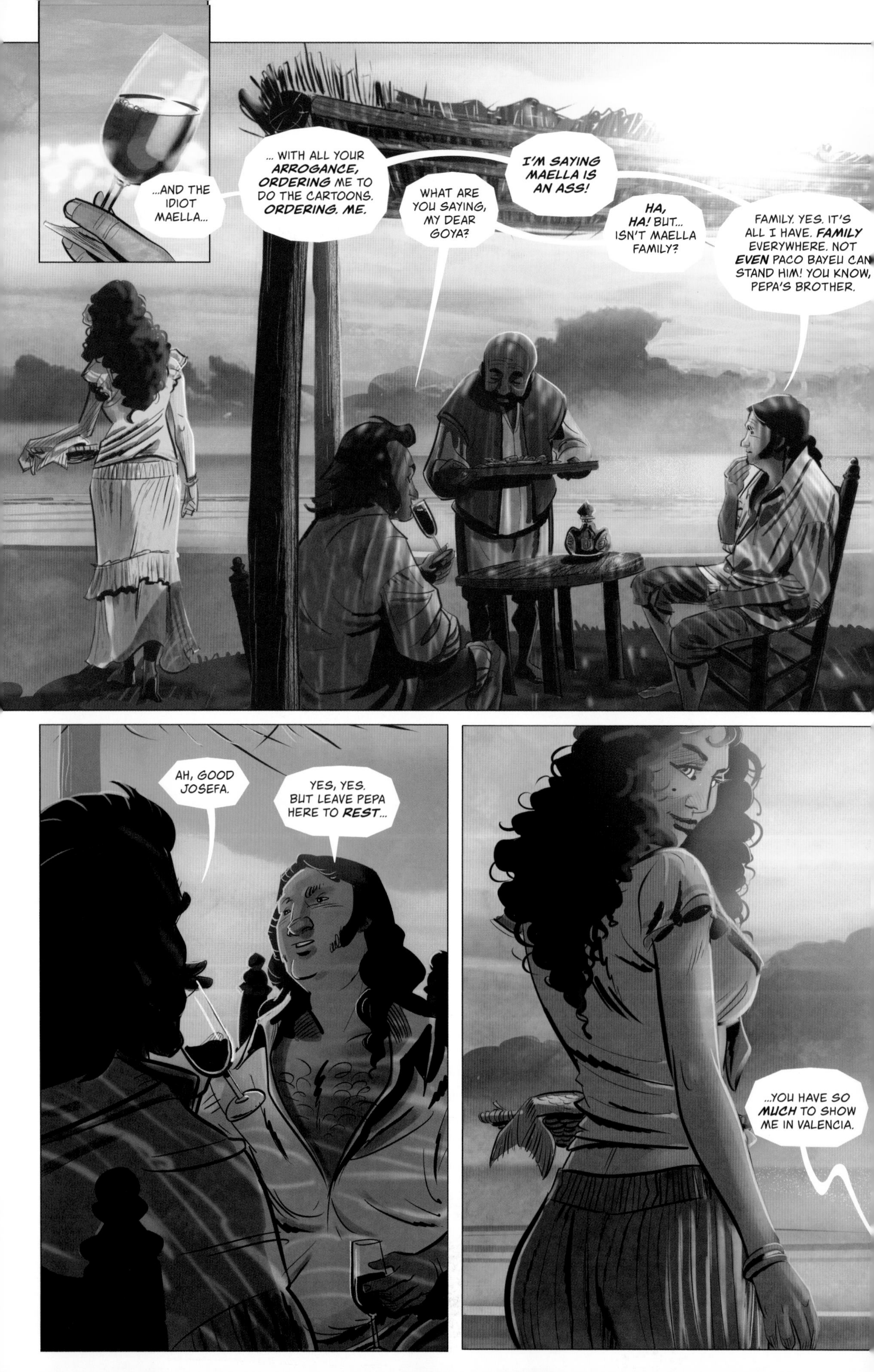
...AND THE IDIOT MAELLA...
... WITH ALL YOUR ARROGANCE, ORDERING ME TO DO THE CARTOONS. ORDERING. ME.
WHAT ARE YOU SAYING, MY DEAR GOYA?
I'M SAYING MAELLA IS AN ASS!
HA, HA! BUT... ISN'T MAELLA FAMILY?
FAMILY. YES. IT'S ALL I HAVE. FAMILY EVERYWHERE. NOT EVEN PACO BAYEU CAN STAND HIM! YOU KNOW, PEPA'S BROTHER.
AH, GOOD JOSEFA.
YES, YES. BUT LEAVE PEPA HERE TO REST...
...YOU HAVE SO MUCH TO SHOW ME IN VALENCIA.

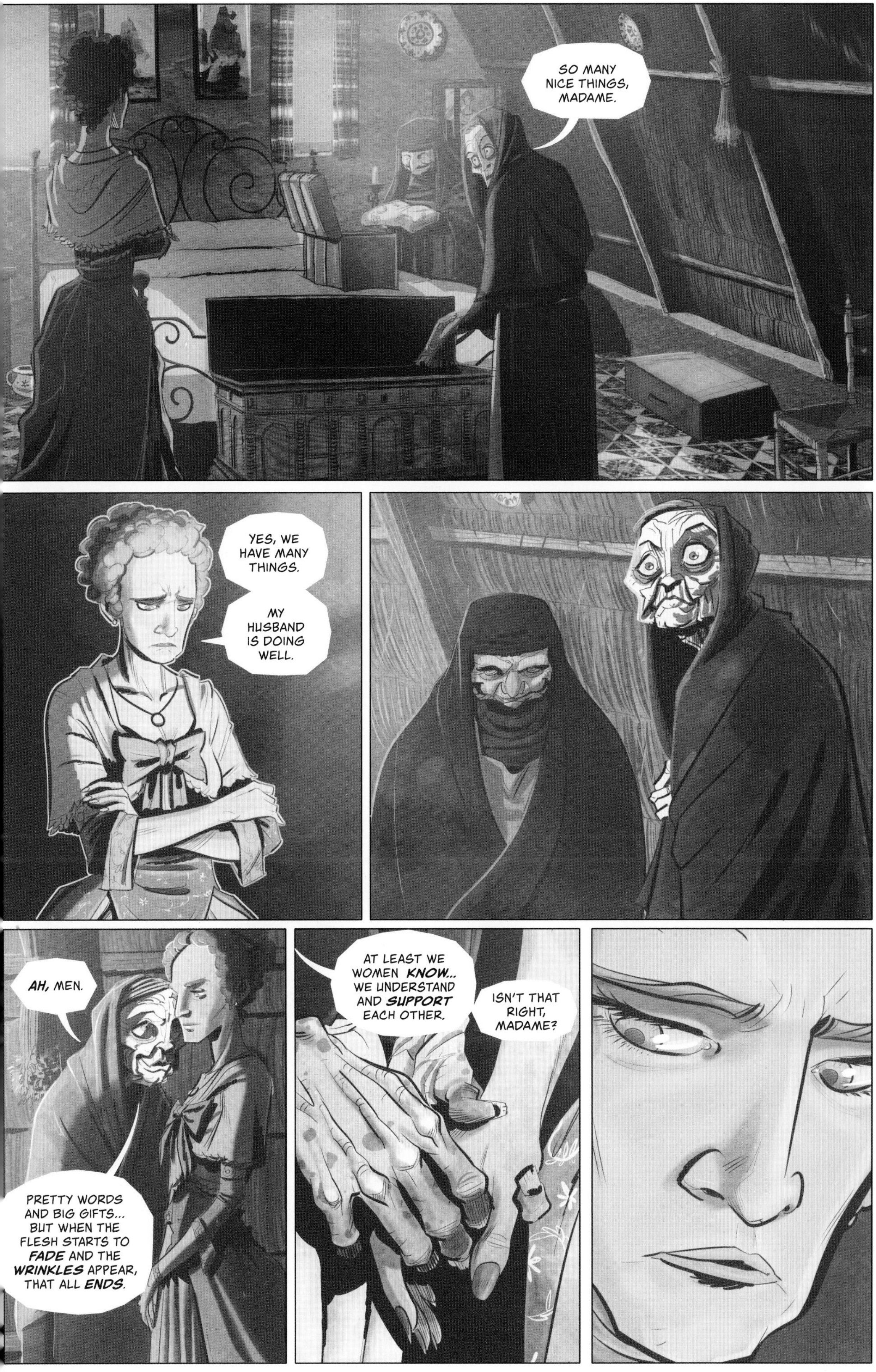
SO MANY NICE THINGS, MADAME.
YES, WE HAVE MANY THINGS.
MY HUSBAND IS DOING WELL.
AH, MEN.
PRETTY WORDS AND BIG GIFTS... BUT WHEN THE FLESH STARTS TO FADE AND THE WRINKLES APPEAR, THAT ALL ENDS.
AT LEAST WE WOMEN KNOW... WE UNDERSTAND AND SUPPORT EACH OTHER.
ISN'T THAT RIGHT, MADAME?

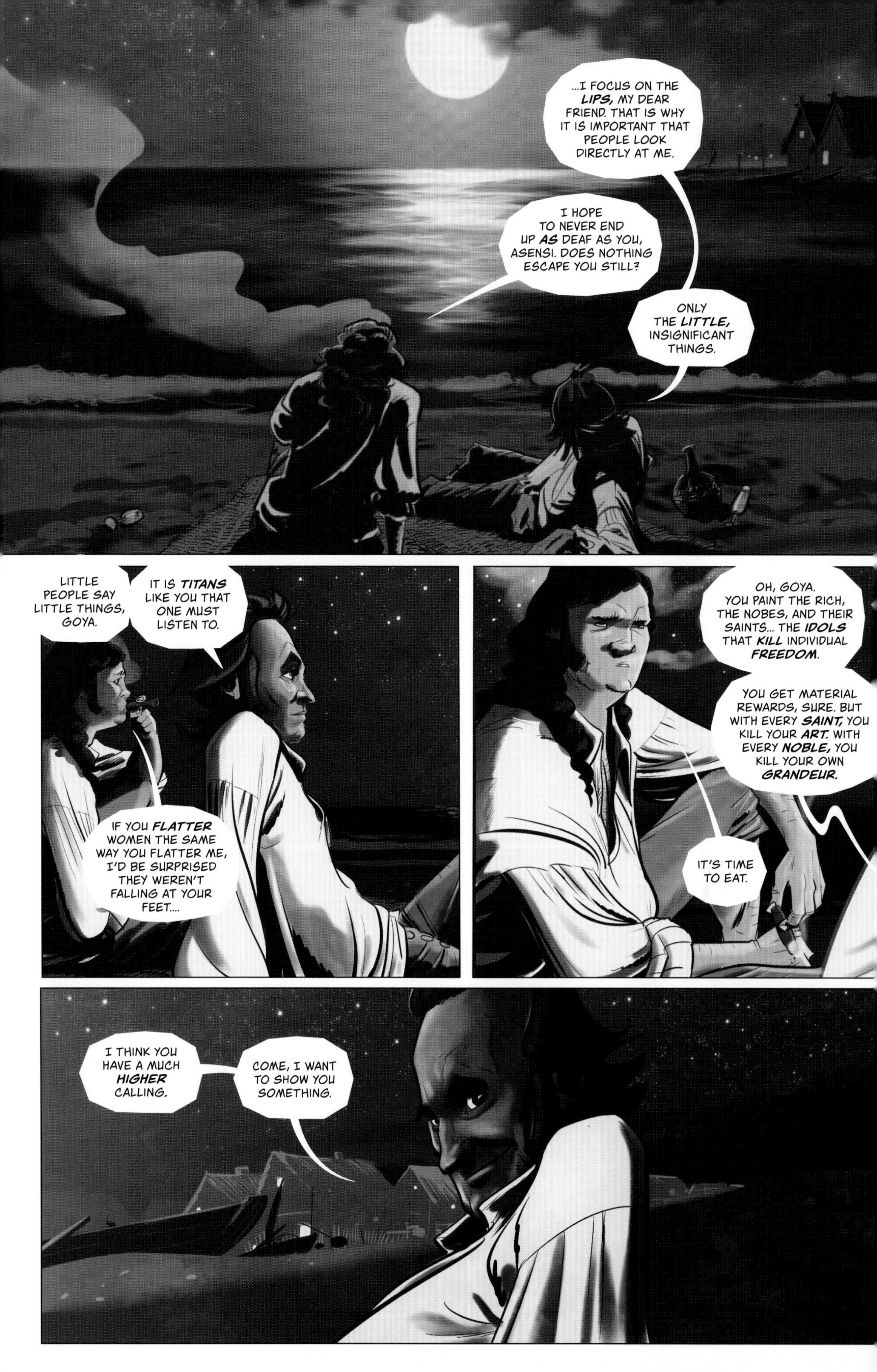
...I FOCUS ON THE LIPS, MY DEAR FRIEND. THAT IS WHY IT IS IMPORTANT THAT PEOPLE LOOK DIRECTLY AT ME.
I HOPE TO NEVER END UP AS DEAF AS YOU, ASENSI. DOES NOTHING ESCAPE YOU STILL?
ONLY THE LITTLE, INSIGNIFICANT THINGS.
LITTLE PEOPLE SAY LITTLE THINGS, GOYA.
IT IS TITANS LIKE YOU THAT ONE MUST LISTEN TO.
IF YOU FLATTER WOMEN THE SAME WAY YOU FLATTER ME, I'D BE SURPRISED THEY WEREN'T FALLING AT YOUR FEET....
OH, GOYA. YOU PAINT THE RICH, THE NOBES, AND THEIR SAINTS... THE IDOLS THAT KILL INDIVIDUAL FREEDOM.
YOU GET MATERIAL REWARDS, SURE. BUT WITH EVERY SAINT, YOU KILL YOUR ART. WITH EVERY NOBLE, YOU KILL YOUR OWN GRANDEUR.
IT'S TIME TO EAT.
I THINK YOU HAVE A MUCH HIGHER CALLING.
COME, I WANT TO SHOW YOU SOMETHING.

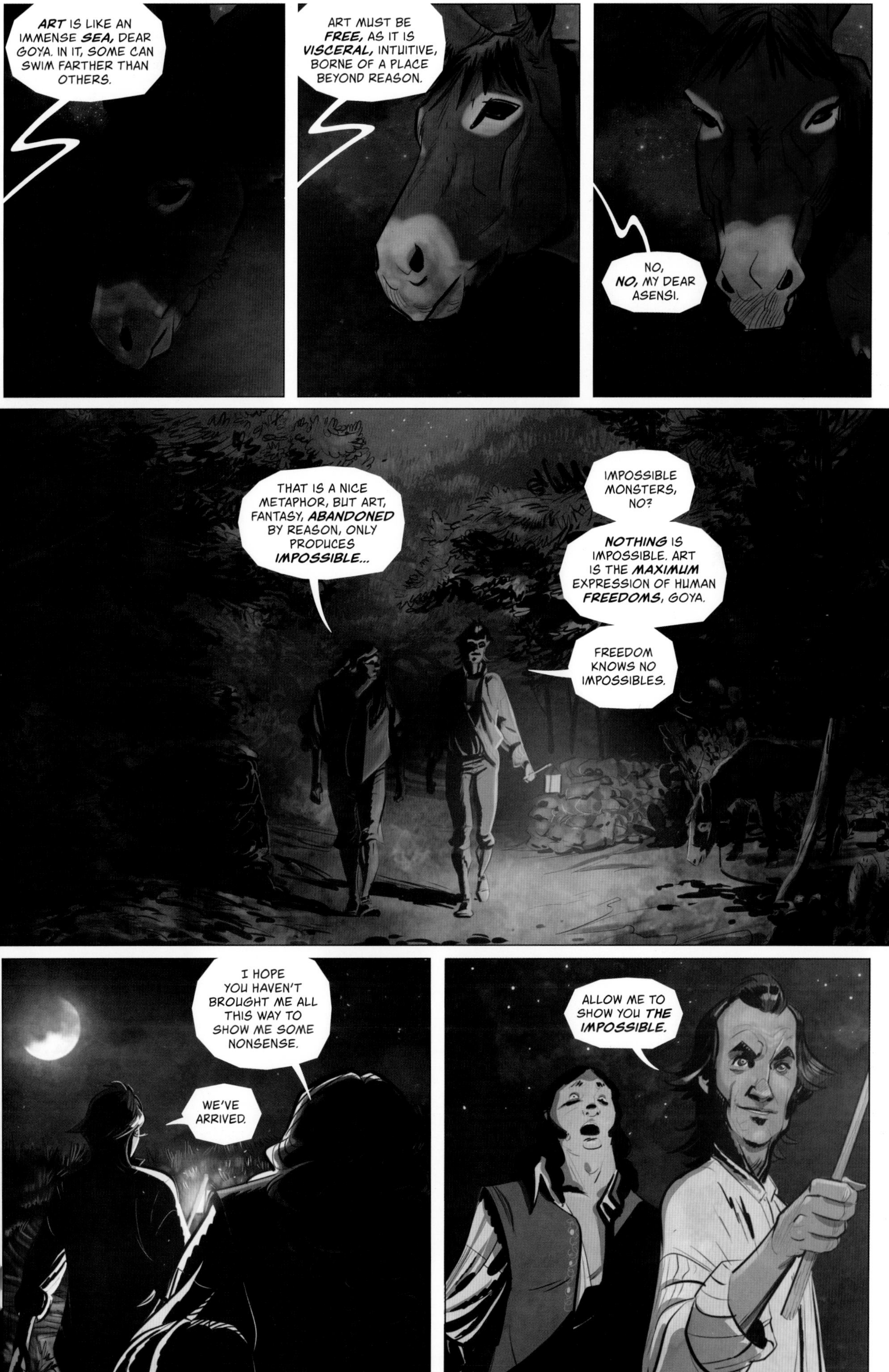

ART IS LIKE AN IMMENSE SEA, DEAR GOYA. IN IT, SOME CAN SWIM FARTHER THAN OTHERS.
ART MUST BE FREE, AS IT IS VISCERAL, INTUITIVE, BORNE OF A PLACE BEYOND REASON.
NO, NO, MY DEAR ASENSI.
THAT IS A NICE METAPHOR, BUT ART, FANTASY, ABANDONED BY REASON, ONLY PRODUCES IMPOSSIBLE...
IMPOSSIBLE MONSTERS, NO?
NOTHING IS IMPOSSIBLE. ART IS THE MAXIMUM EXPRESSION OF HUMAN FREEDOMS, GOYA.
FREEDOM KNOWS NO IMPOSSIBLES.
I HOPE YOU HAVEN'T BROUGHT ME ALL THIS WAY TO SHOW ME SOME NONSENSE.
WE'VE ARRIVED.
ALLOW ME TO SHOW YOU THE IMPOSSIBLE.

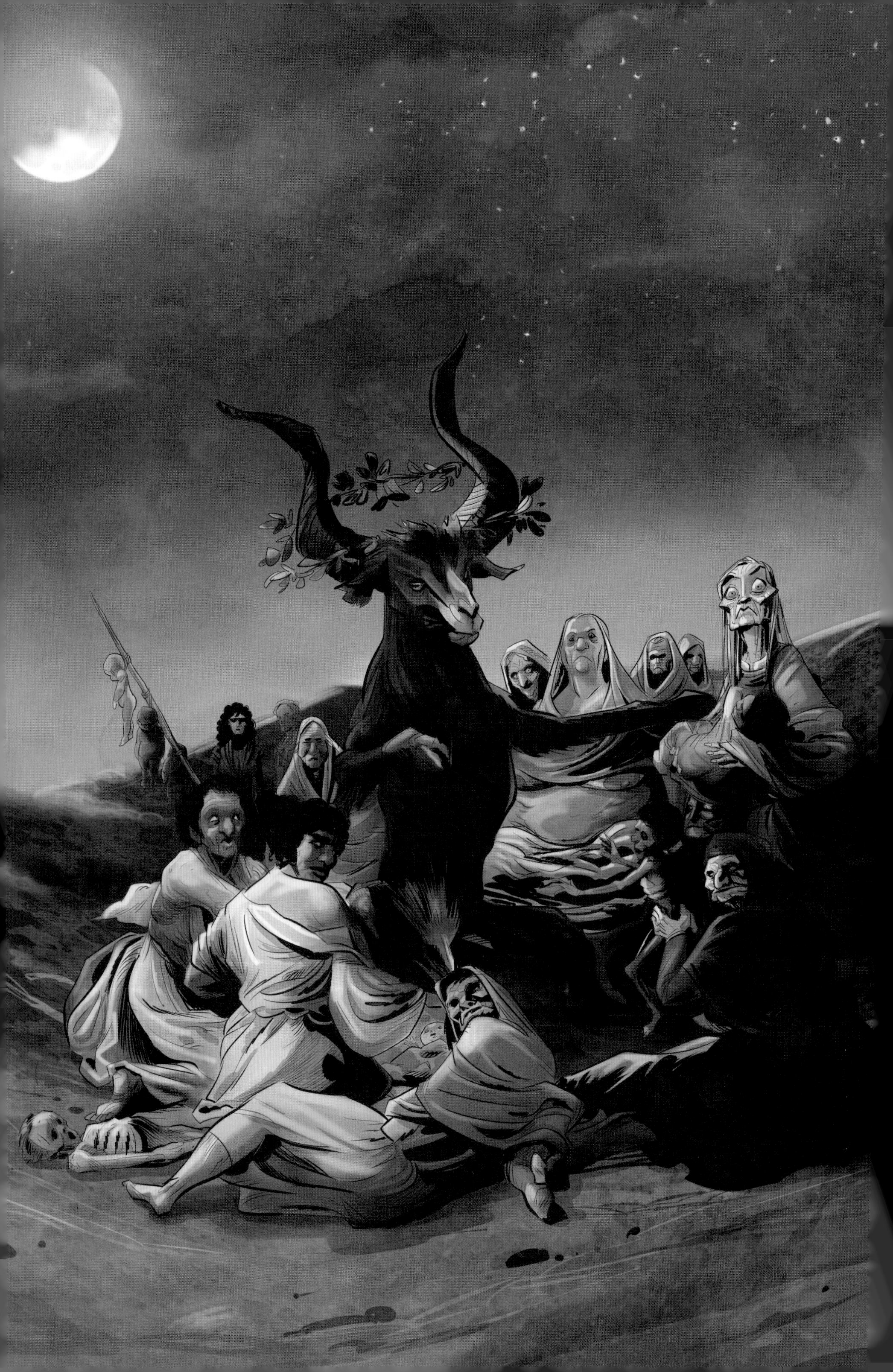

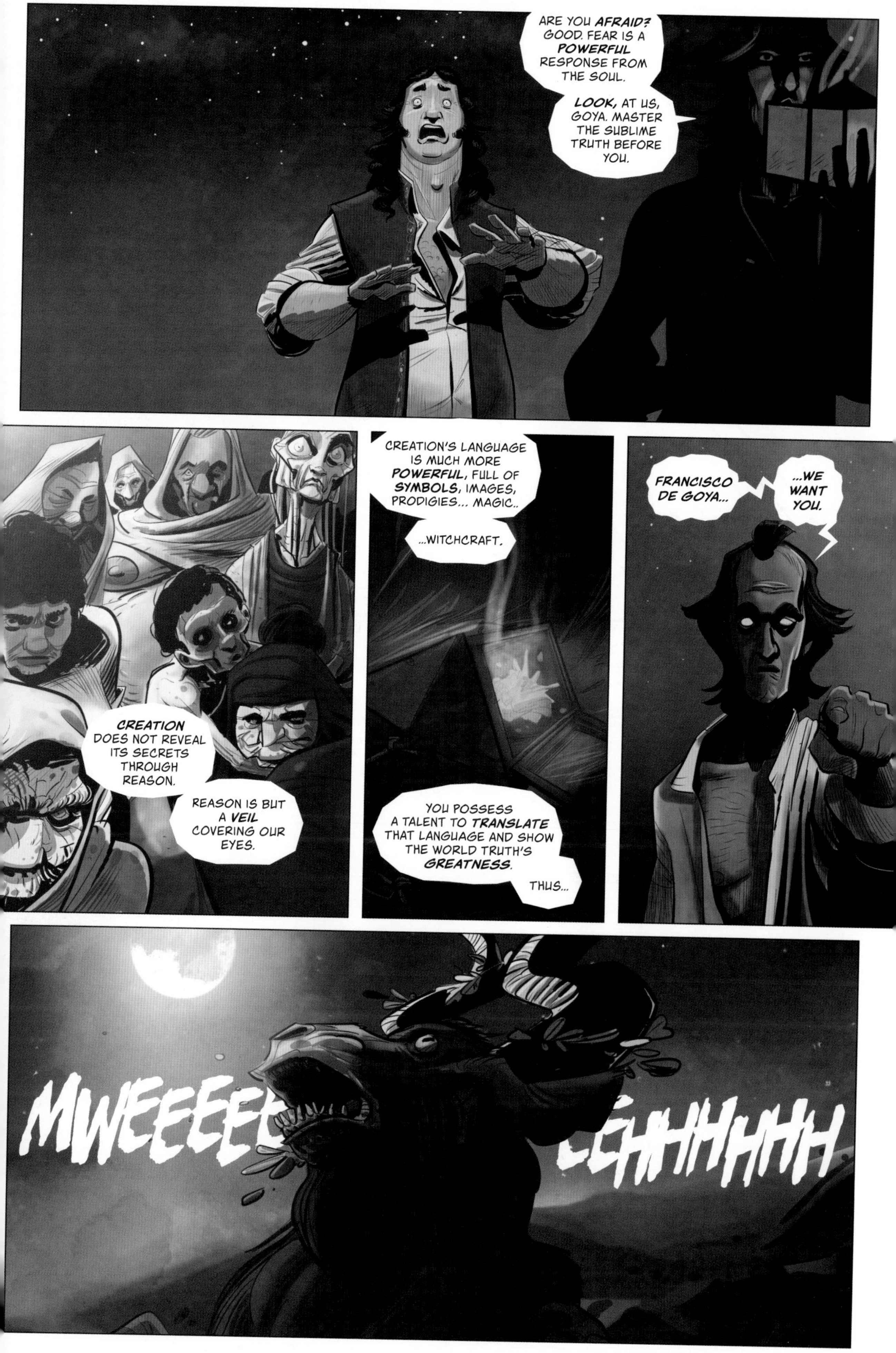

ARE YOU AFRAID? GOOD. FEAR IS A POWERFUL RESPONSE FROM THE SOUL.
LOOK, AT US, GOYA. MASTER THE SUBLIME TRUTH BEFORE YOU.
CREATION DOES NOT REVEAL ITS SECRETS THROUGH REASON.
REASON IS BUT A VEIL COVERING OUR EYES.
CREATION'S LANGUAGE IS MUCH MORE POWERFUL, FULL OF SYMBOLS, IMAGES, PRODIGIES... MAGIC..
...WITCHCRAFT.
YOU POSSESS A TALENT TO TRANSLATE THAT LANGUAGE AND SHOW THE WORLD TRUTH'S GREATNESS.
THUS...
FRANCISCO DE GOYA...
...WE WANT YOU.
MWEEEEE EEHHHHHH

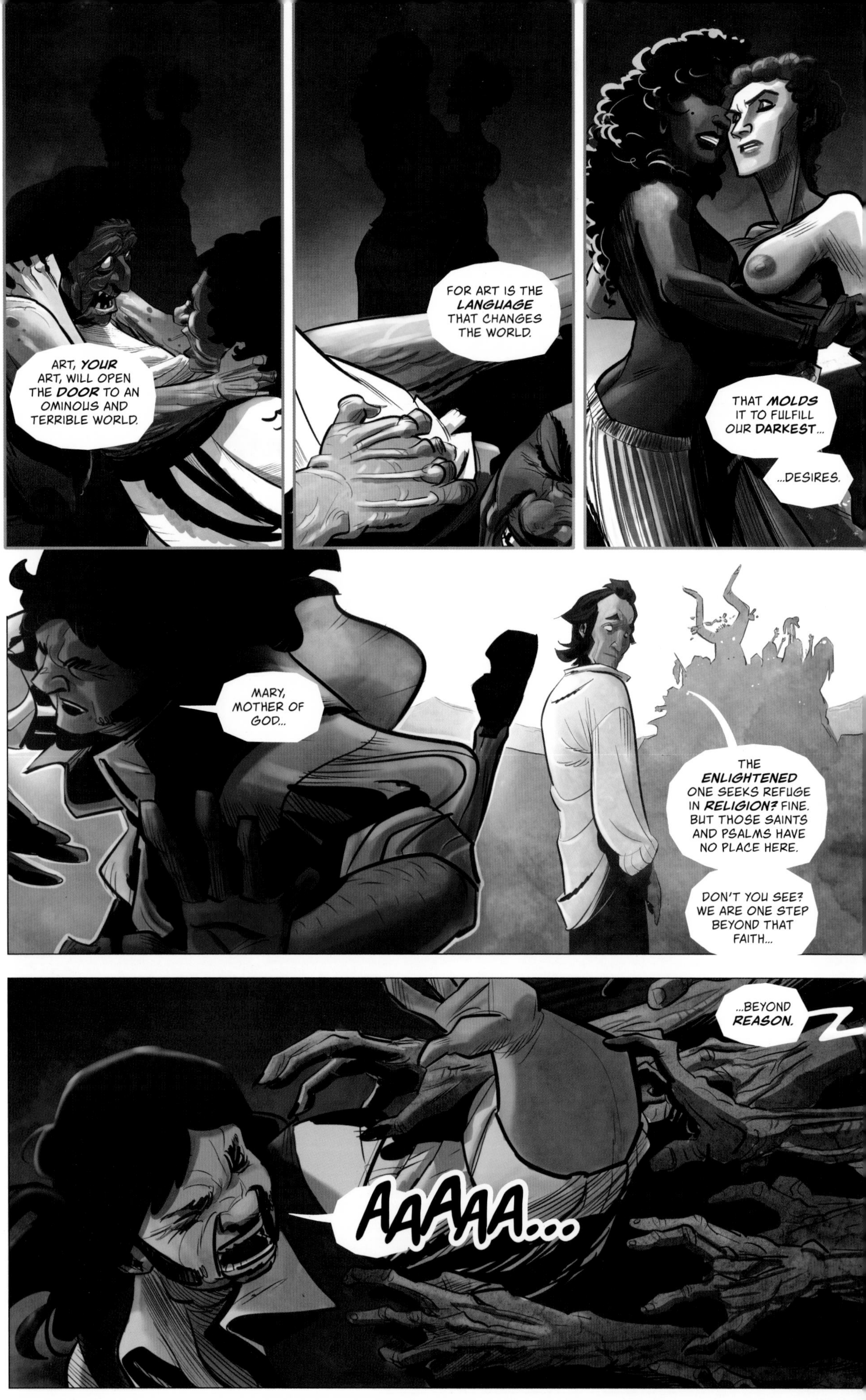

ART, YOUR ART, WILL OPEN THE DOOR TO AN OMINOUS AND TERRIBLE WORLD.
FOR ART IS THE LANGUAGE THAT CHANGES THE WORLD.
THAT MOLDS IT TO FULFILL OUR DARKEST...
...DESIRES.
MARY, MOTHER OF GOD...
THE ENLIGHTENED ONE SEEKS REFUGE IN RELIGION? FINE. BUT THOSE SAINTS AND PSALMS HAVE NO PLACE HERE.
DON'T YOU SEE? WE ARE ONE STEP BEYOND THAT FAITH...
...BEYOND REASON.
AAAAA...

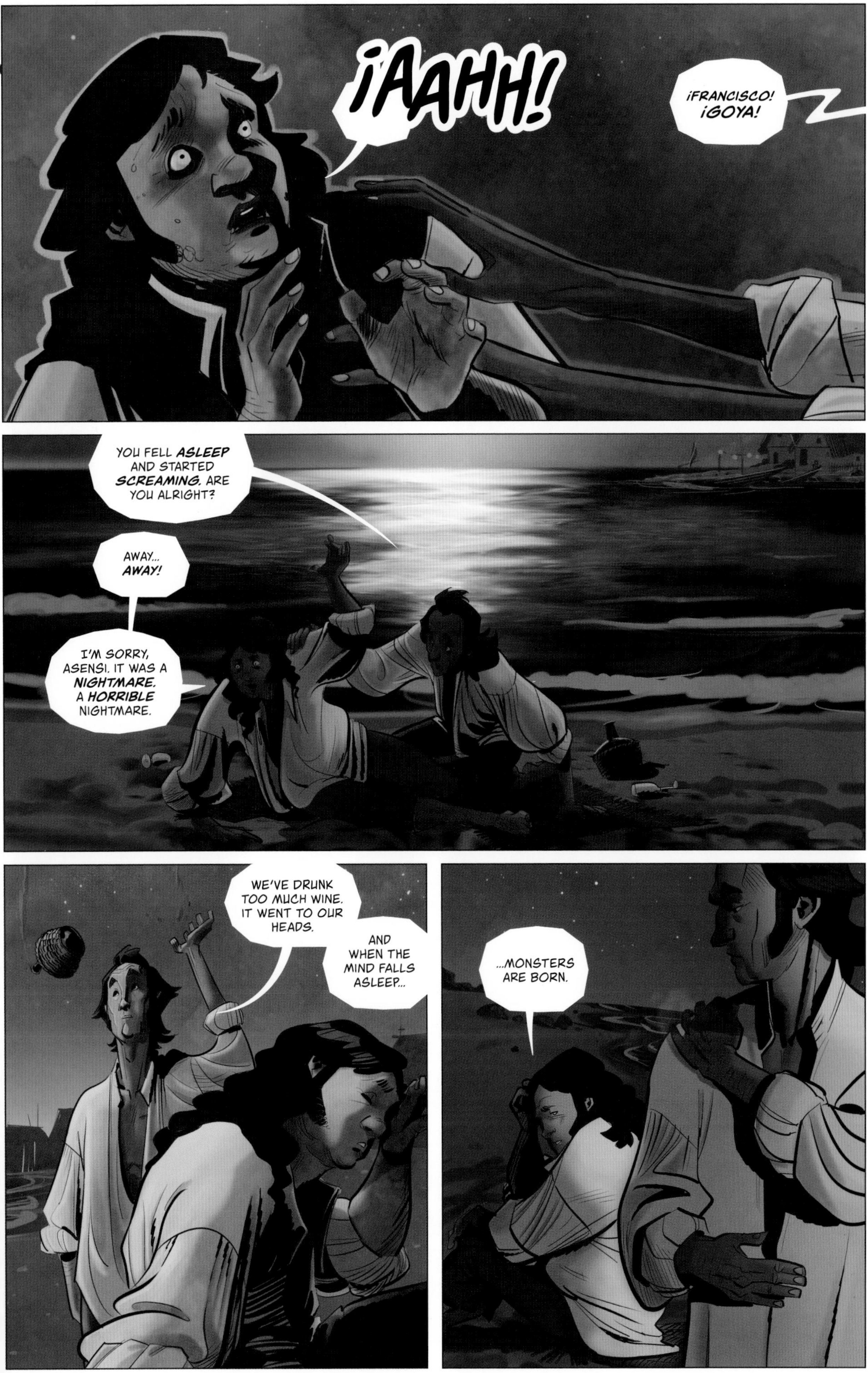
¡AAHH!
¡FRANCISCO! ¡GOYA!
YOU FELL ASLEEP AND STARTED SCREAMING. ARE YOU ALRIGHT?
AWAY... AWAY!
I'M SORRY, ASENSI. IT WAS A NIGHTMARE. A HORRIBLE NIGHTMARE.
WE'VE DRUNK TOO MUCH WINE. IT WENT TO OUR HEADS.
AND WHEN THE MIND FALLS ASLEEP...
...MONSTERS ARE BORN.

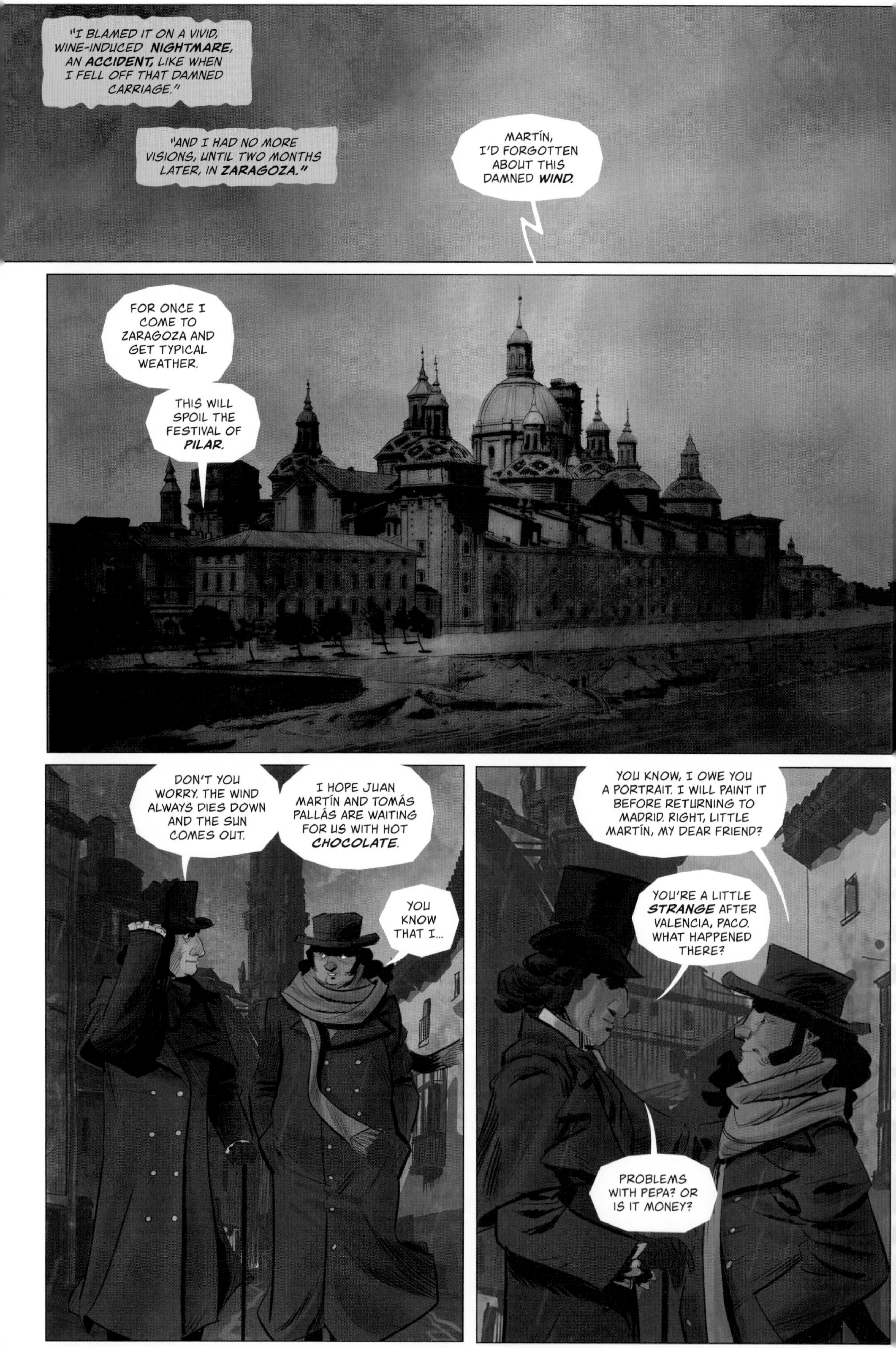
"I BLAMED IT ON A VIVID, WINE-INDUCED NIGHTMARE, AN ACCIDENT, LIKE WHEN I FELL OFF THAT DAMNED CARRIAGE."
"AND I HAD NO MORE VISIONS, UNTIL TWO MONTHS LATER, IN ZARAGOZA."
MARTÍN, I'D FORGOTTEN ABOUT THIS DAMNED WIND.
FOR ONCE I COME TO ZARAGOZA AND GET TYPICAL WEATHER.
THIS WILL SPOIL THE FESTIVAL OF PILAR.
DON'T YOU WORRY. THE WIND ALWAYS DIES DOWN AND THE SUN COMES OUT.
I HOPE JUAN MARTÍN AND TOMÁS PALLÁS ARE WAITING FOR US WITH HOT CHOCOLATE.
YOU KNOW THAT I...
YOU KNOW, I OWE YOU A PORTRAIT. I WILL PAINT IT BEFORE RETURNING TO MADRID. RIGHT, LITTLE MARTÍN, MY DEAR FRIEND?
YOU'RE A LITTLE STRANGE AFTER VALENCIA, PACO. WHAT HAPPENED THERE?
PROBLEMS WITH PEPA? OR IS IT MONEY?

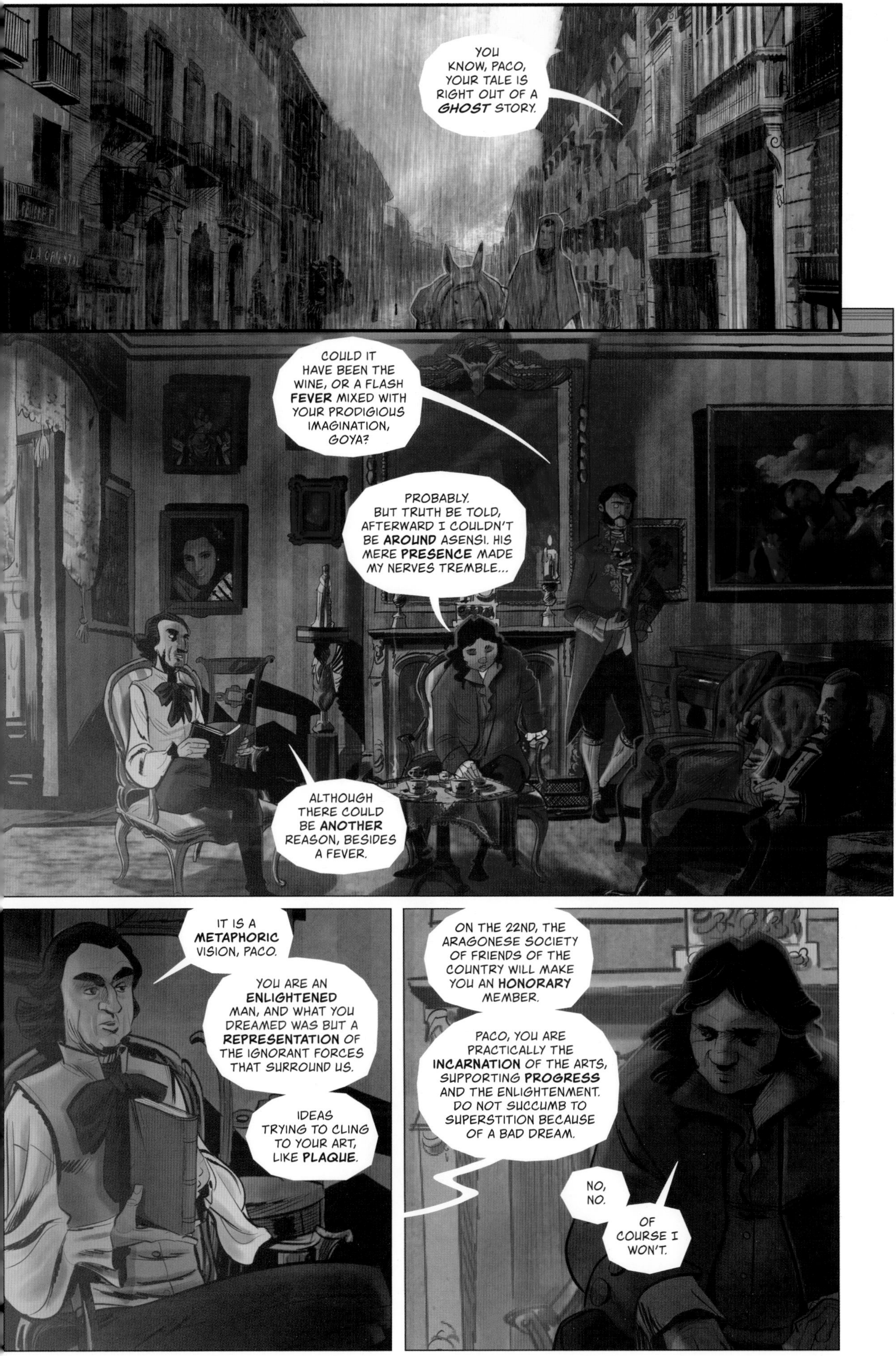
YOU KNOW, PACO, YOUR TALE IS RIGHT OUT OF A **GHOST** STORY.
LA ORIENTAL
COULD IT HAVE BEEN THE WINE, OR A FLASH **FEVER** MIXED WITH YOUR PRODIGIOUS IMAGINATION, GOYA?
PROBABLY. BUT TRUTH BE TOLD, AFTERWARD I COULDN'T BE **AROUND** ASENSI. HIS MERE **PRESENCE** MADE MY NERVES TREMBLE...
ALTHOUGH THERE COULD BE **ANOTHER** REASON, BESIDES A FEVER.
IT IS A **METAPHORIC** VISION, PACO.
YOU ARE AN **ENLIGHTENED** MAN, AND WHAT YOU DREAMED WAS BUT A **REPRESENTATION** OF THE IGNORANT FORCES THAT SURROUND US.
IDEAS TRYING TO CLING TO YOUR ART, LIKE **PLAQUE**.
ON THE 22ND, THE ARAGONESE SOCIETY OF FRIENDS OF THE COUNTRY WILL MAKE YOU AN **HONORARY** MEMBER.
PACO, YOU ARE PRACTICALLY THE **INCARNATION** OF THE ARTS, SUPPORTING **PROGRESS** AND THE ENLIGHTENMENT. DO NOT SUCCUMB TO SUPERSTITION BECAUSE OF A BAD DREAM.
NO, NO.
OF COURSE I WON'T.

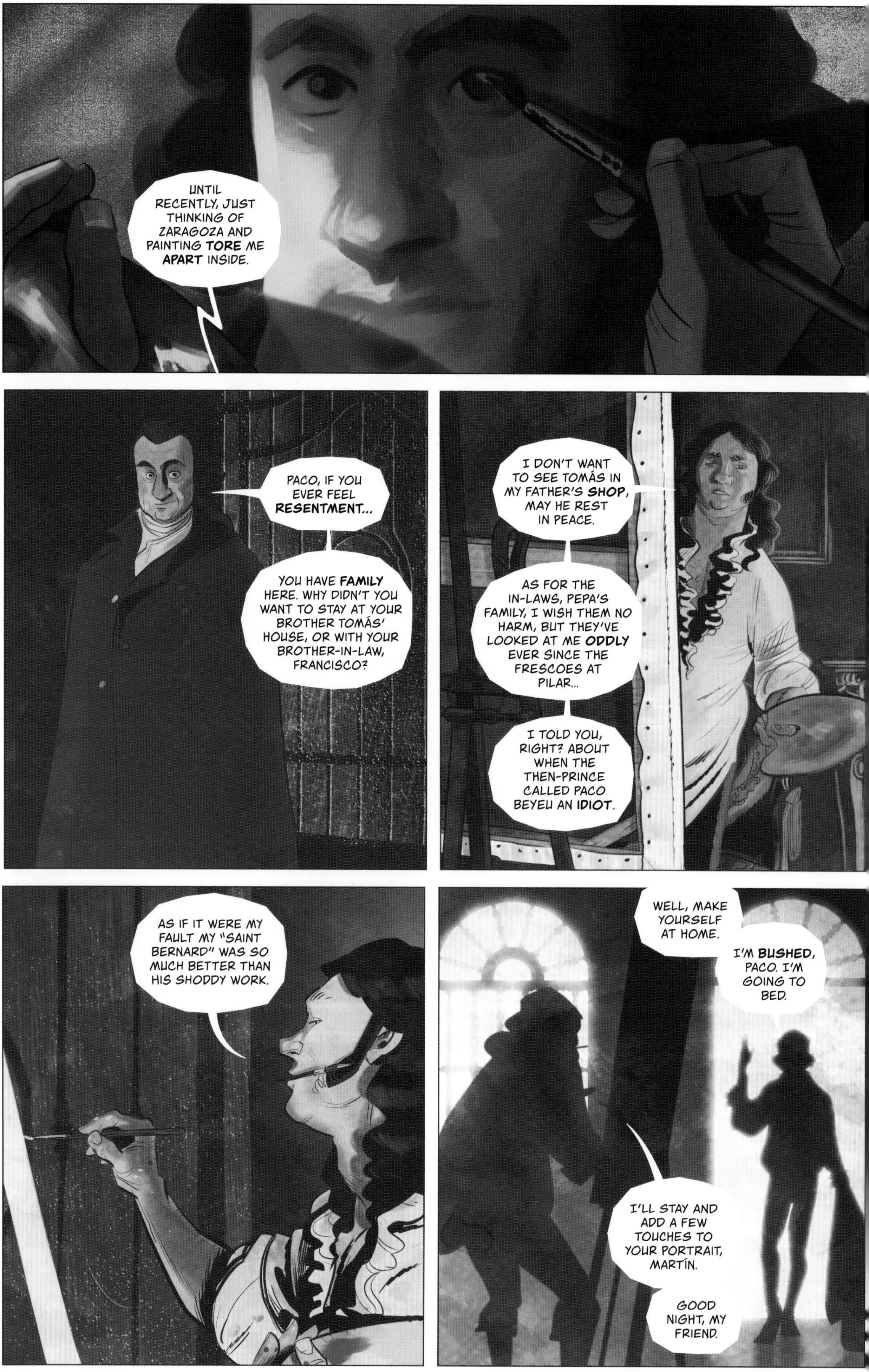
UNTIL RECENTLY, JUST THINKING OF ZARAGOZA AND PAINTING TORE ME APART INSIDE.
PACO, IF YOU EVER FEEL RESENTMENT...
YOU HAVE FAMILY HERE. WHY DIDN'T YOU WANT TO STAY AT YOUR BROTHER TOMÁS' HOUSE, OR WITH YOUR BROTHER-IN-LAW, FRANCISCO?
I DON'T WANT TO SEE TOMÁS IN MY FATHER'S SHOP, MAY HE REST IN PEACE.
AS FOR THE IN-LAWS, PEPA'S FAMILY, I WISH THEM NO HARM, BUT THEY'VE LOOKED AT ME ODDLY EVER SINCE THE FRESCOES AT PILAR...
I TOLD YOU, RIGHT? ABOUT WHEN THE THEN-PRINCE CALLED PACO BEYEU AN IDIOT.
AS IF IT WERE MY FAULT MY "SAINT BERNARD" WAS SO MUCH BETTER THAN HIS SHODDY WORK.
WELL, MAKE YOURSELF AT HOME.
I'M BUSHED, PACO. I'M GOING TO BED.
I'LL STAY AND ADD A FEW TOUCHES TO YOUR PORTRAIT, MARTÍN.
GOOD NIGHT, MY FRIEND.

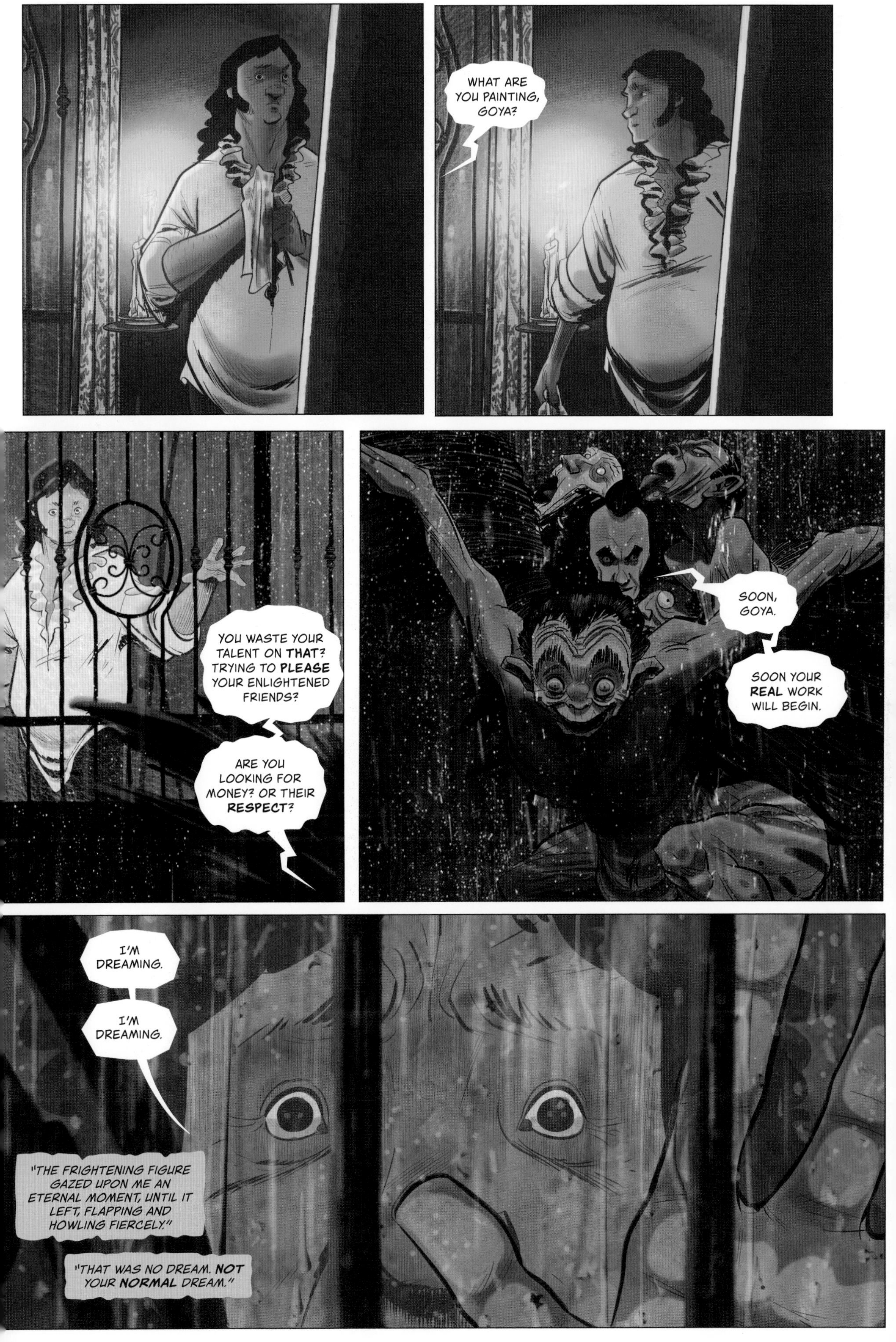
WHAT ARE YOU PAINTING, GOYA?
YOU WASTE YOUR TALENT ON **THAT**? TRYING TO **PLEASE** YOUR ENLIGHTENED FRIENDS?
ARE YOU LOOKING FOR MONEY? OR THEIR **RESPECT**?
SOON, GOYA.
SOON YOUR **REAL** WORK WILL BEGIN.
I'M DREAMING.
I'M DREAMING.
"THE FRIGHTENING FIGURE GAZED UPON ME AN ETERNAL MOMENT, UNTIL IT LEFT, FLAPPING AND HOWLING FIERCELY."
"THAT WAS NO DREAM. **NOT** YOUR **NORMAL** DREAM."

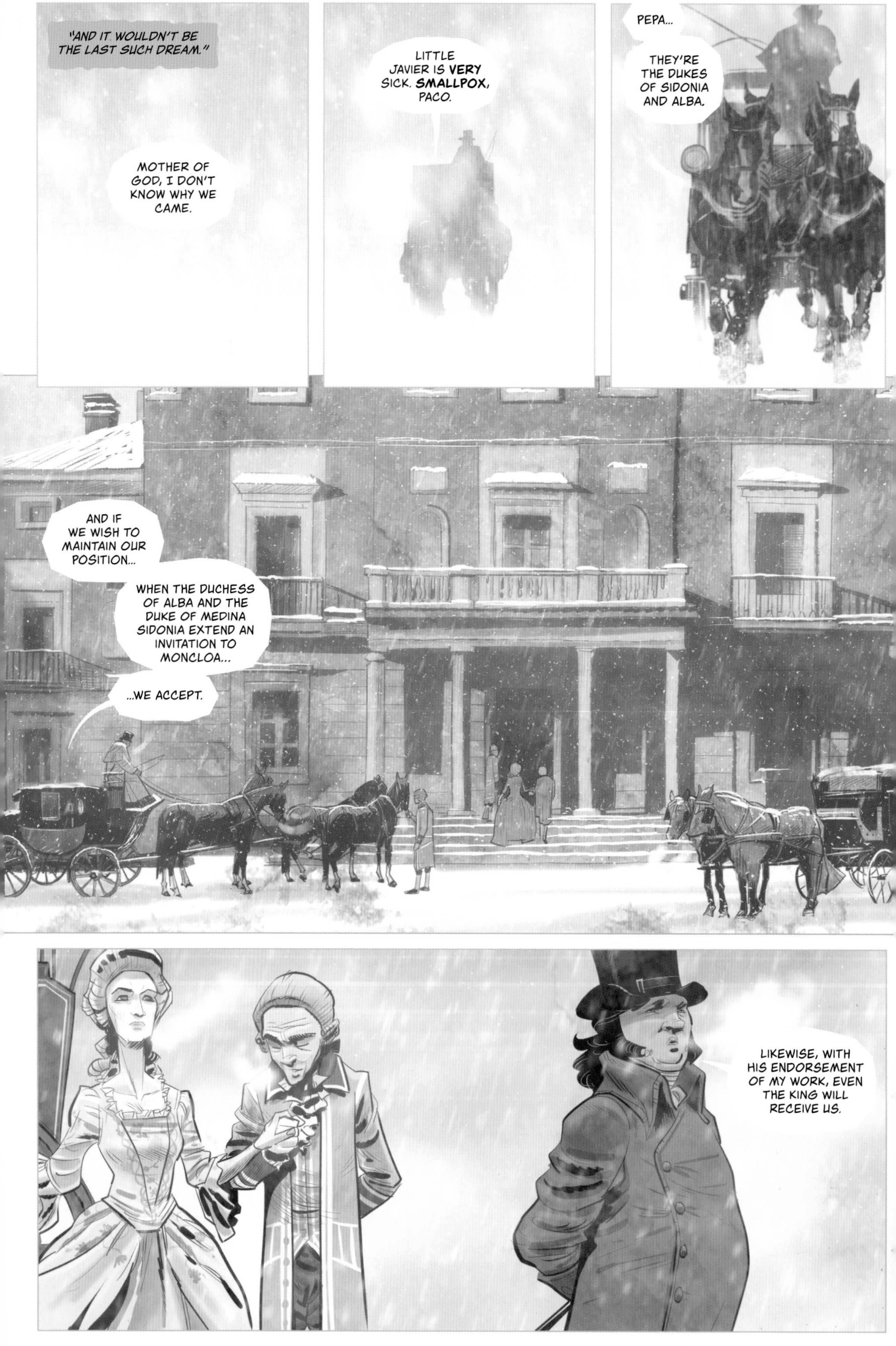
"AND IT WOULDN'T BE THE LAST SUCH DREAM."
MOTHER OF GOD, I DON'T KNOW WHY WE CAME.
LITTLE JAVIER IS **VERY** SICK. **SMALLPOX**, PACO.
PEPA...
THEY'RE THE DUKES OF SIDONIA AND ALBA.
AND IF WE WISH TO MAINTAIN OUR POSITION...
WHEN THE DUCHESS OF ALBA AND THE DUKE OF MEDINA SIDONIA EXTEND AN INVITATION TO MONCLOA...
...WE ACCEPT.
LIKEWISE, WITH HIS ENDORSEMENT OF MY WORK, EVEN THE KING WILL RECEIVE US.

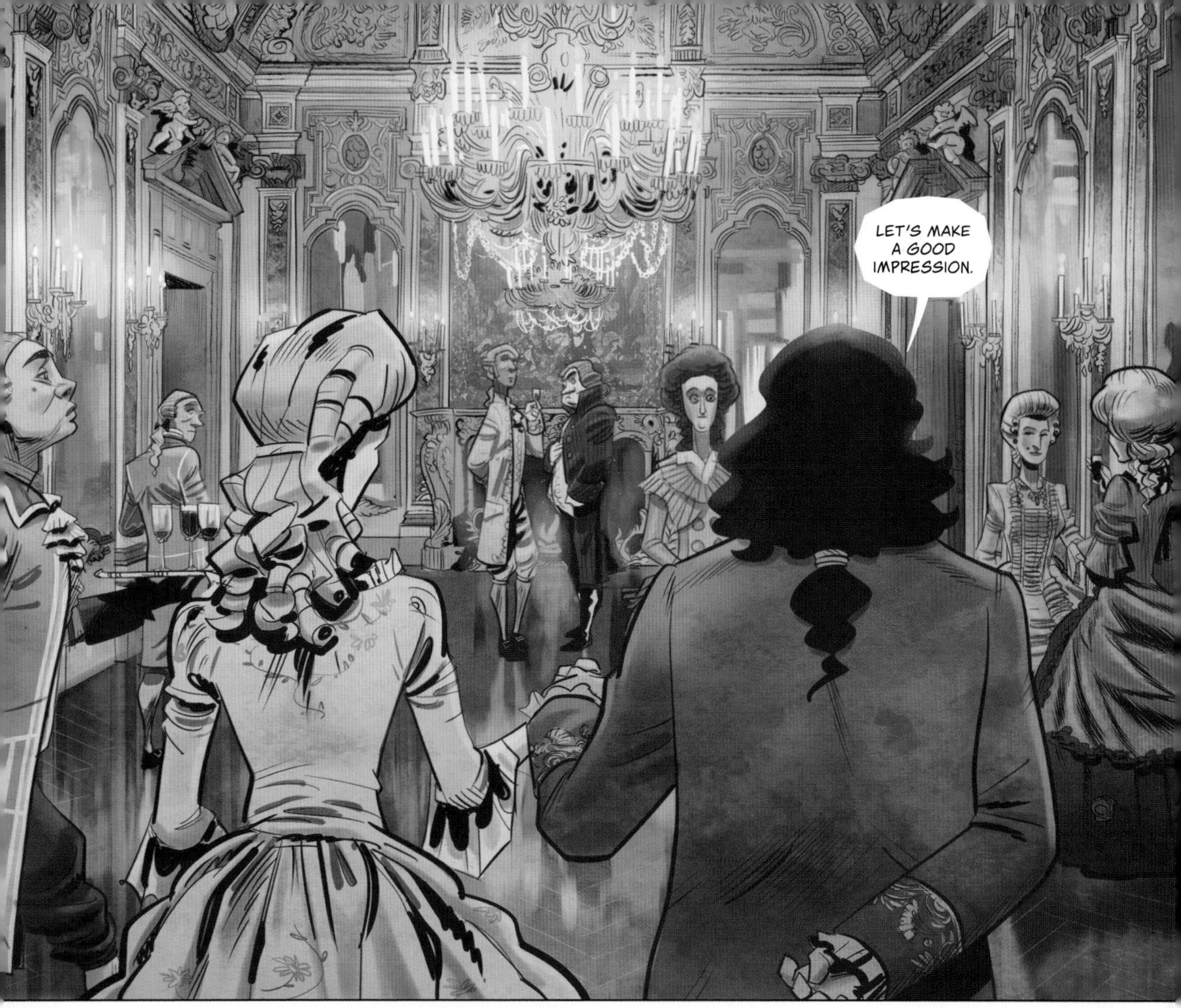
LET'S MAKE A GOOD IMPRESSION.

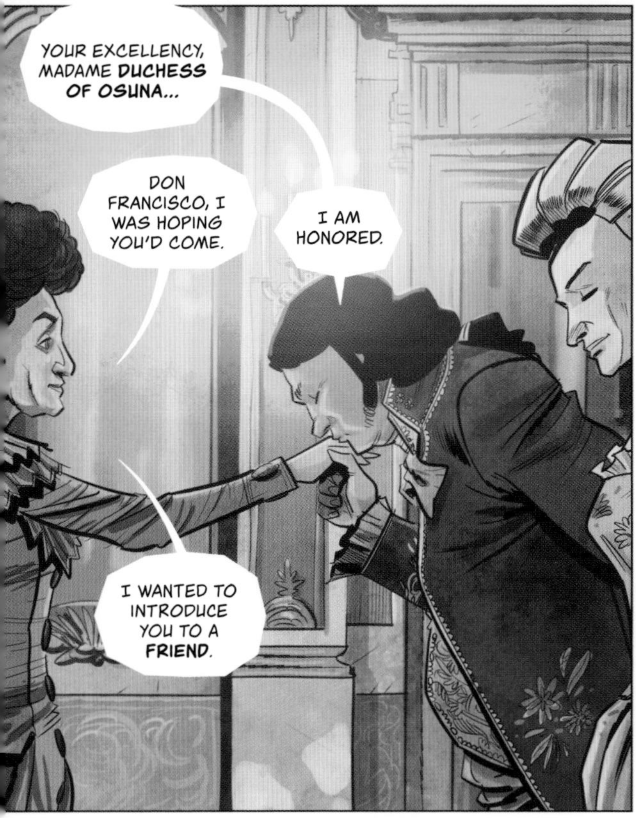
YOUR EXCELLENCY, MADAME **DUCHESS OF OSUNA...**
I AM HONORED.
DON FRANCISCO, I WAS HOPING YOU'D COME.
I WANTED TO INTRODUCE YOU TO A **FRIEND**.

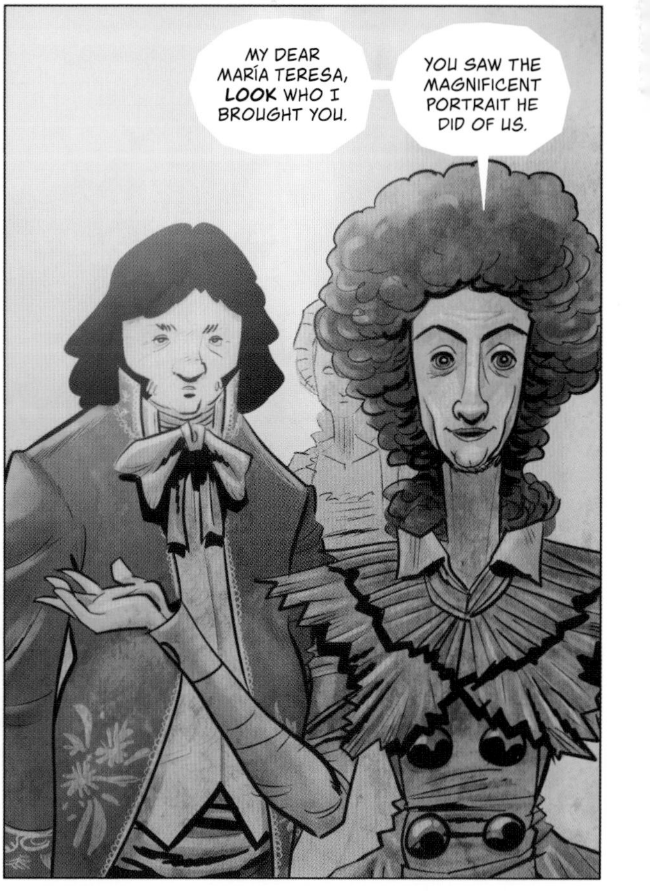
MY DEAR MARÍA TERESA, **LOOK** WHO I BROUGHT YOU.
YOU SAW THE MAGNIFICENT PORTRAIT HE DID OF US.

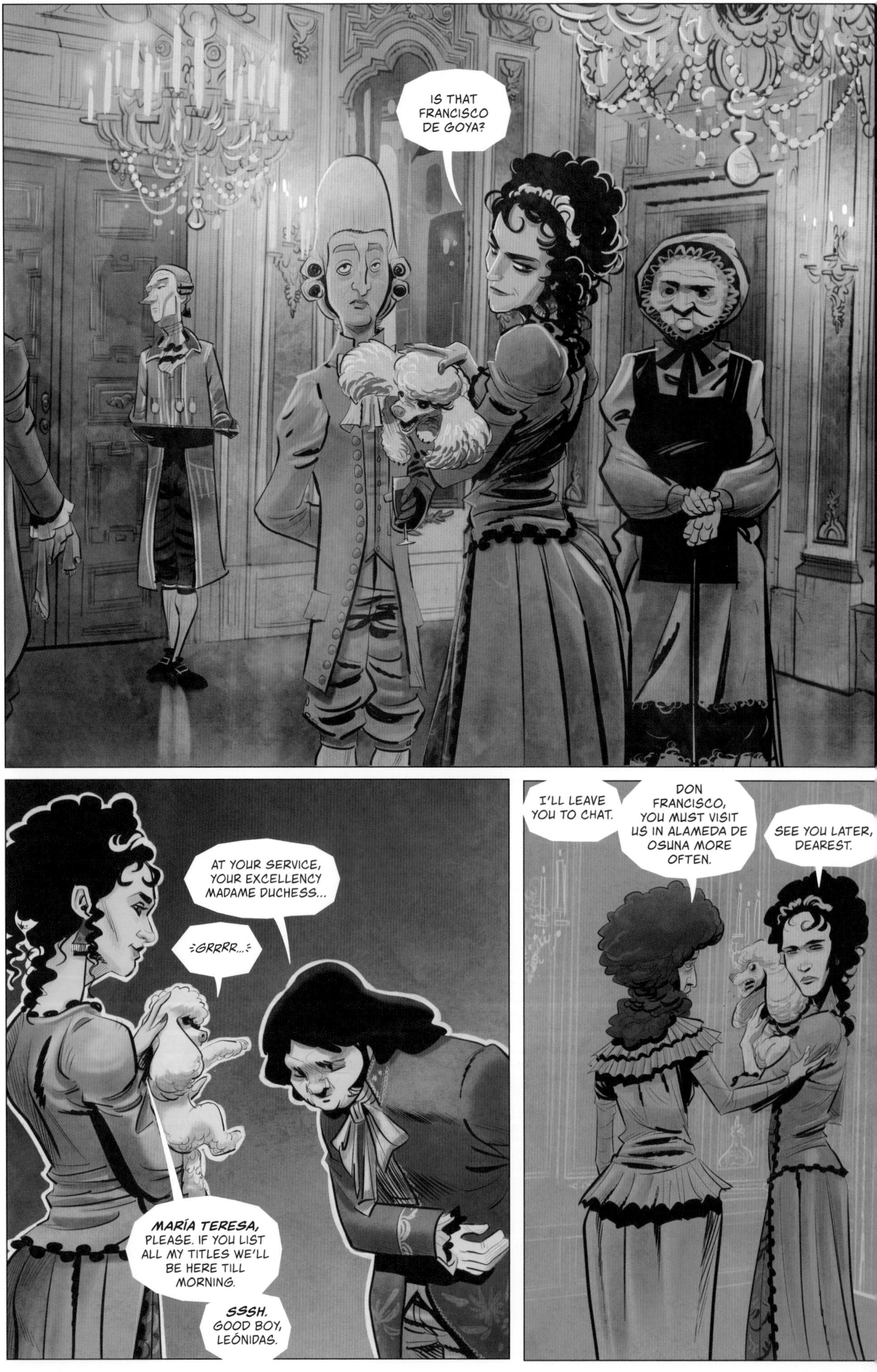
IS THAT FRANCISCO DE GOYA?
AT YOUR SERVICE, YOUR EXCELLENCY MADAME DUCHESS...
GRRRR...
MARÍA TERESA, PLEASE. IF YOU LIST ALL MY TITLES WE'LL BE HERE TILL MORNING.
SSSH. GOOD BOY, LEÓNIDAS.
I'LL LEAVE YOU TO CHAT.
DON FRANCISCO, YOU MUST VISIT US IN ALAMEDA DE OSUNA MORE OFTEN.
SEE YOU LATER, DEAREST.

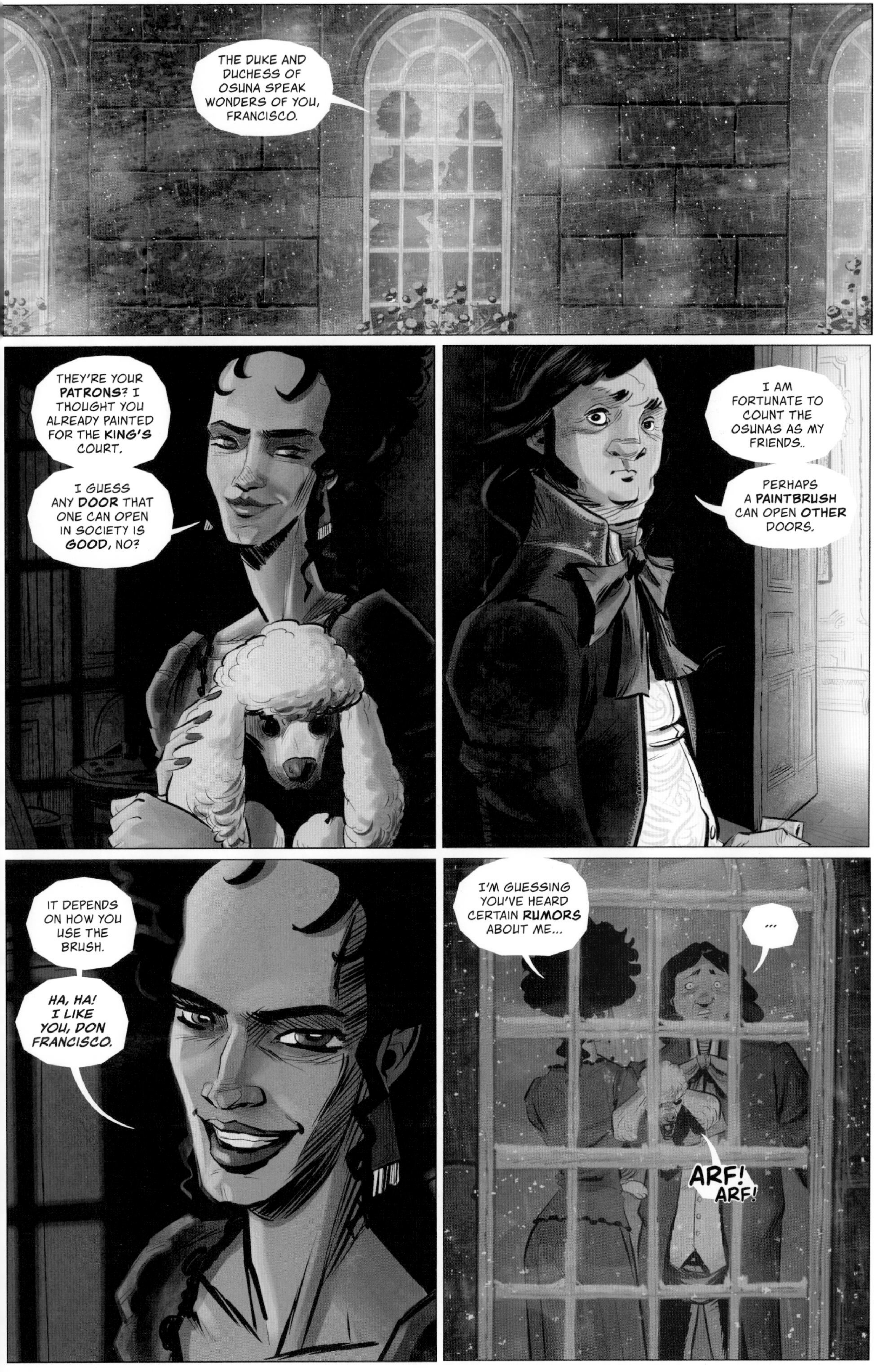
THE DUKE AND DUCHESS OF OSUNA SPEAK WONDERS OF YOU, FRANCISCO.
THEY'RE YOUR **PATRONS**? I THOUGHT YOU ALREADY PAINTED FOR THE **KING'S** COURT.
I GUESS ANY **DOOR** THAT ONE CAN OPEN IN SOCIETY IS **GOOD**, NO?
I AM FORTUNATE TO COUNT THE OSUNAS AS MY FRIENDS..
PERHAPS A **PAINTBRUSH** CAN OPEN **OTHER** DOORS.
IT DEPENDS ON HOW YOU USE THE BRUSH.
***HA, HA! I LIKE YOU, DON FRANCISCO.***
I'M GUESSING YOU'VE HEARD CERTAIN **RUMORS** ABOUT ME...
...
ARF! ARF!

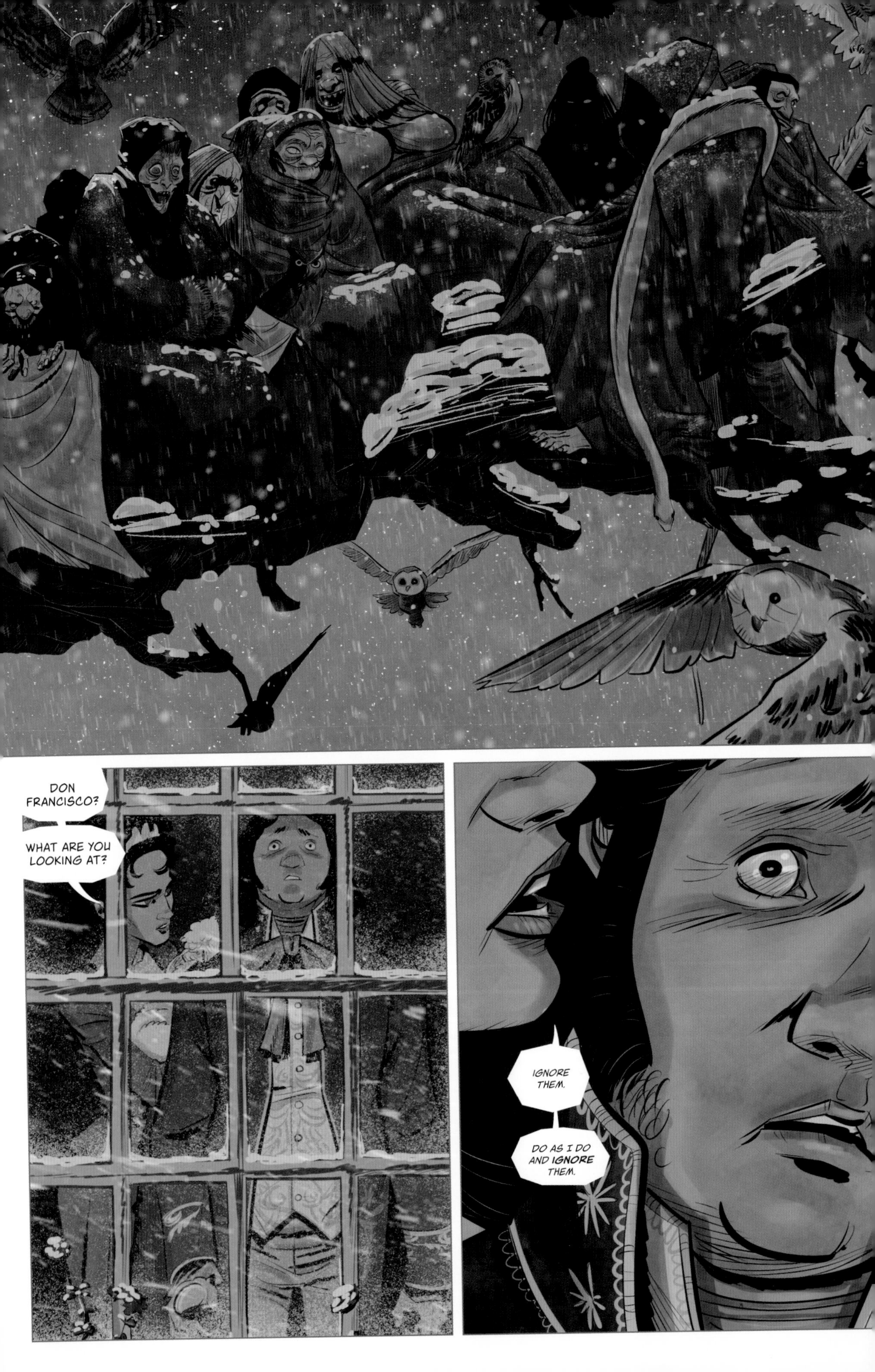
DON FRANCISCO?
WHAT ARE YOU LOOKING AT?
IGNORE THEM.
DO AS I DO AND **IGNORE** THEM.

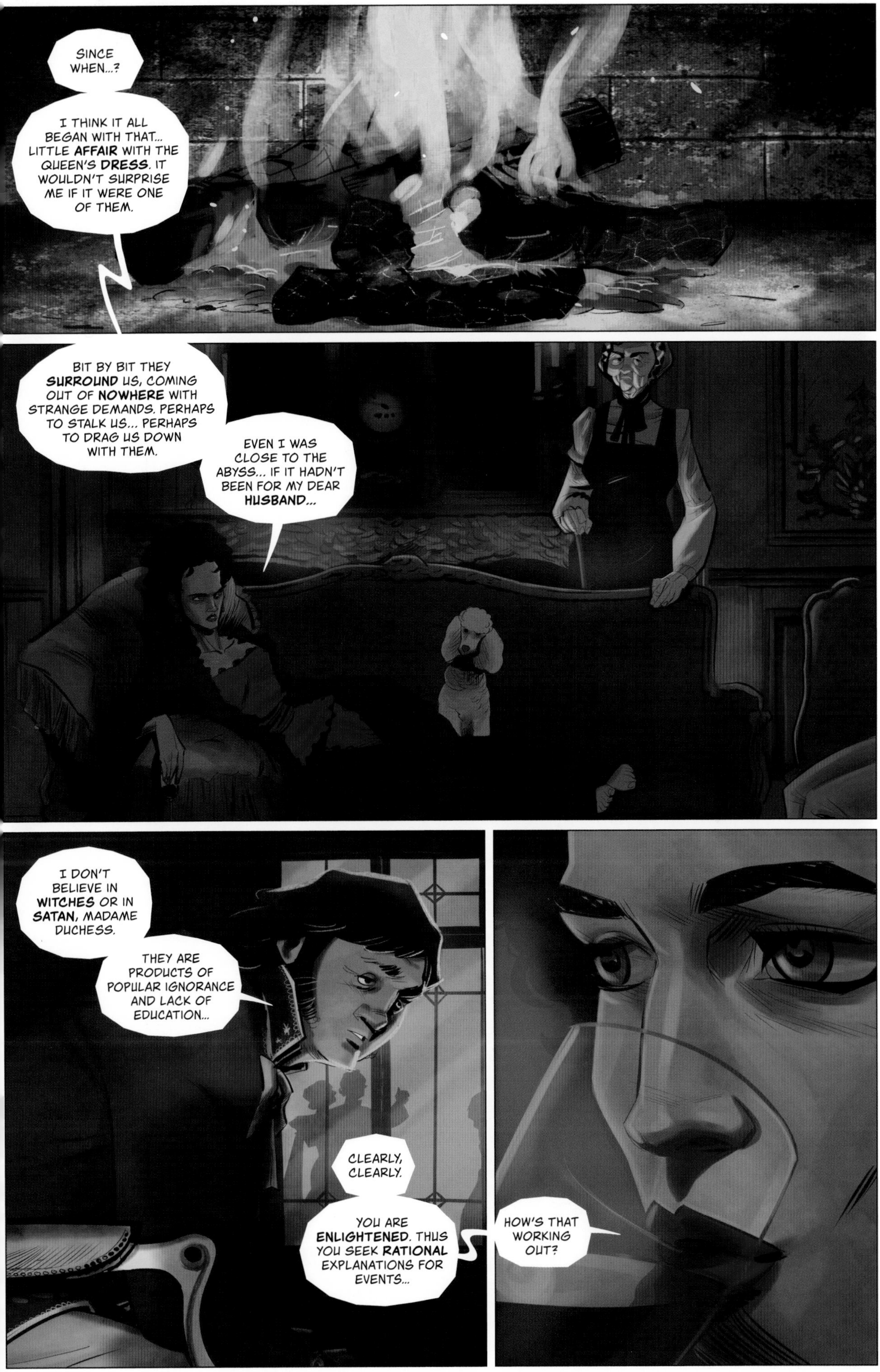
SINCE WHEN...?
I THINK IT ALL BEGAN WITH THAT... LITTLE AFFAIR WITH THE QUEEN'S DRESS. IT WOULDN'T SURPRISE ME IF IT WERE ONE OF THEM.
BIT BY BIT THEY SURROUND US, COMING OUT OF NOWHERE WITH STRANGE DEMANDS. PERHAPS TO STALK US... PERHAPS TO DRAG US DOWN WITH THEM.
EVEN I WAS CLOSE TO THE ABYSS... IF IT HADN'T BEEN FOR MY DEAR HUSBAND...
I DON'T BELIEVE IN WITCHES OR IN SATAN, MADAME DUCHESS.
THEY ARE PRODUCTS OF POPULAR IGNORANCE AND LACK OF EDUCATION...
CLEARLY, CLEARLY.
YOU ARE ENLIGHTENED. THUS YOU SEEK RATIONAL EXPLANATIONS FOR EVENTS...
HOW'S THAT WORKING OUT?

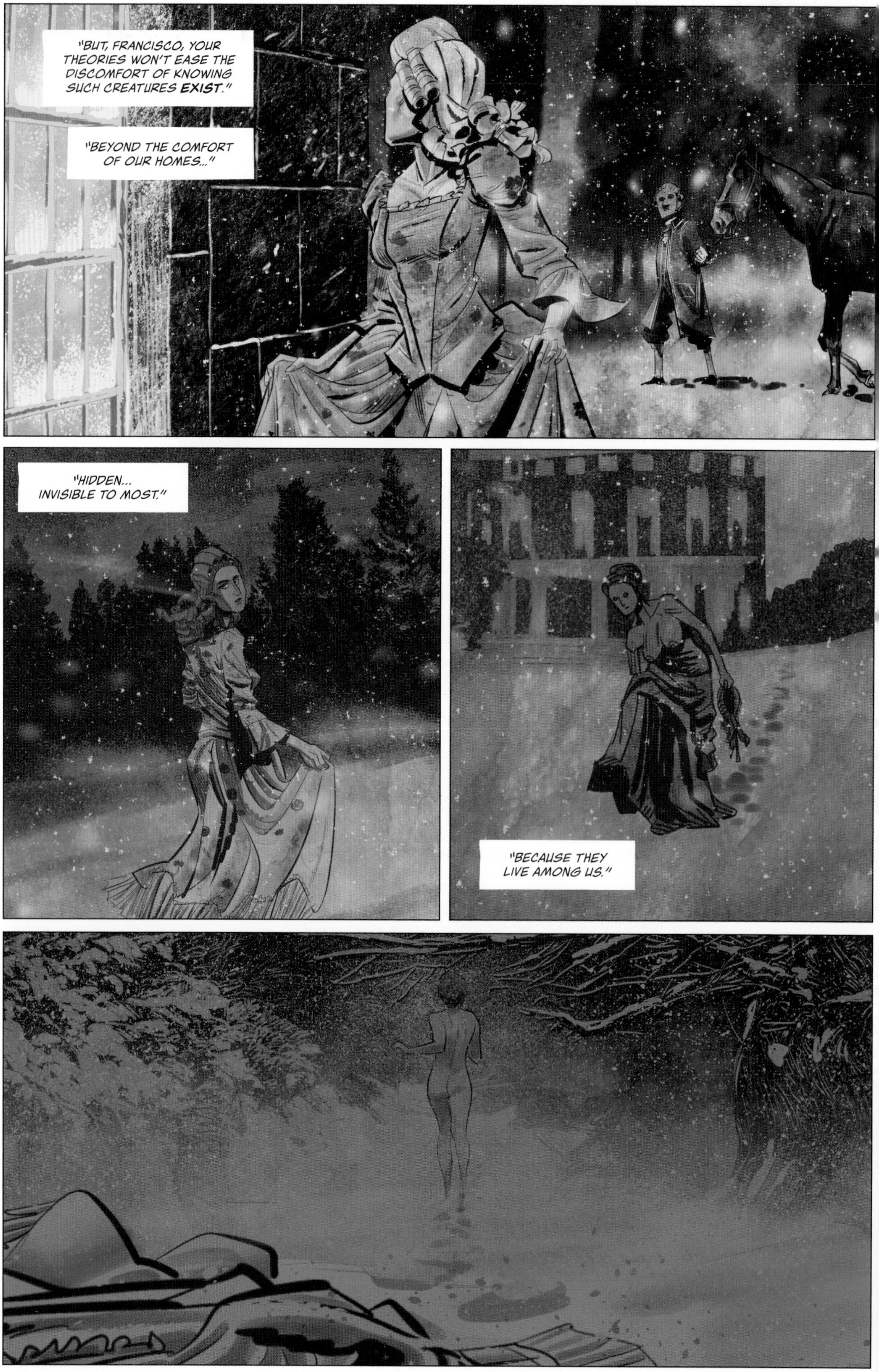
"BUT, FRANCISCO, YOUR THEORIES WON'T EASE THE DISCOMFORT OF KNOWING SUCH CREATURES **EXIST**."
"BEYOND THE COMFORT OF OUR HOMES..."
"HIDDEN... INVISIBLE TO MOST."
"BECAUSE THEY LIVE AMONG US."

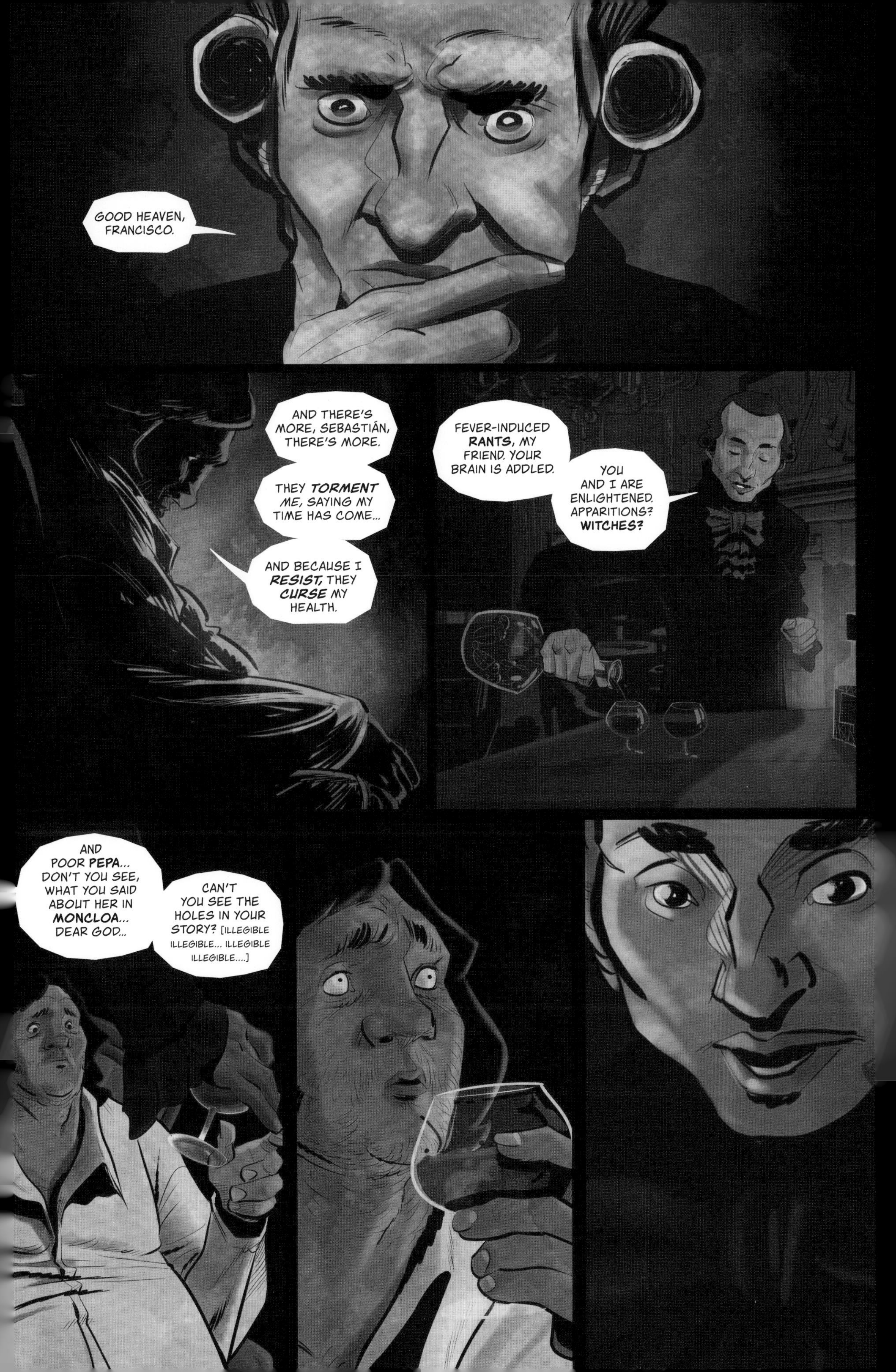
GOOD HEAVEN, FRANCISCO.
AND THERE'S MORE, SEBASTIÁN, THERE'S MORE.
THEY *TORMENT* ME, SAYING MY TIME HAS COME...
AND BECAUSE I *RESIST,* THEY *CURSE* MY HEALTH.
FEVER-INDUCED **RANTS**, MY FRIEND. YOUR BRAIN IS ADDLED.
YOU AND I ARE ENLIGHTENED. APPARITIONS? **WITCHES?**
AND POOR **PEPA**... DON'T YOU SEE, WHAT YOU SAID ABOUT HER IN **MONCLOA**... DEAR GOD...
CAN'T YOU SEE THE HOLES IN YOUR STORY? [ILLEGIBLE ILLEGIBLE... ILLEGIBLE ILLEGIBLE....]

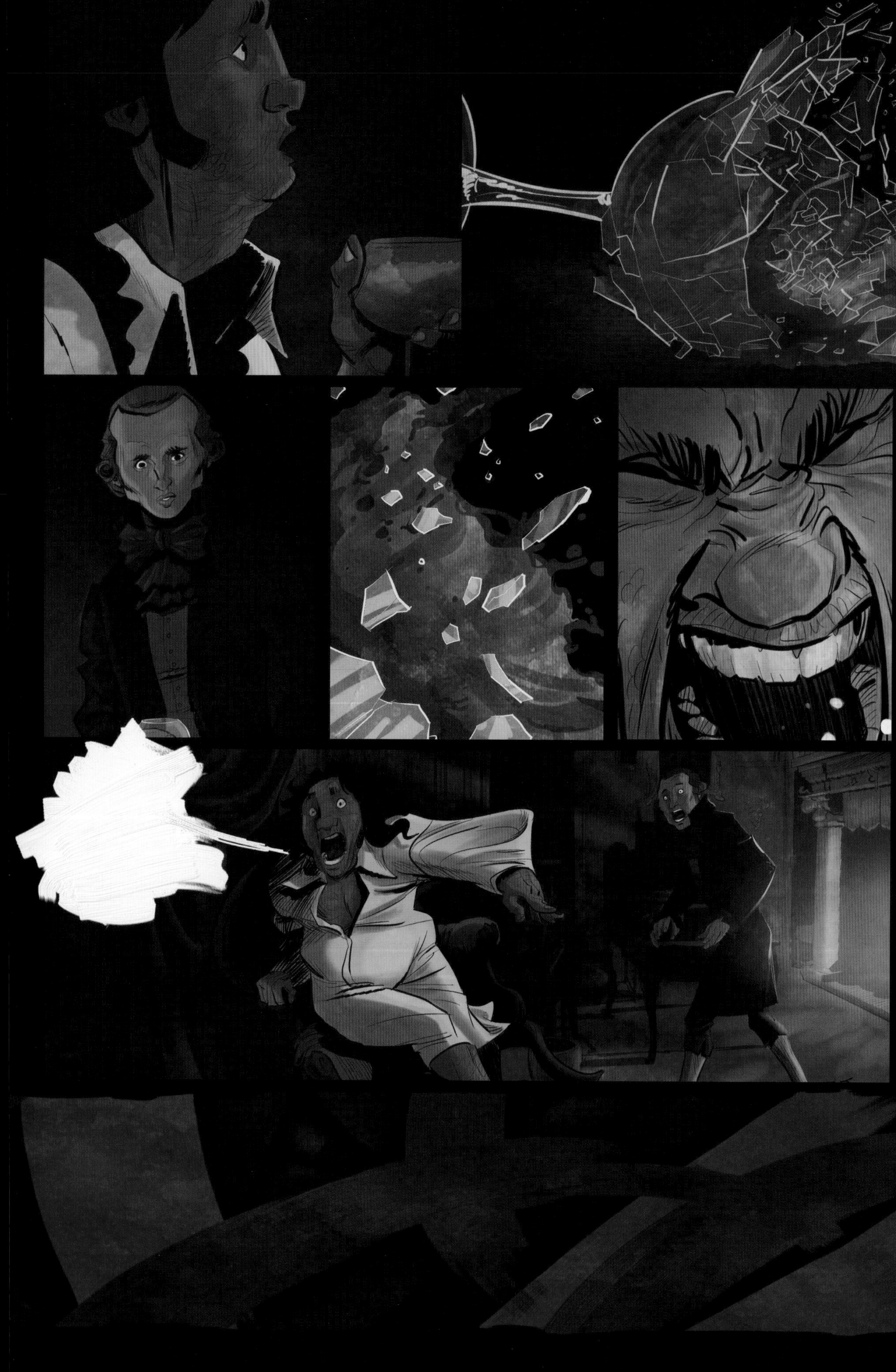

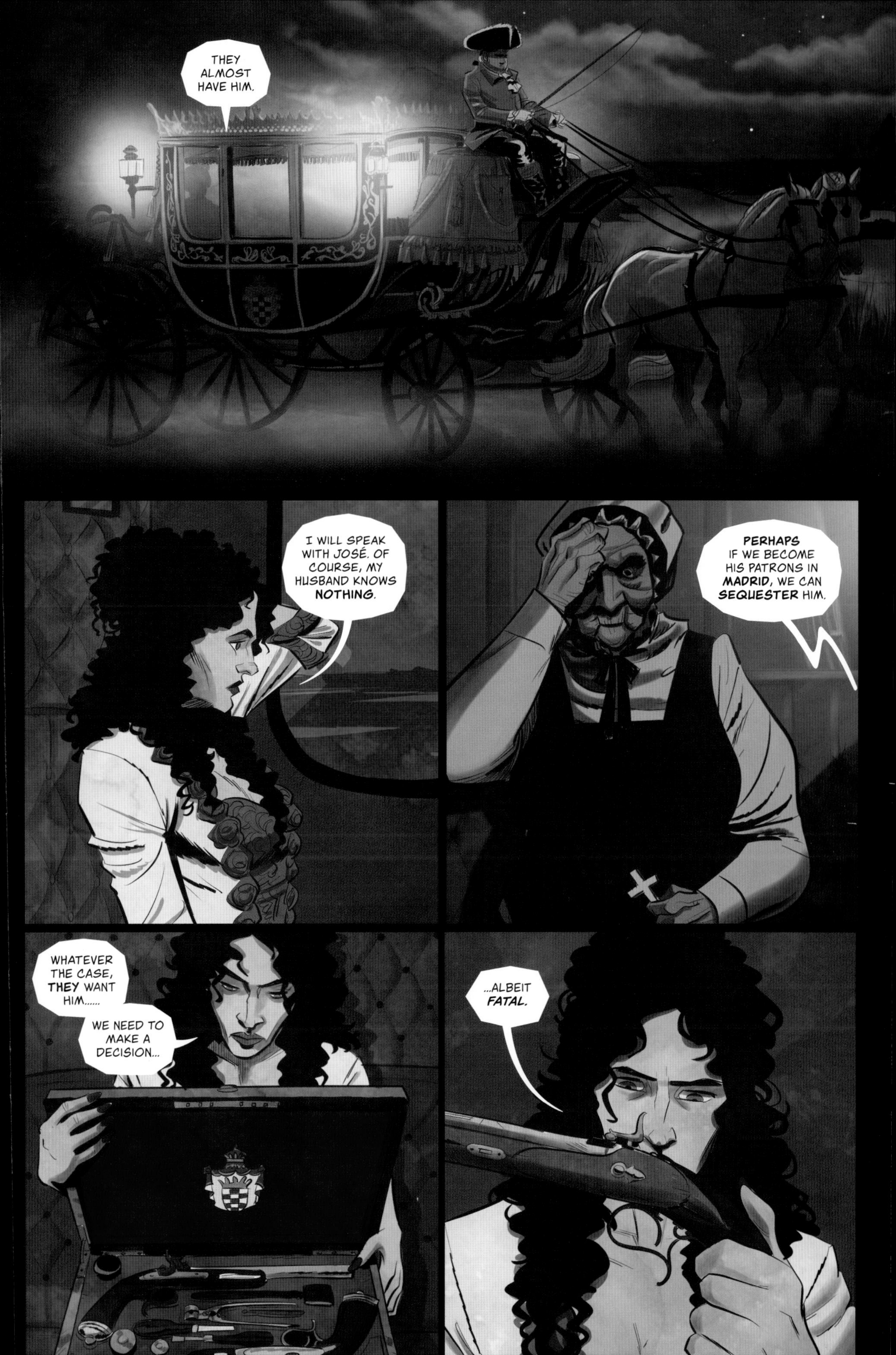
THEY ALMOST HAVE HIM.
I WILL SPEAK WITH JOSÉ. OF COURSE, MY HUSBAND KNOWS **NOTHING**.
**PERHAPS** IF WE BECOME HIS PATRONS IN **MADRID**, WE CAN **SEQUESTER** HIM.
WHATEVER THE CASE, **THEY** WANT HIM......
WE NEED TO MAKE A DECISION...
...ALBEIT ***FATAL.***

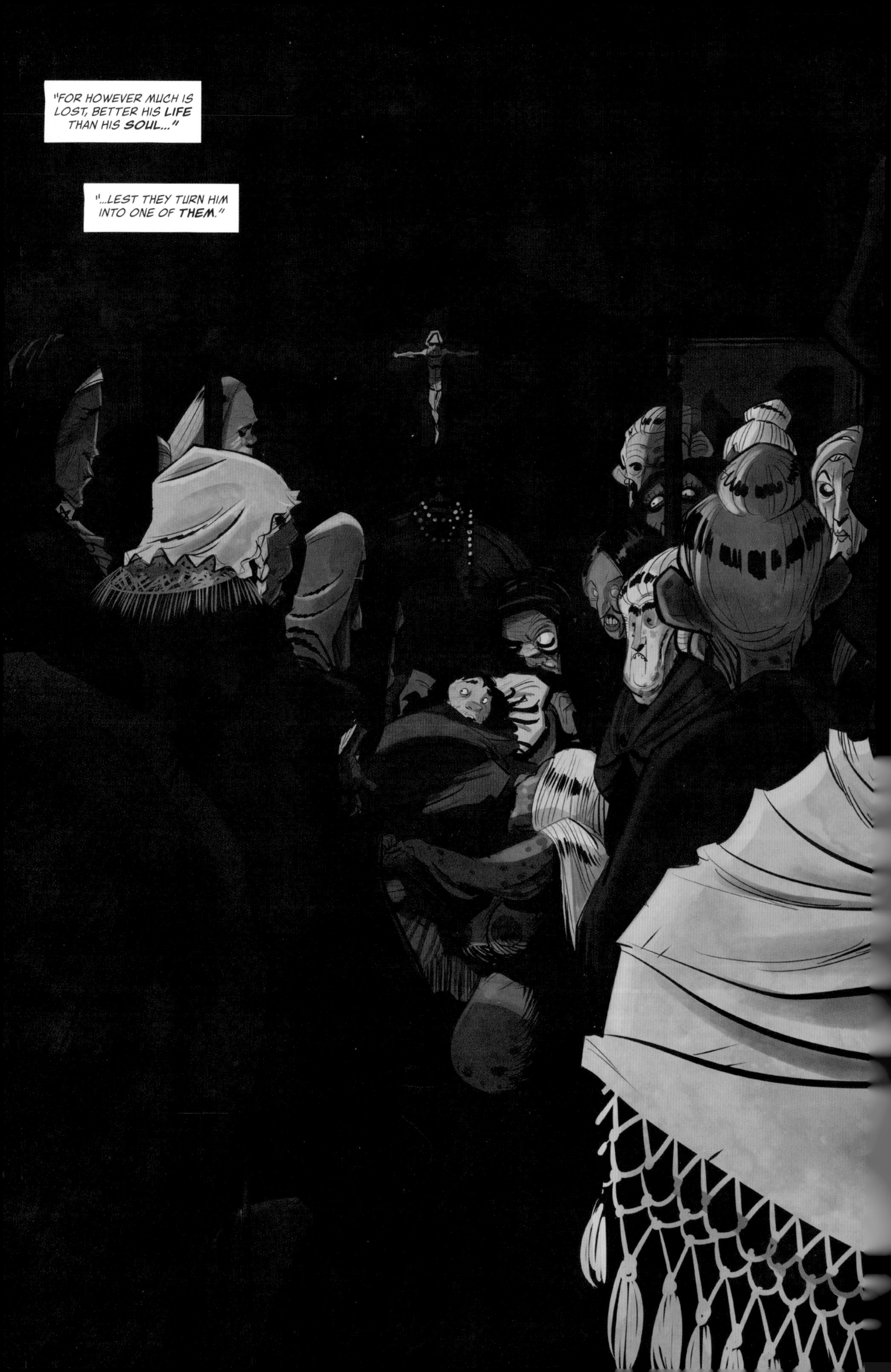
"FOR HOWEVER MUCH IS LOST, BETTER HIS LIFE THAN HIS SOUL..."
"...LEST THEY TURN HIM INTO ONE OF THEM."

# Second act
## María Teresa

Madrid, 1794

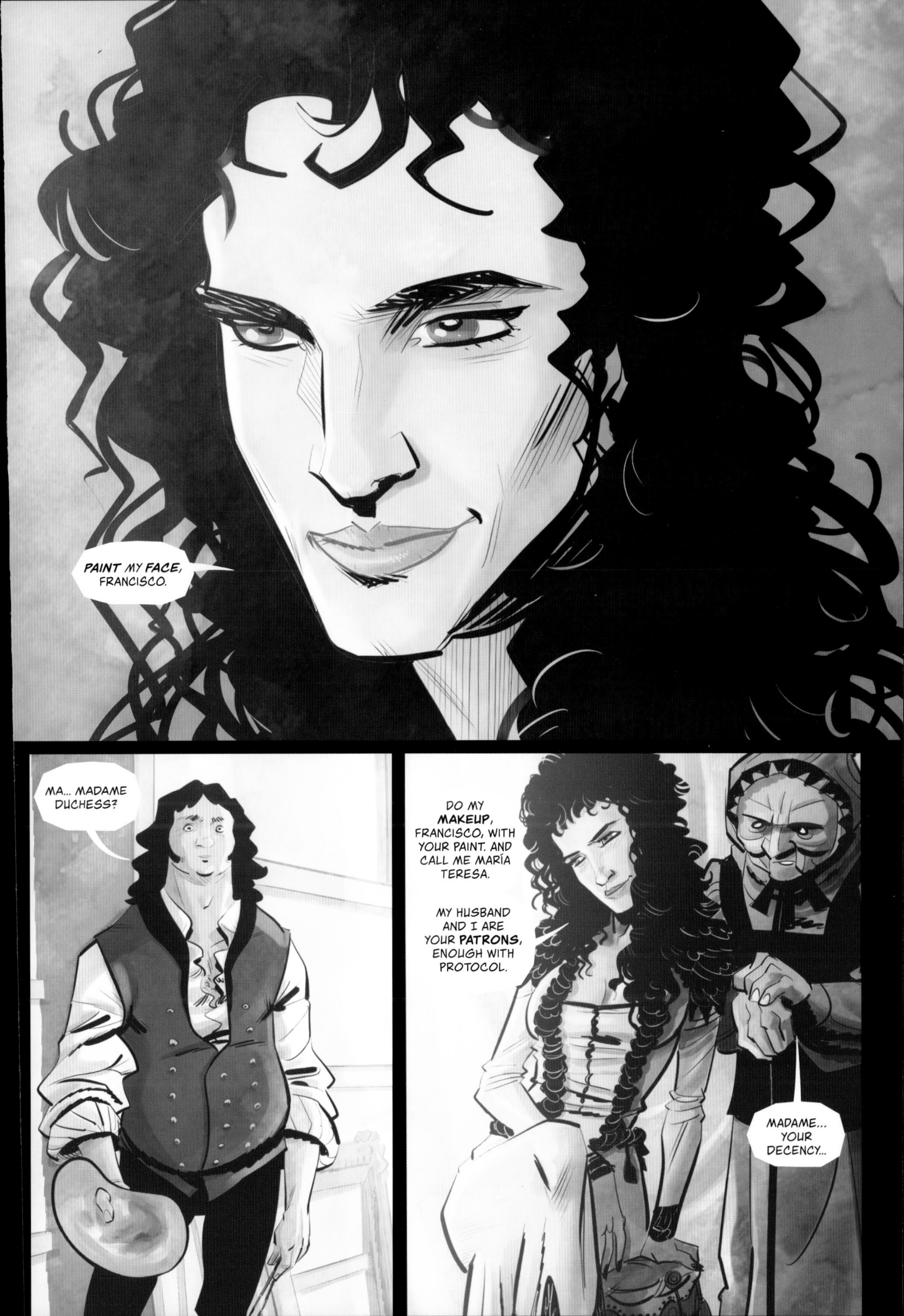
PAINT MY FACE, FRANCISCO.
MA... MADAME DUCHESS?
DO MY MAKEUP, FRANCISCO, WITH YOUR PAINT. AND CALL ME MARÍA TERESA.
MY HUSBAND AND I ARE YOUR PATRONS, ENOUGH WITH PROTOCOL.
MADAME... YOUR DECENCY...

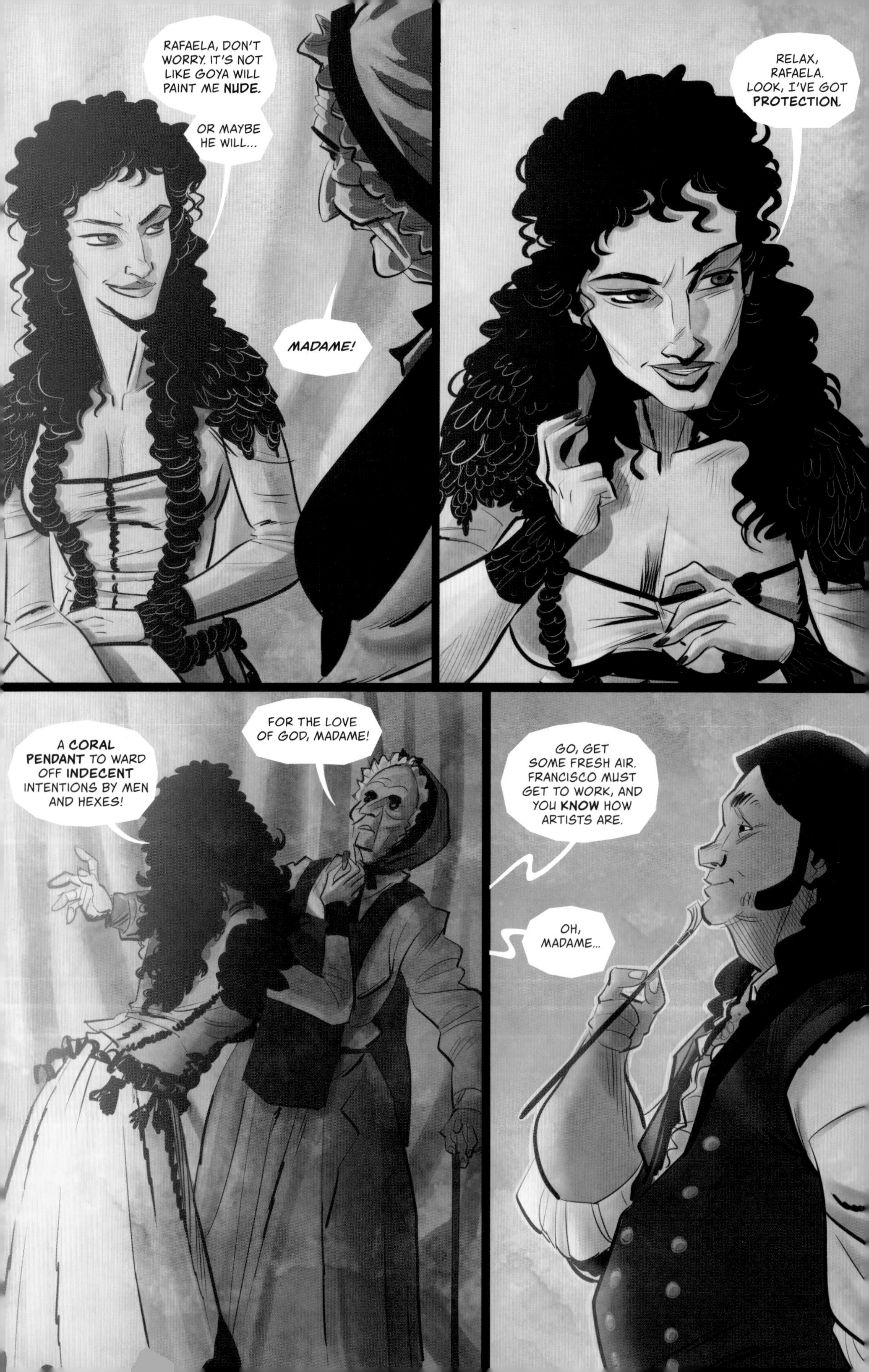
RAFAELA, DON'T WORRY. IT'S NOT LIKE GOYA WILL PAINT ME **NUDE.**
OR MAYBE HE WILL...
*MADAME!*
RELAX, RAFAELA. LOOK, I'VE GOT **PROTECTION.**
A **CORAL PENDANT** TO WARD OFF **INDECENT** INTENTIONS BY MEN AND HEXES!
FOR THE LOVE OF GOD, MADAME!
GO, GET SOME FRESH AIR. FRANCISCO MUST GET TO WORK, AND YOU **KNOW** HOW ARTISTS ARE.
OH, MADAME...

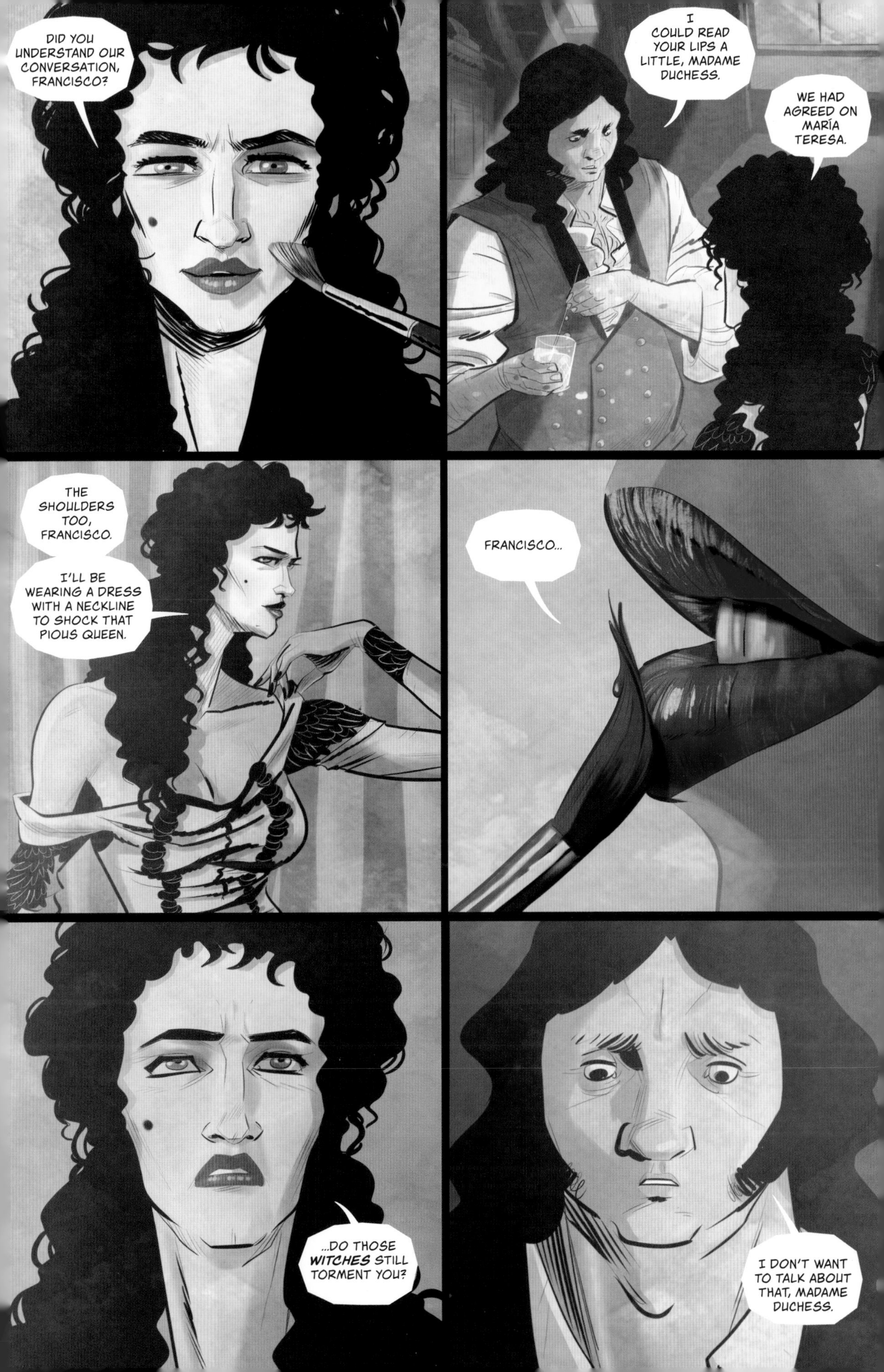
DID YOU UNDERSTAND OUR CONVERSATION, FRANCISCO?
I COULD READ YOUR LIPS A LITTLE, MADAME DUCHESS.
WE HAD AGREED ON MARÍA TERESA.
THE SHOULDERS TOO, FRANCISCO.
I'LL BE WEARING A DRESS WITH A NECKLINE TO SHOCK THAT PIOUS QUEEN.
FRANCISCO...
...DO THOSE *WITCHES* STILL TORMENT YOU?
I DON'T WANT TO TALK ABOUT THAT, MADAME DUCHESS.

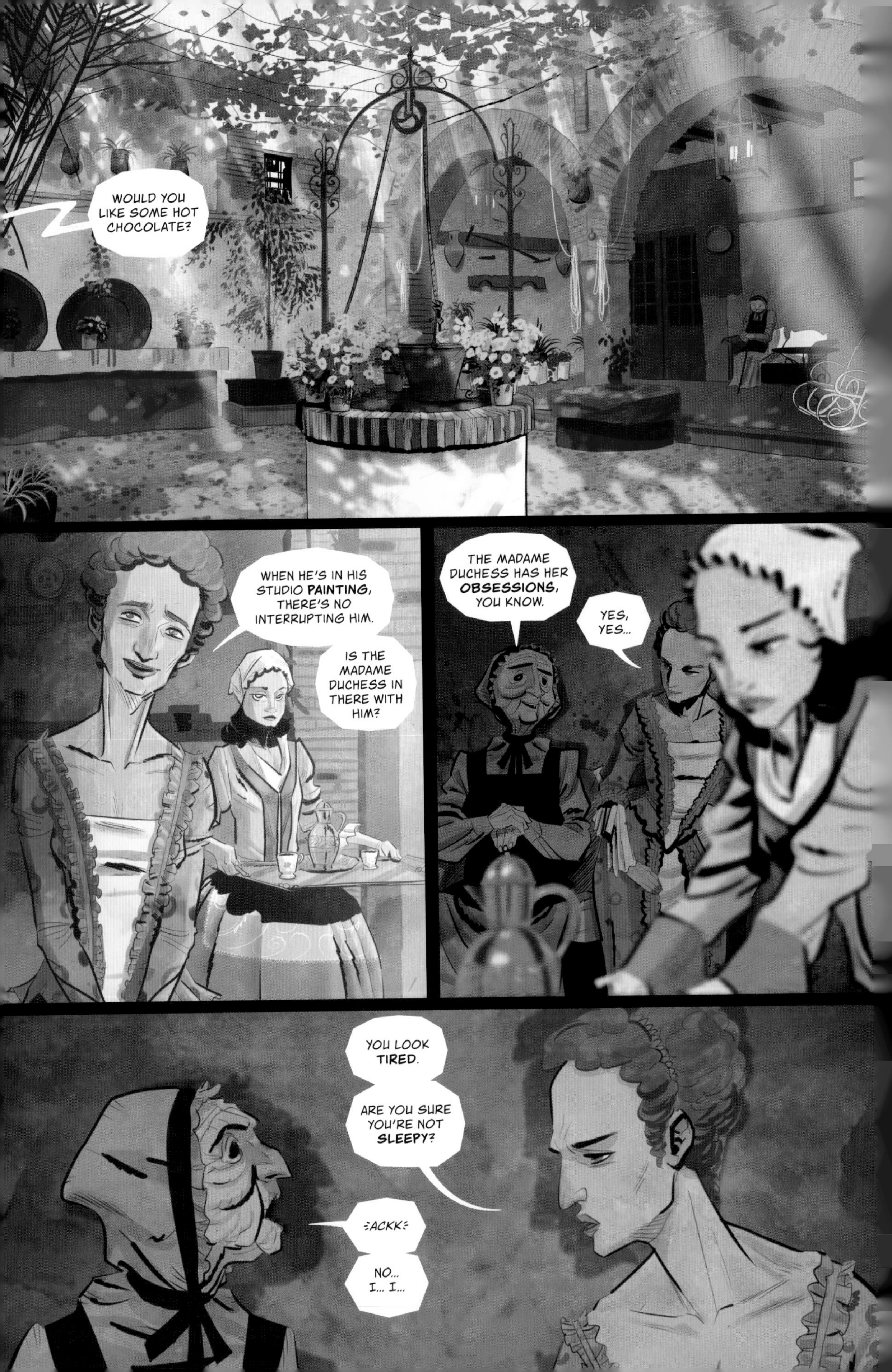
WOULD YOU LIKE SOME HOT CHOCOLATE?
WHEN HE'S IN HIS STUDIO PAINTING, THERE'S NO INTERRUPTING HIM.
IS THE MADAME DUCHESS IN THERE WITH HIM?
THE MADAME DUCHESS HAS HER OBSESSIONS, YOU KNOW.
YES, YES...
YOU LOOK TIRED.
ARE YOU SURE YOU'RE NOT SLEEPY?
ACKK
NO... I... I...

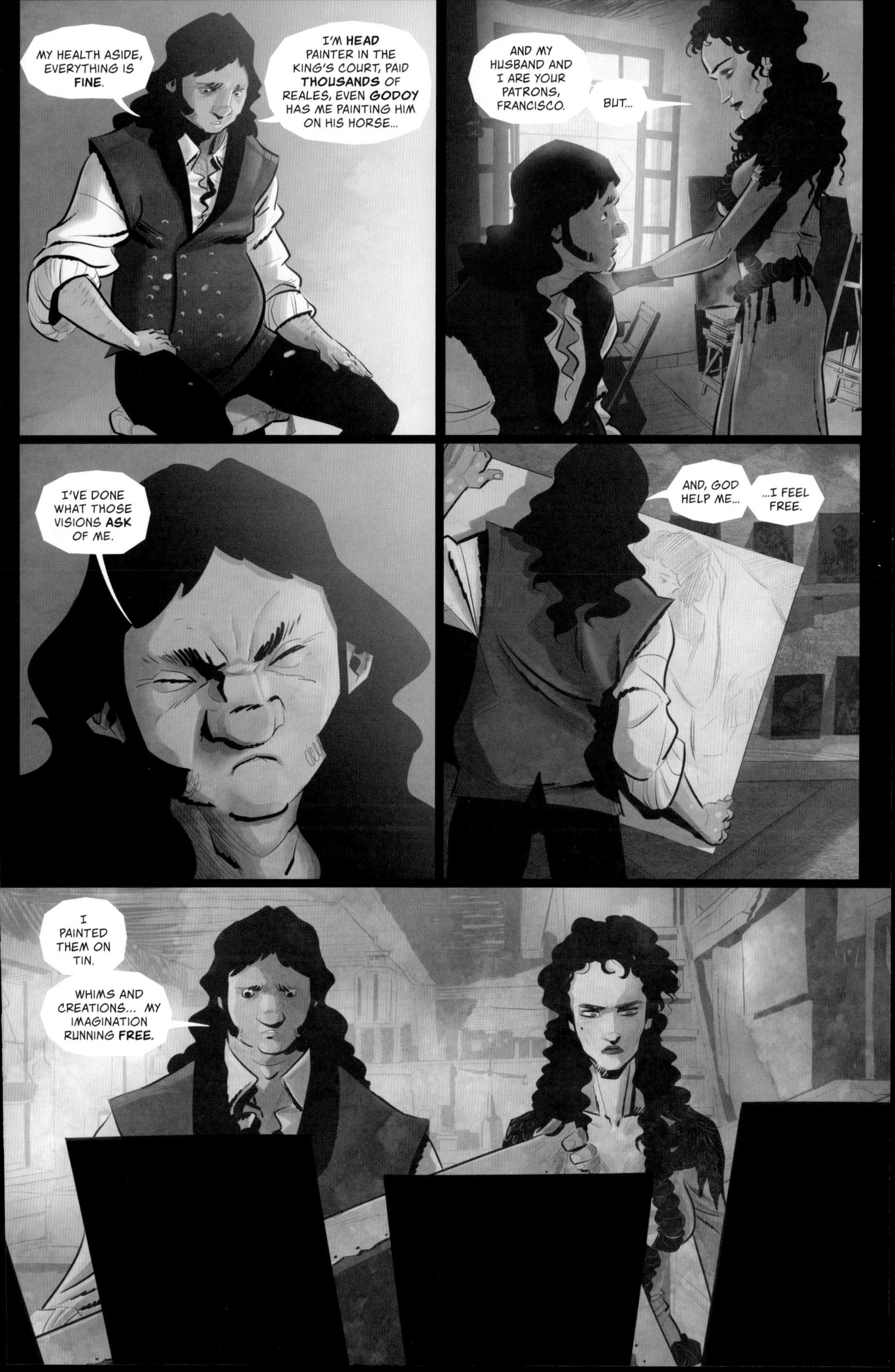
MY HEALTH ASIDE, EVERYTHING IS FINE.
I'M HEAD PAINTER IN THE KING'S COURT, PAID THOUSANDS OF REALES, EVEN GODOY HAS ME PAINTING HIM ON HIS HORSE...
AND MY HUSBAND AND I ARE YOUR PATRONS, FRANCISCO.
BUT...
I'VE DONE WHAT THOSE VISIONS ASK OF ME.
AND, GOD HELP ME...
...I FEEL FREE.
I PAINTED THEM ON TIN.
WHIMS AND CREATIONS... MY IMAGINATION RUNNING FREE.

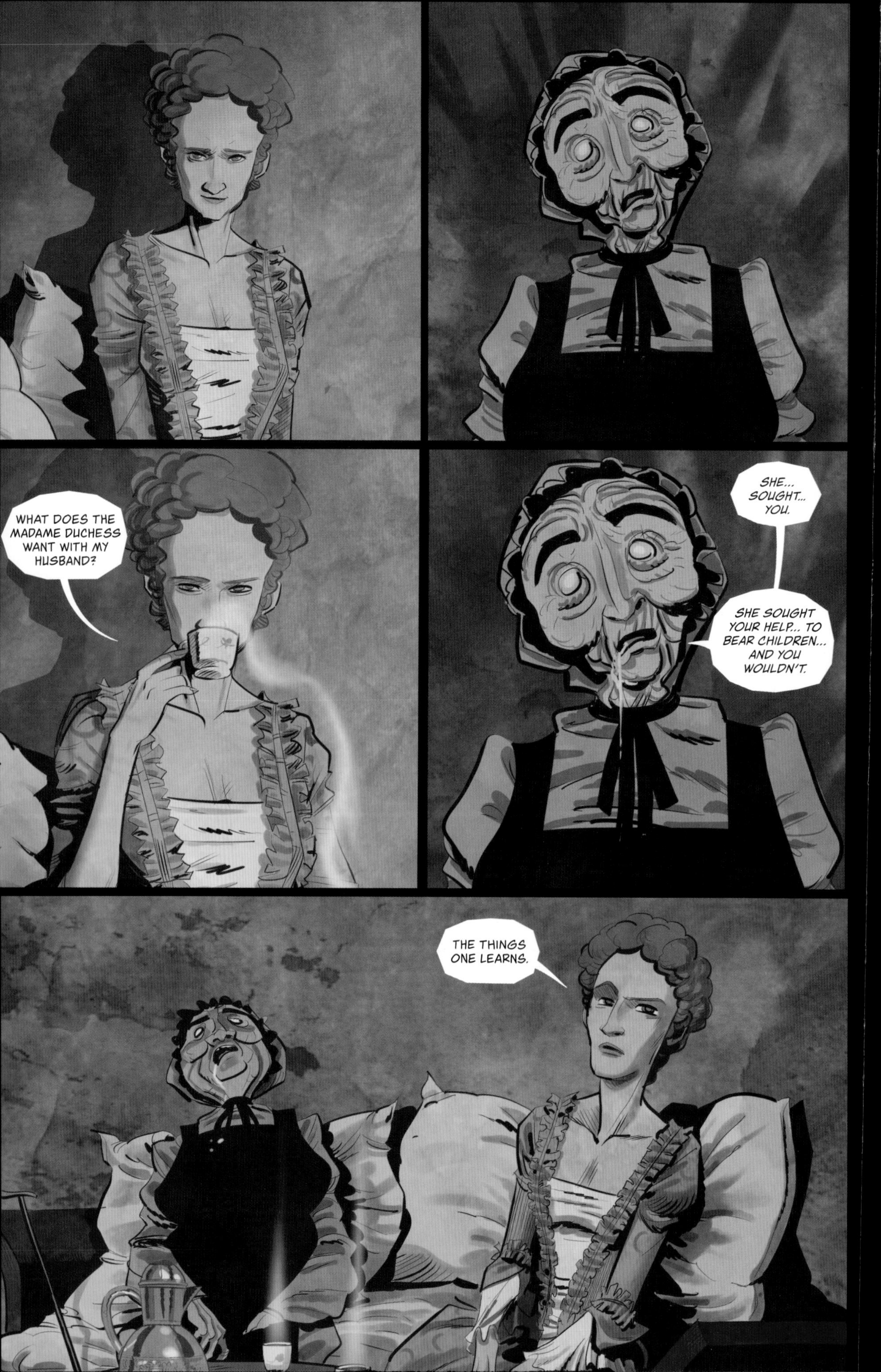
WHAT DOES THE MADAME DUCHESS WANT WITH MY HUSBAND?
SHE... SOUGHT... YOU.
SHE SOUGHT YOUR HELP... TO BEAR CHILDREN... AND YOU WOULDN'T.
THE THINGS ONE LEARNS.

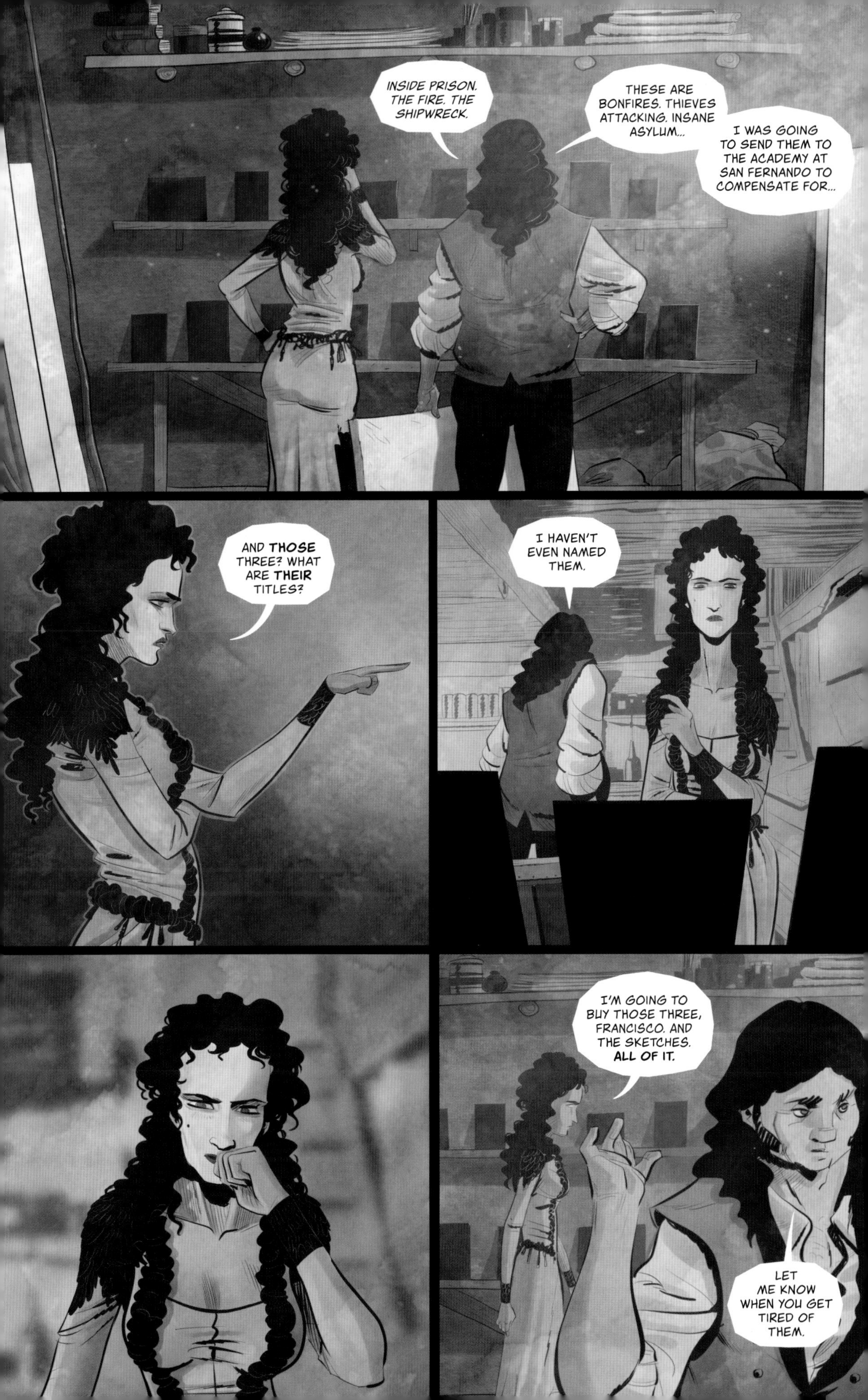
INSIDE PRISON. THE FIRE. THE SHIPWRECK.
THESE ARE BONFIRES. THIEVES ATTACKING. INSANE ASYLUM...
I WAS GOING TO SEND THEM TO THE ACADEMY AT SAN FERNANDO TO COMPENSATE FOR...
AND **THOSE** THREE? WHAT ARE **THEIR** TITLES?
I HAVEN'T EVEN NAMED THEM.
I'M GOING TO BUY THOSE THREE, FRANCISCO. AND THE SKETCHES. **ALL OF IT.**
LET ME KNOW WHEN YOU GET TIRED OF THEM.

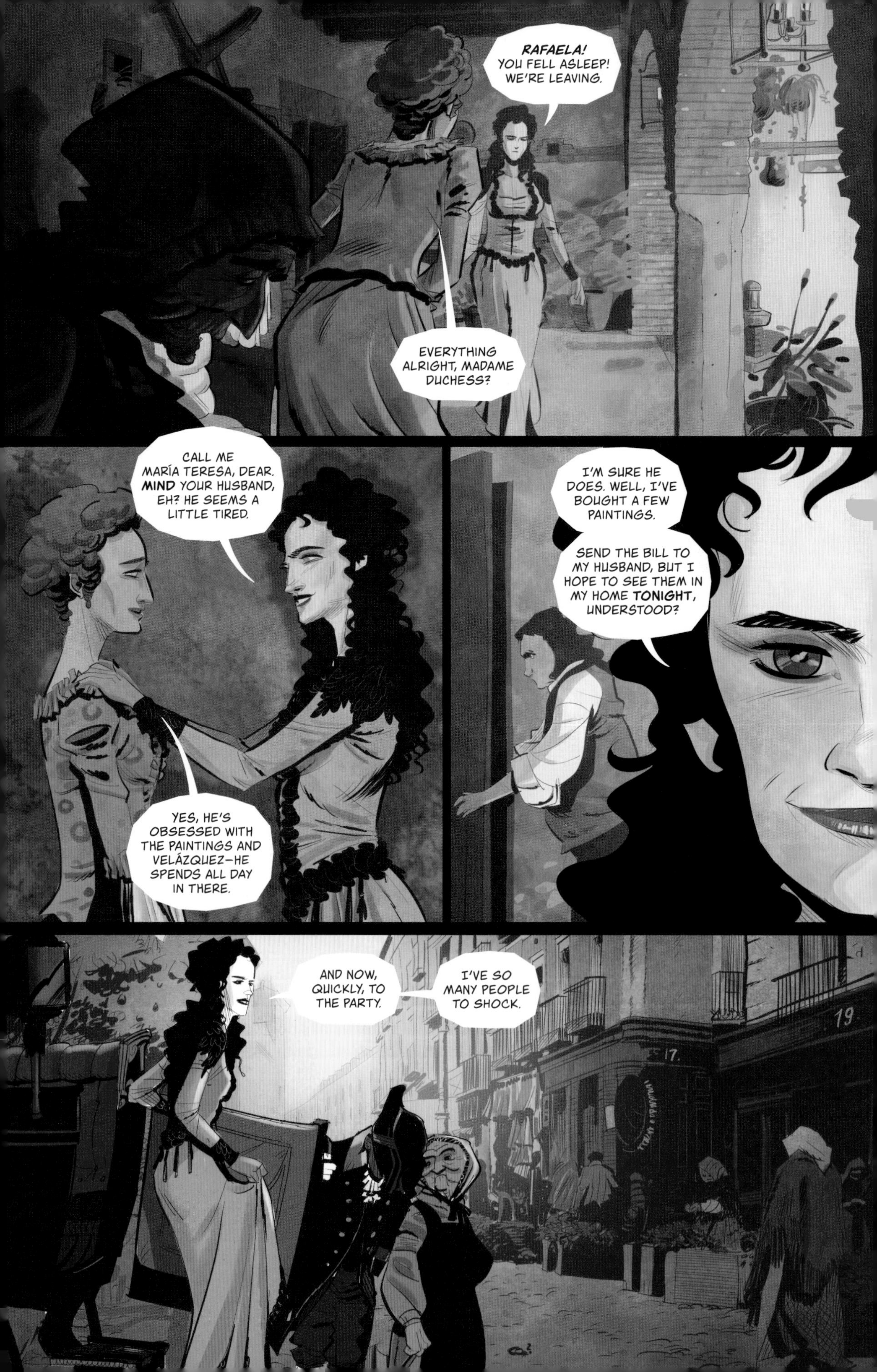

RAFAELA! YOU FELL ASLEEP! WE'RE LEAVING.
EVERYTHING ALRIGHT, MADAME DUCHESS?
CALL ME MARÍA TERESA, DEAR. MIND YOUR HUSBAND, EH? HE SEEMS A LITTLE TIRED.
YES, HE'S OBSESSED WITH THE PAINTINGS AND VELÁZQUEZ—HE SPENDS ALL DAY IN THERE.
I'M SURE HE DOES. WELL, I'VE BOUGHT A FEW PAINTINGS.
SEND THE BILL TO MY HUSBAND, BUT I HOPE TO SEE THEM IN MY HOME TONIGHT, UNDERSTOOD?
AND NOW, QUICKLY, TO THE PARTY.
I'VE SO MANY PEOPLE TO SHOCK.
17.
19.

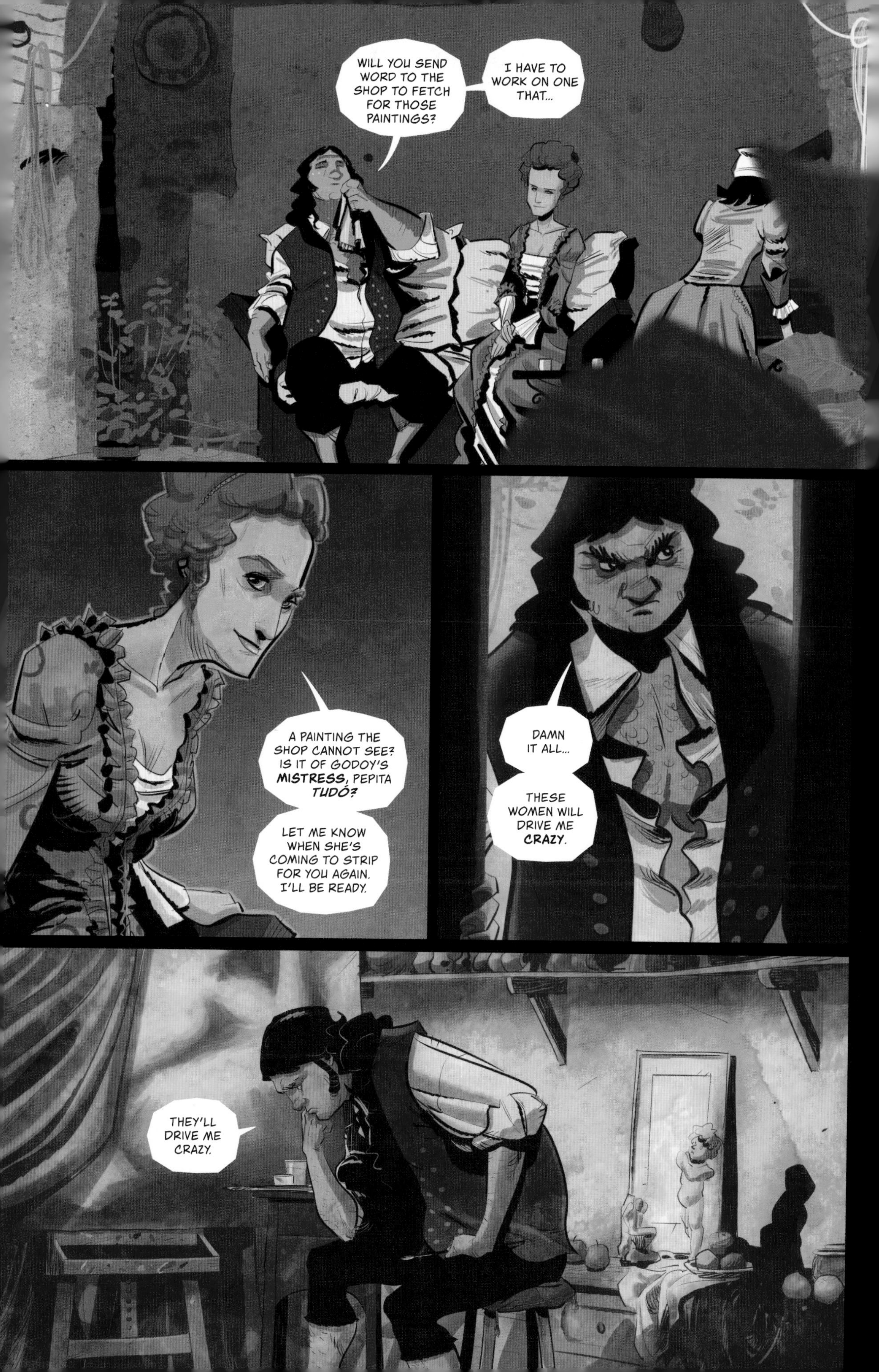
WILL YOU SEND WORD TO THE SHOP TO FETCH FOR THOSE PAINTINGS?
I HAVE TO WORK ON ONE THAT...
A PAINTING THE SHOP CANNOT SEE? IS IT OF GODOY'S **MISTRESS,** PEPITA ***TUDÓ?***
LET ME KNOW WHEN SHE'S COMING TO STRIP FOR YOU AGAIN. I'LL BE READY.
DAMN IT ALL...
THESE WOMEN WILL DRIVE ME **CRAZY**.
THEY'LL DRIVE ME CRAZY.

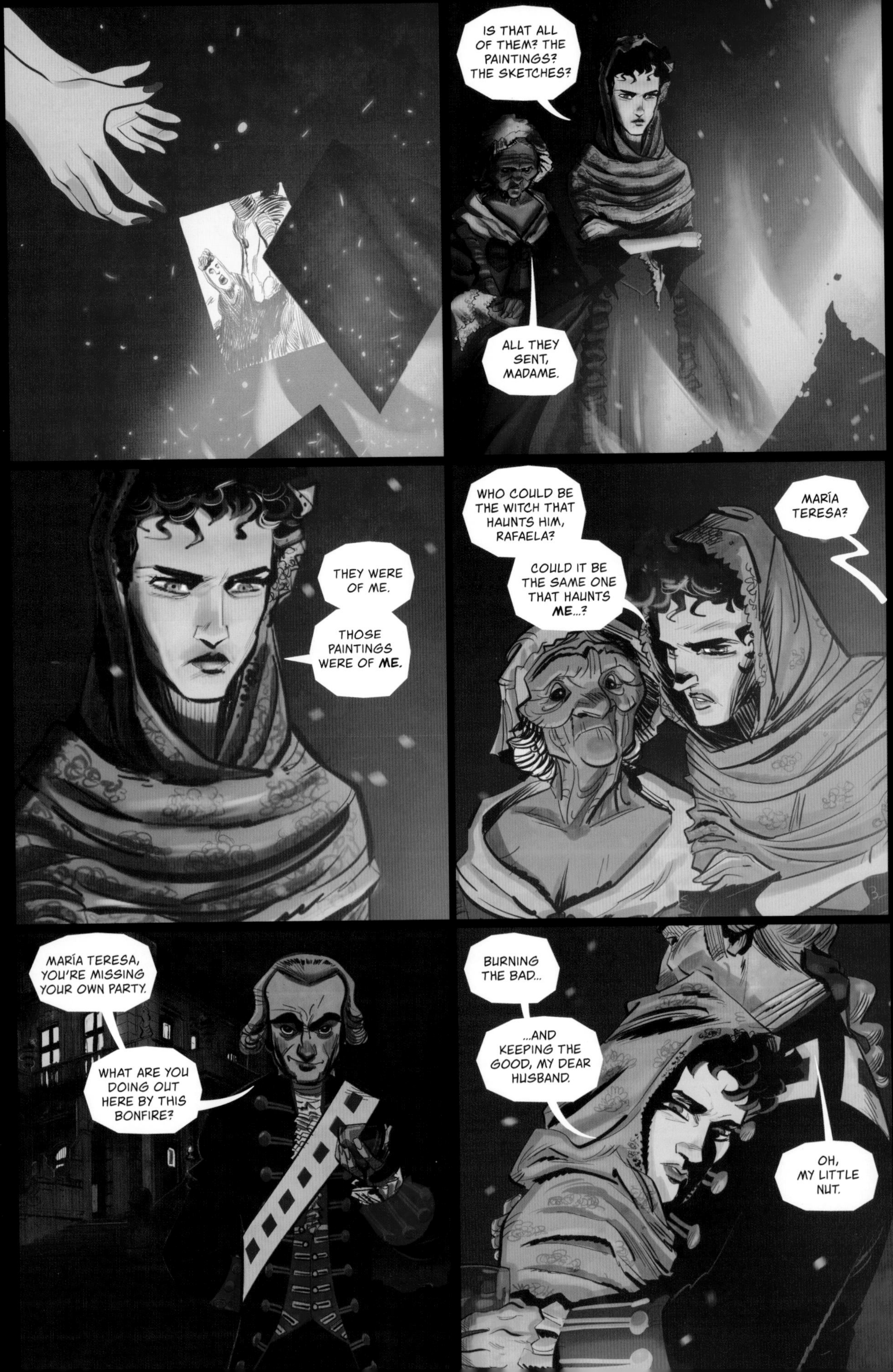
IS THAT ALL OF THEM? THE PAINTINGS? THE SKETCHES?
ALL THEY SENT, MADAME.
THEY WERE OF ME.
THOSE PAINTINGS WERE OF **ME.**
WHO COULD BE THE WITCH THAT HAUNTS HIM, RAFAELA?
COULD IT BE THE SAME ONE THAT HAUNTS **ME**...?
MARÍA TERESA?
MARÍA TERESA, YOU'RE MISSING YOUR OWN PARTY.
WHAT ARE YOU DOING OUT HERE BY THIS BONFIRE?
BURNING THE BAD...
...AND KEEPING THE GOOD, MY DEAR HUSBAND.
OH, MY LITTLE NUT.

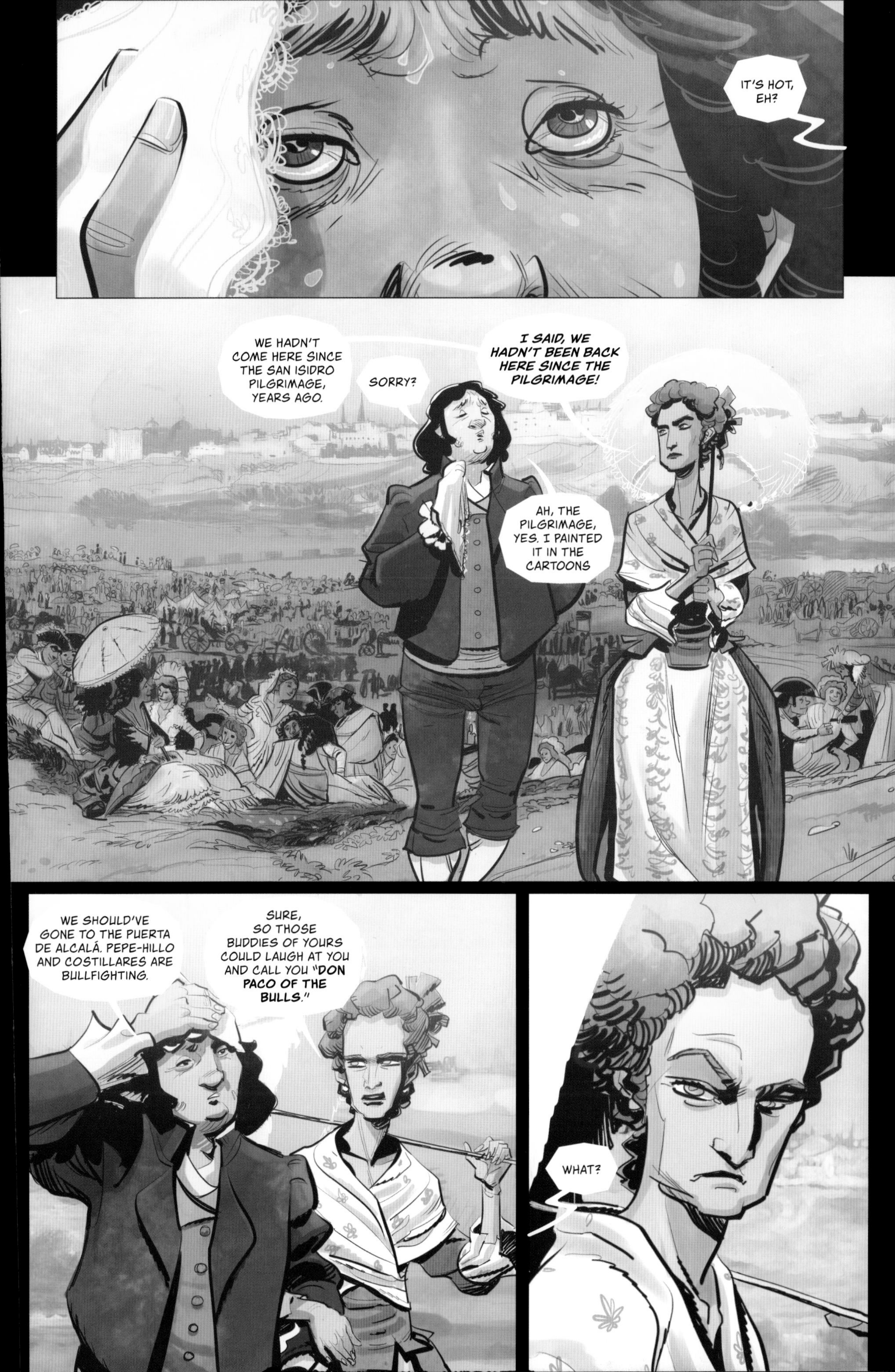
IT'S HOT, EH?
WE HADN'T COME HERE SINCE THE SAN ISIDRO PILGRIMAGE, YEARS AGO.
SORRY?
I SAID, WE HADN'T BEEN BACK HERE SINCE THE PILGRIMAGE!
AH, THE PILGRIMAGE, YES. I PAINTED IT IN THE CARTOONS
WE SHOULD'VE GONE TO THE PUERTA DE ALCALÁ. PEPE-HILLO AND COSTILLARES ARE BULLFIGHTING.
SURE, SO THOSE BUDDIES OF YOURS COULD LAUGH AT YOU AND CALL YOU "DON PACO OF THE BULLS."
WHAT?

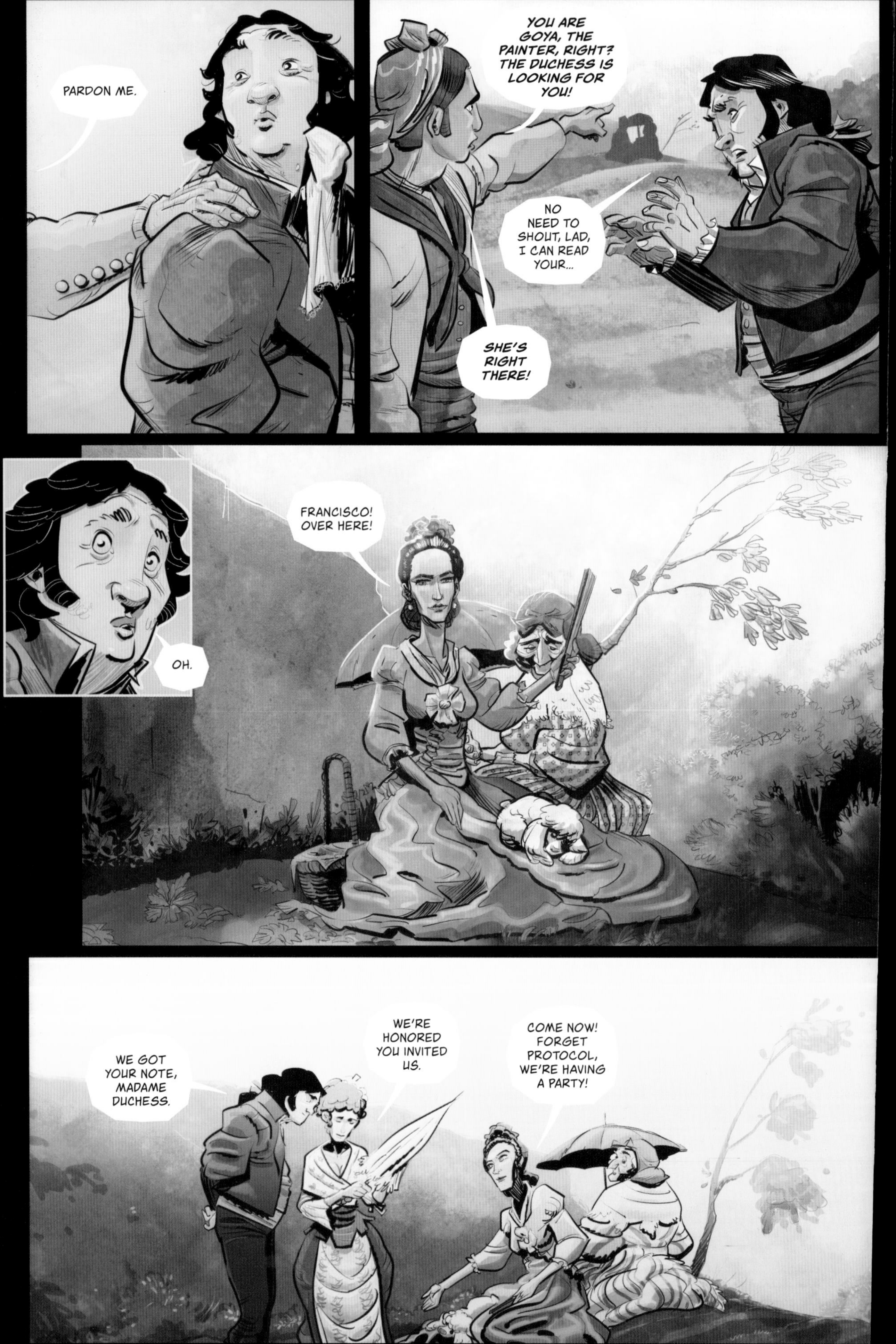
PARDON ME.
YOU ARE GOYA, THE PAINTER, RIGHT? THE DUCHESS IS LOOKING FOR YOU!
NO NEED TO SHOUT, LAD, I CAN READ YOUR...
SHE'S RIGHT THERE!
OH.
FRANCISCO! OVER HERE!
WE GOT YOUR NOTE, MADAME DUCHESS.
WE'RE HONORED YOU INVITED US.
COME NOW! FORGET PROTOCOL, WE'RE HAVING A PARTY!

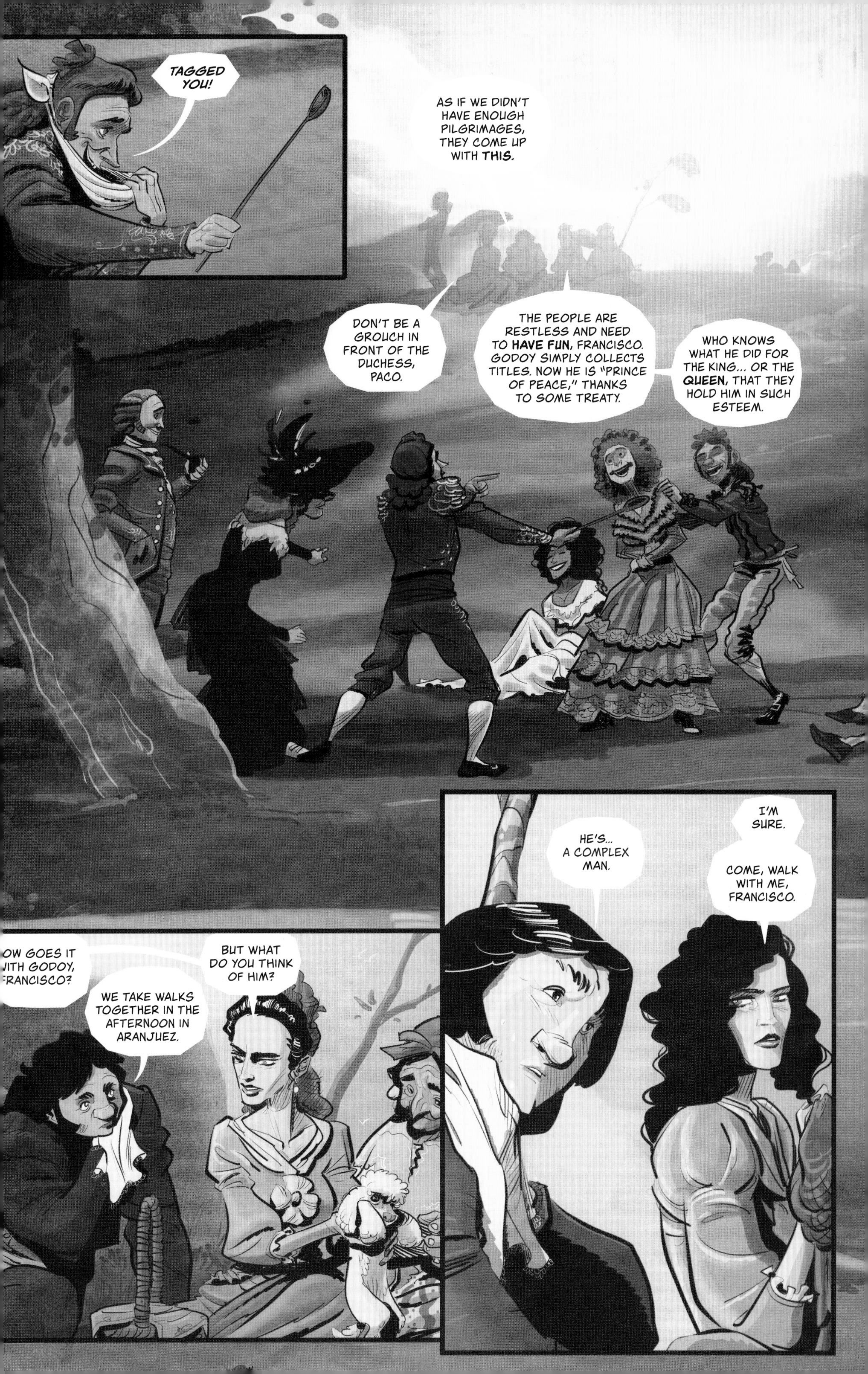

TAGGED YOU!
AS IF WE DIDN'T HAVE ENOUGH PILGRIMAGES, THEY COME UP WITH **THIS.**
DON'T BE A GROUCH IN FRONT OF THE DUCHESS, PACO.
THE PEOPLE ARE RESTLESS AND NEED TO **HAVE FUN**, FRANCISCO. GODOY SIMPLY COLLECTS TITLES. NOW HE IS "PRINCE OF PEACE," THANKS TO SOME TREATY.
WHO KNOWS WHAT HE DID FOR THE KING... OR THE **QUEEN**, THAT THEY HOLD HIM IN SUCH ESTEEM.
OW GOES IT WITH GODOY, FRANCISCO?
WE TAKE WALKS TOGETHER IN THE AFTERNOON IN ARANJUEZ.
BUT WHAT DO YOU THINK OF HIM?
HE'S... A COMPLEX MAN.
I'M SURE.
COME, WALK WITH ME, FRANCISCO.

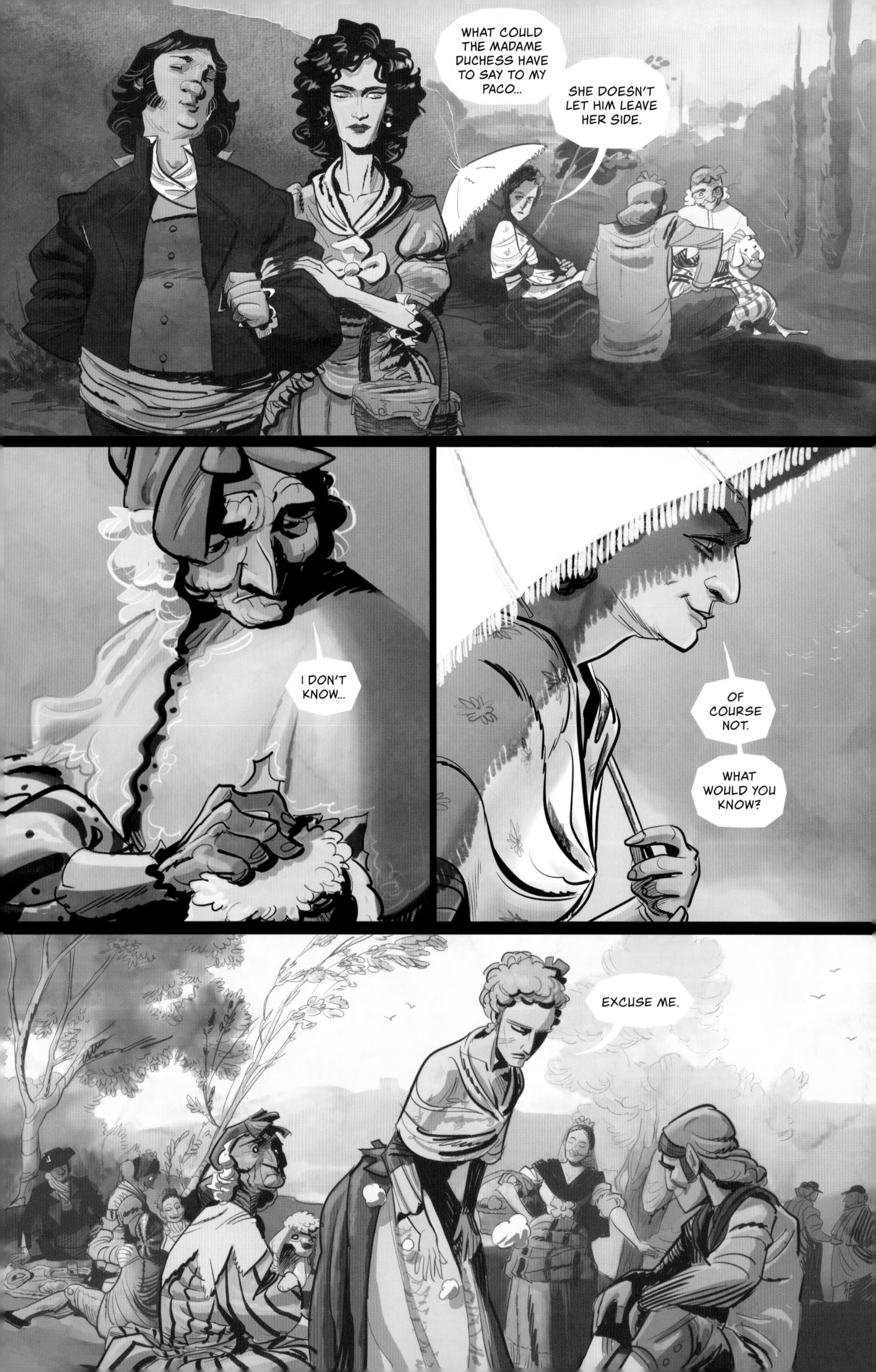

WHAT COULD THE MADAME DUCHESS HAVE TO SAY TO MY PACO...
SHE DOESN'T LET HIM LEAVE HER SIDE.
I DON'T KNOW...
OF COURSE NOT.
WHAT WOULD YOU KNOW?
EXCUSE ME.

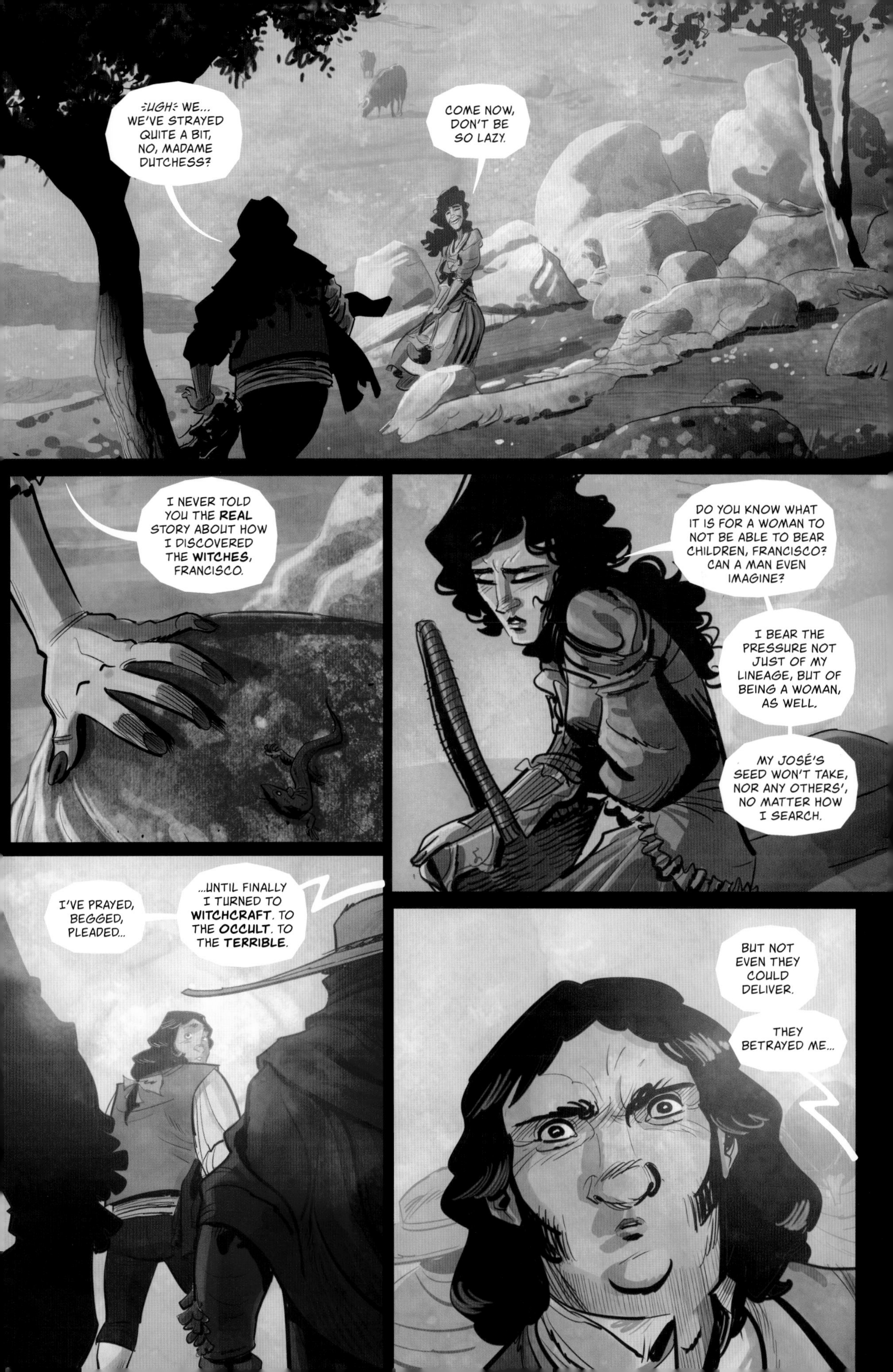

=UGH= WE... WE'VE STRAYED QUITE A BIT, NO, MADAME DUTCHESS?
COME NOW, DON'T BE SO LAZY.
I NEVER TOLD YOU THE **REAL** STORY ABOUT HOW I DISCOVERED THE **WITCHES**, FRANCISCO.
DO YOU KNOW WHAT IT IS FOR A WOMAN TO NOT BE ABLE TO BEAR CHILDREN, FRANCISCO? CAN A MAN EVEN IMAGINE?
I BEAR THE PRESSURE NOT JUST OF MY LINEAGE, BUT OF BEING A WOMAN, AS WELL.
MY JOSÉ'S SEED WON'T TAKE, NOR ANY OTHERS', NO MATTER HOW I SEARCH.
I'VE PRAYED, BEGGED, PLEADED...
...UNTIL FINALLY I TURNED TO **WITCHCRAFT**. TO THE **OCCULT**. TO THE **TERRIBLE**.
BUT NOT EVEN THEY COULD DELIVER.
THEY BETRAYED ME...

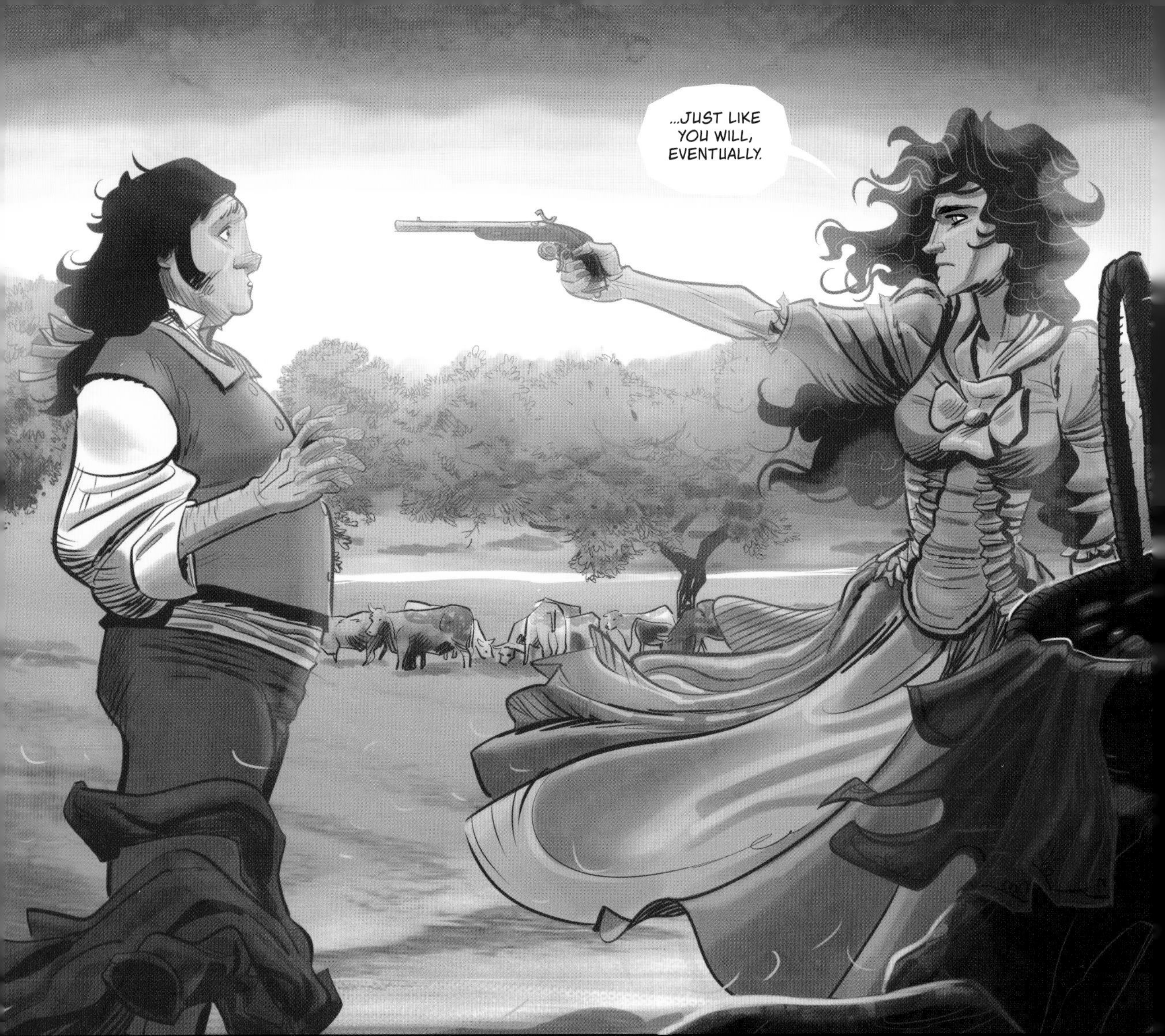
...JUST LIKE YOU WILL, EVENTUALLY.

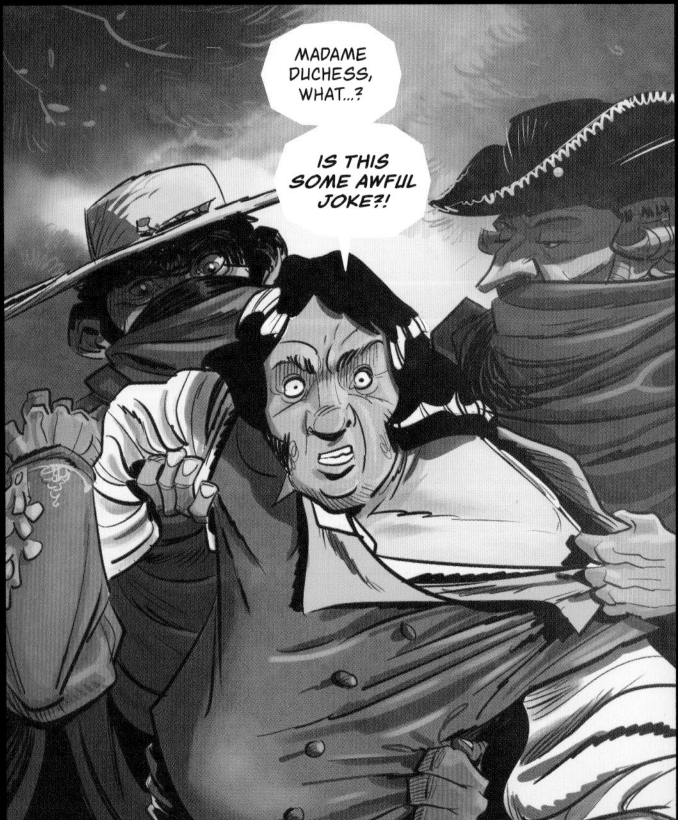
MADAME DUCHESS, WHAT...?
IS THIS SOME AWFUL JOKE?!

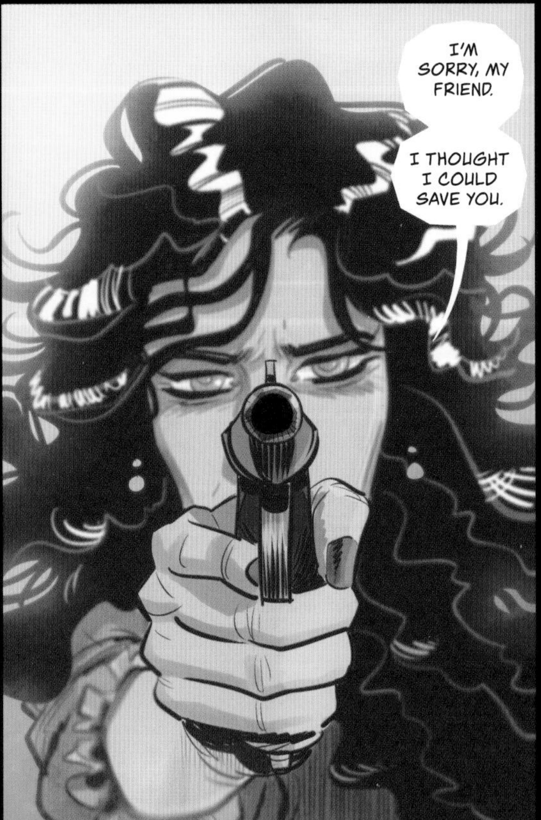
I'M SORRY, MY FRIEND.
I THOUGHT I COULD SAVE YOU.

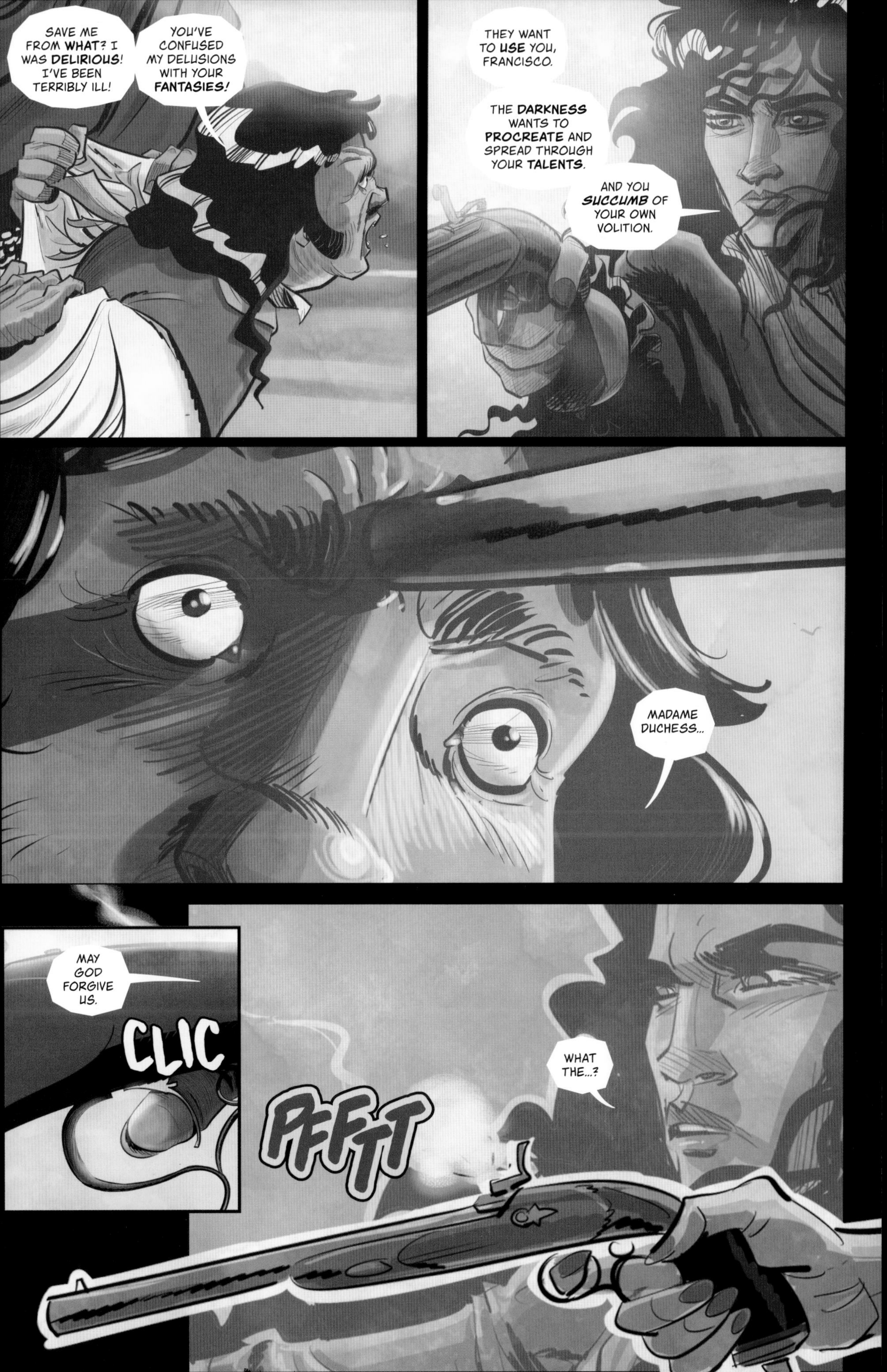
SAVE ME FROM WHAT? I WAS DELIRIOUS! I'VE BEEN TERRIBLY ILL!
YOU'VE CONFUSED MY DELUSIONS WITH YOUR FANTASIES!
THEY WANT TO USE YOU, FRANCISCO.
THE DARKNESS WANTS TO PROCREATE AND SPREAD THROUGH YOUR TALENTS.
AND YOU SUCCUMB OF YOUR OWN VOLITION.
MADAME DUCHESS...
MAY GOD FORGIVE US.
CLIC
PFFTT
WHAT THE...?

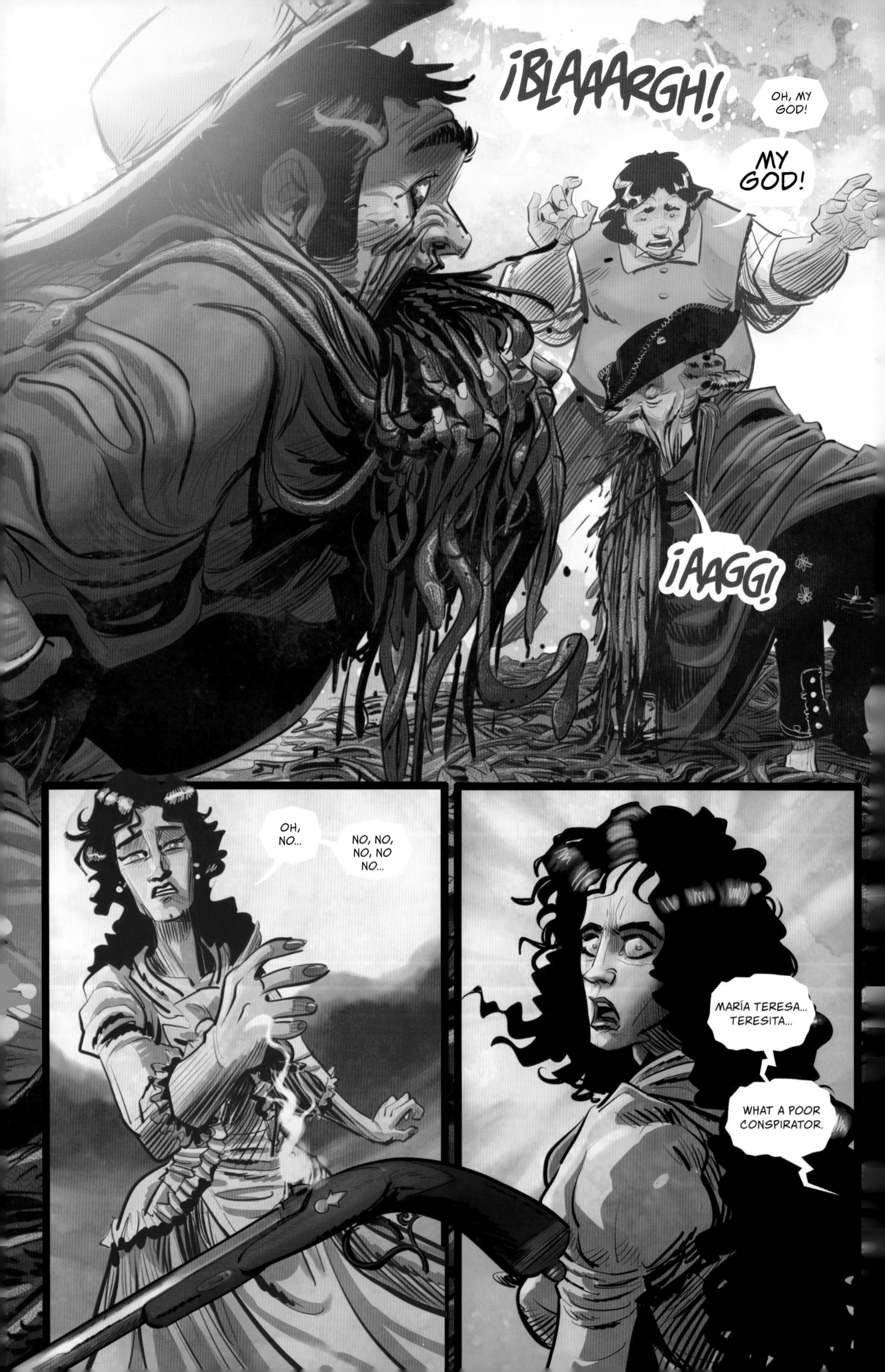
¡BLAAARGH!
OH, MY GOD!
MY GOD!
¡AAGG!
OH, NO...
NO, NO, NO, NO NO...
MARÍA TERESA... TERESITA...
WHAT A POOR CONSPIRATOR.

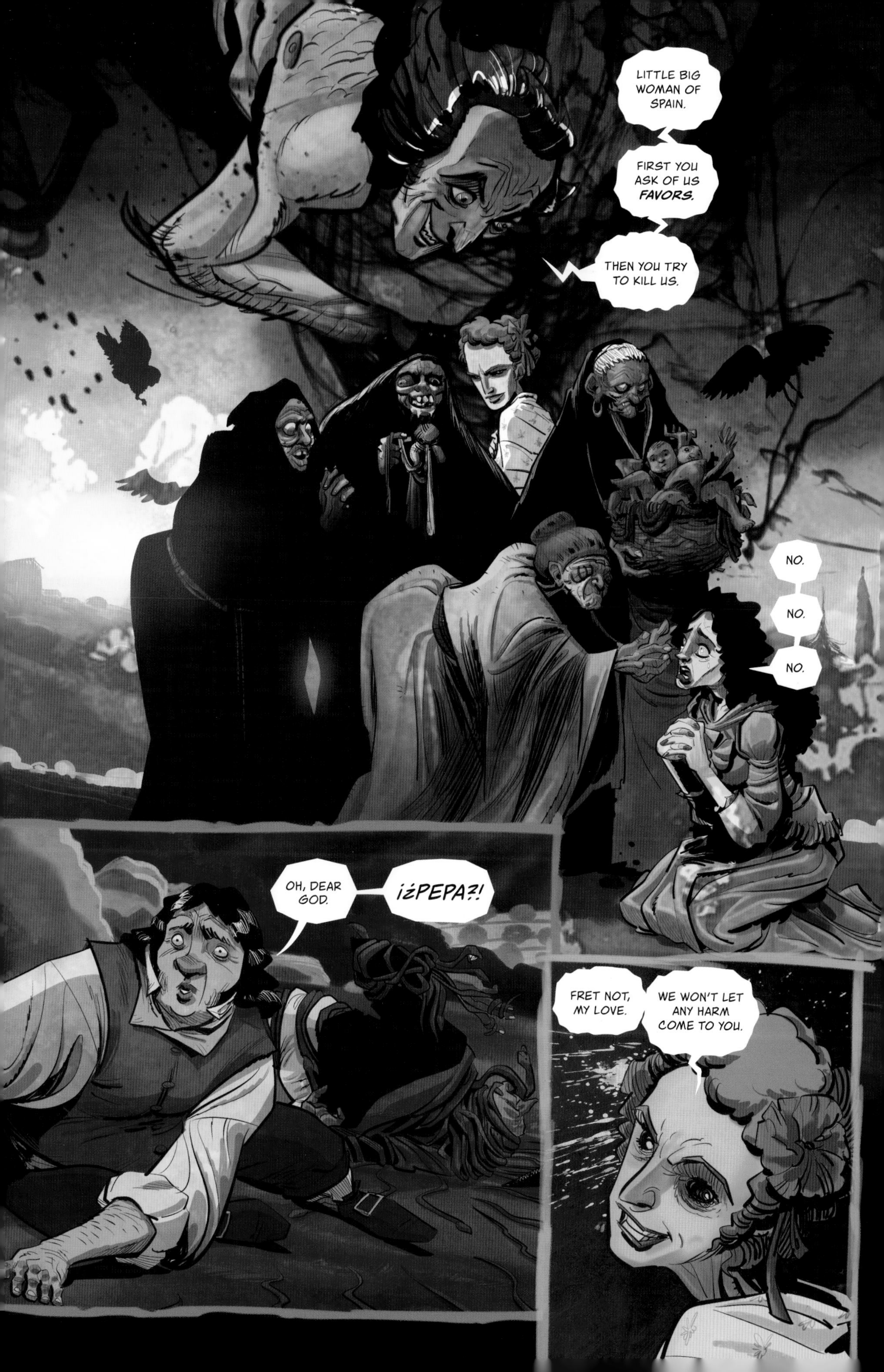
LITTLE BIG WOMAN OF SPAIN.
FIRST YOU ASK OF US FAVORS.
THEN YOU TRY TO KILL US.
NO.
NO.
NO.
OH, DEAR GOD.
¡¿PEPA?!
FRET NOT, MY LOVE.
WE WON'T LET ANY HARM COME TO YOU.

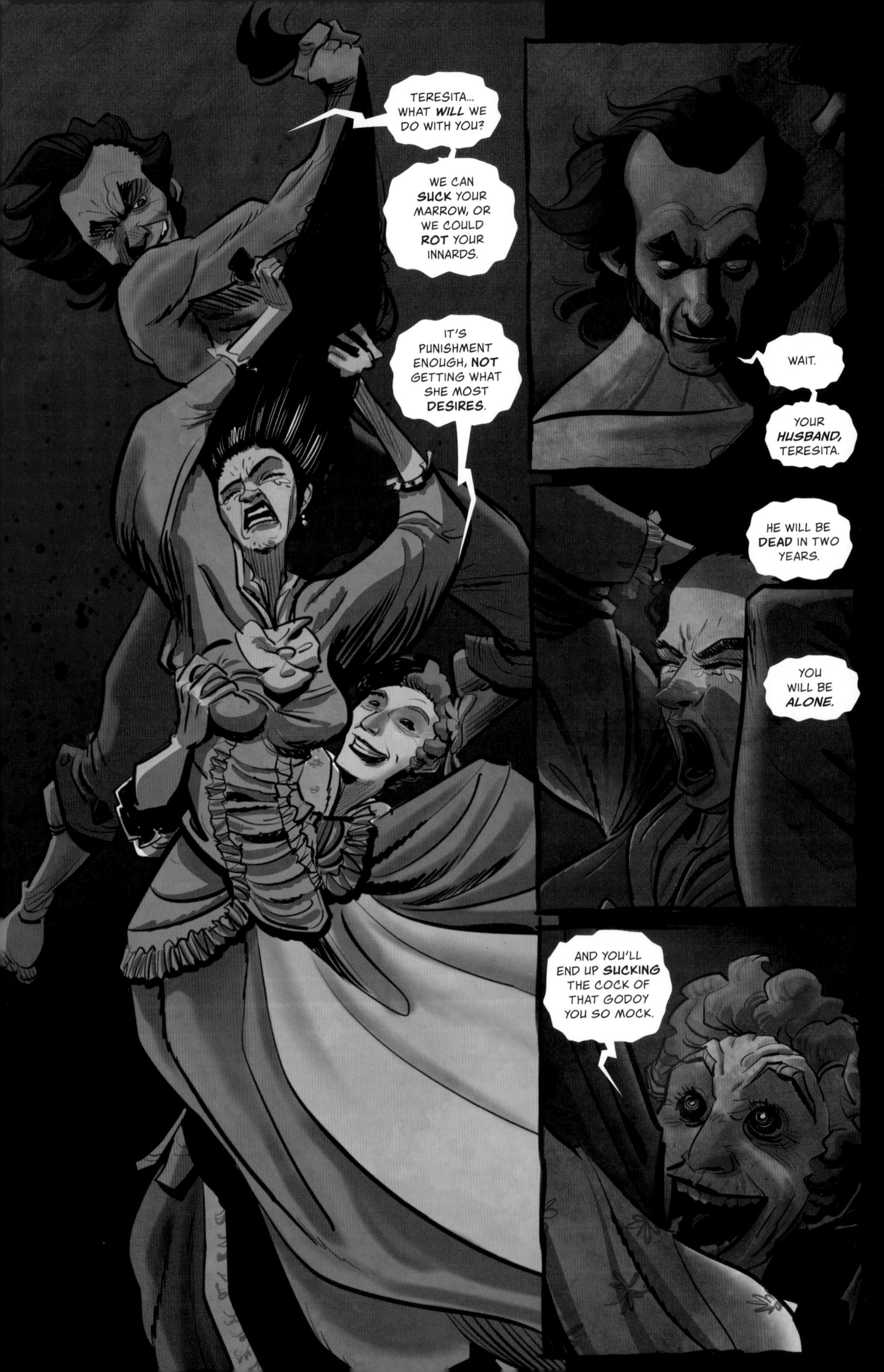
TERESITA... WHAT **WILL** WE DO WITH YOU?
WE CAN **SUCK** YOUR MARROW, OR WE COULD **ROT** YOUR INNARDS.
IT'S PUNISHMENT ENOUGH, **NOT** GETTING WHAT SHE MOST **DESIRES**.
WAIT.
YOUR ***HUSBAND,*** TERESITA.
HE WILL BE **DEAD** IN TWO YEARS.
YOU WILL BE ***ALONE.***
AND YOU'LL END UP **SUCKING** THE COCK OF THAT GODOY YOU SO MOCK.

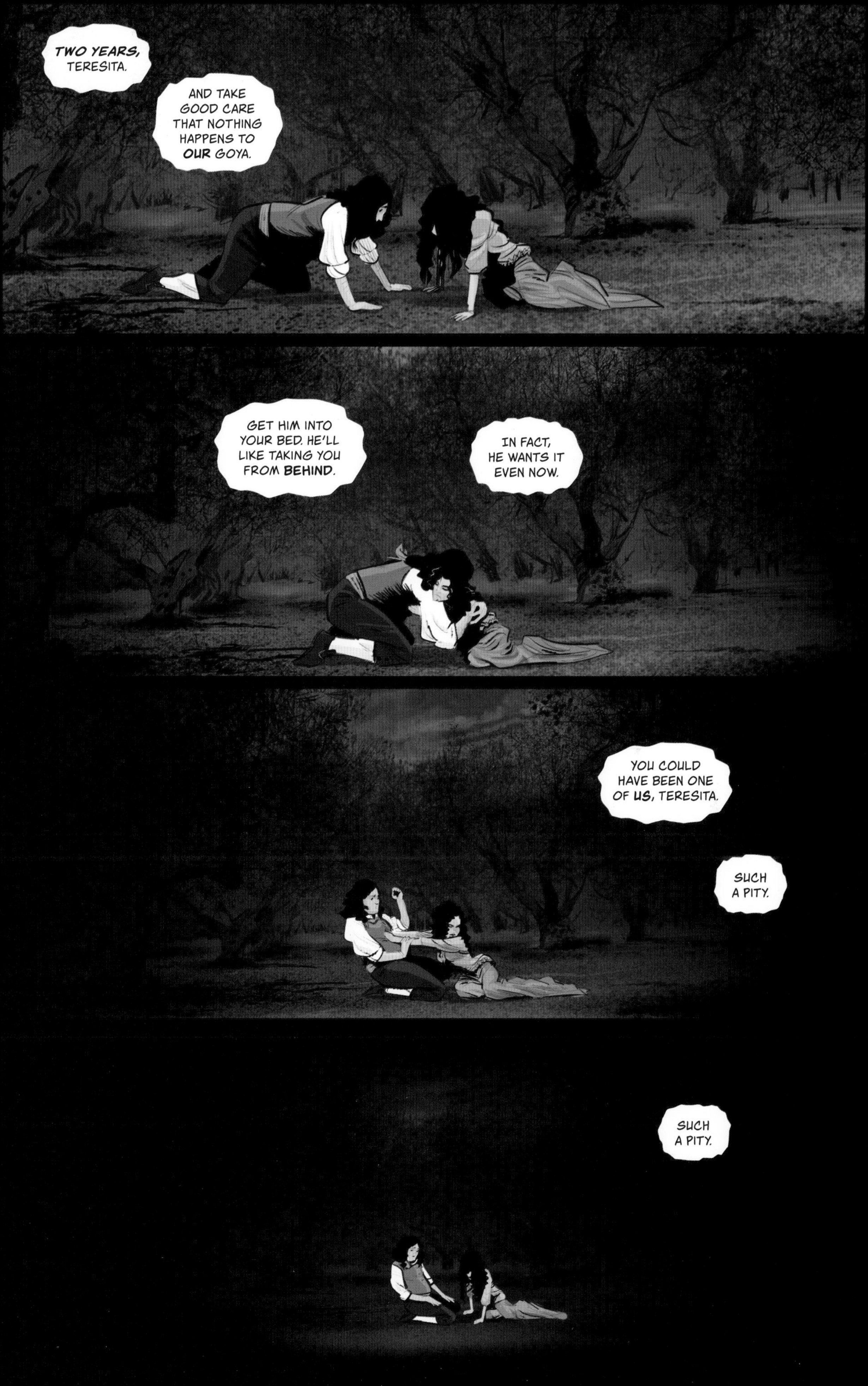

TWO YEARS, TERESITA.
AND TAKE GOOD CARE THAT NOTHING HAPPENS TO OUR GOYA.
GET HIM INTO YOUR BED. HE'LL LIKE TAKING YOU FROM BEHIND.
IN FACT, HE WANTS IT EVEN NOW.
YOU COULD HAVE BEEN ONE OF US, TERESITA.
SUCH A PITY.
SUCH A PITY.

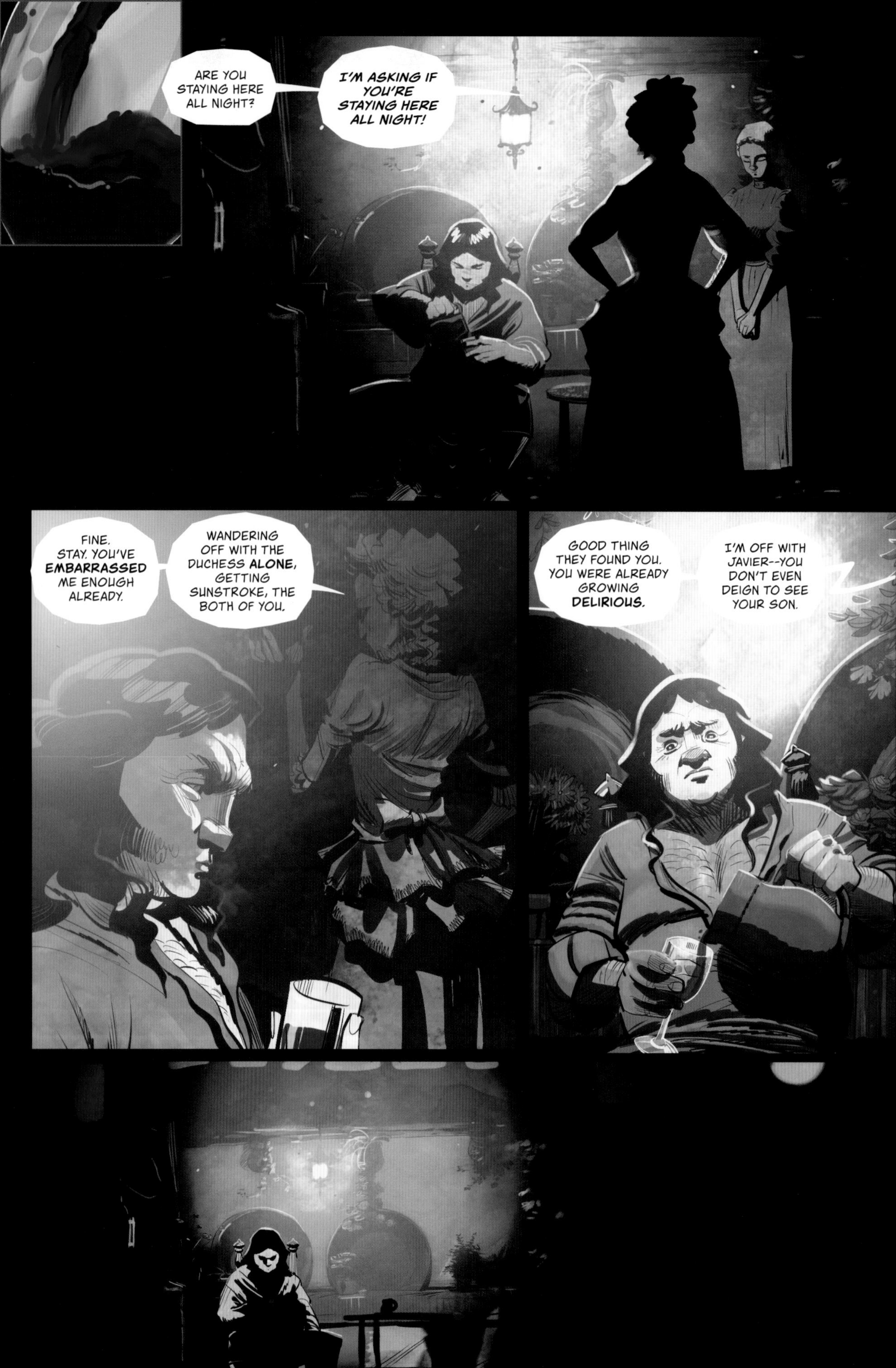
ARE YOU STAYING HERE ALL NIGHT?
I'M ASKING IF YOU'RE STAYING HERE ALL NIGHT!
FINE. STAY. YOU'VE **EMBARRASSED** ME ENOUGH ALREADY.
WANDERING OFF WITH THE DUCHESS **ALONE**, GETTING SUNSTROKE, THE BOTH OF YOU.
GOOD THING THEY FOUND YOU. YOU WERE ALREADY GROWING **DELIRIOUS.**
I'M OFF WITH JAVIER--YOU DON'T EVEN DEIGN TO SEE YOUR SON.

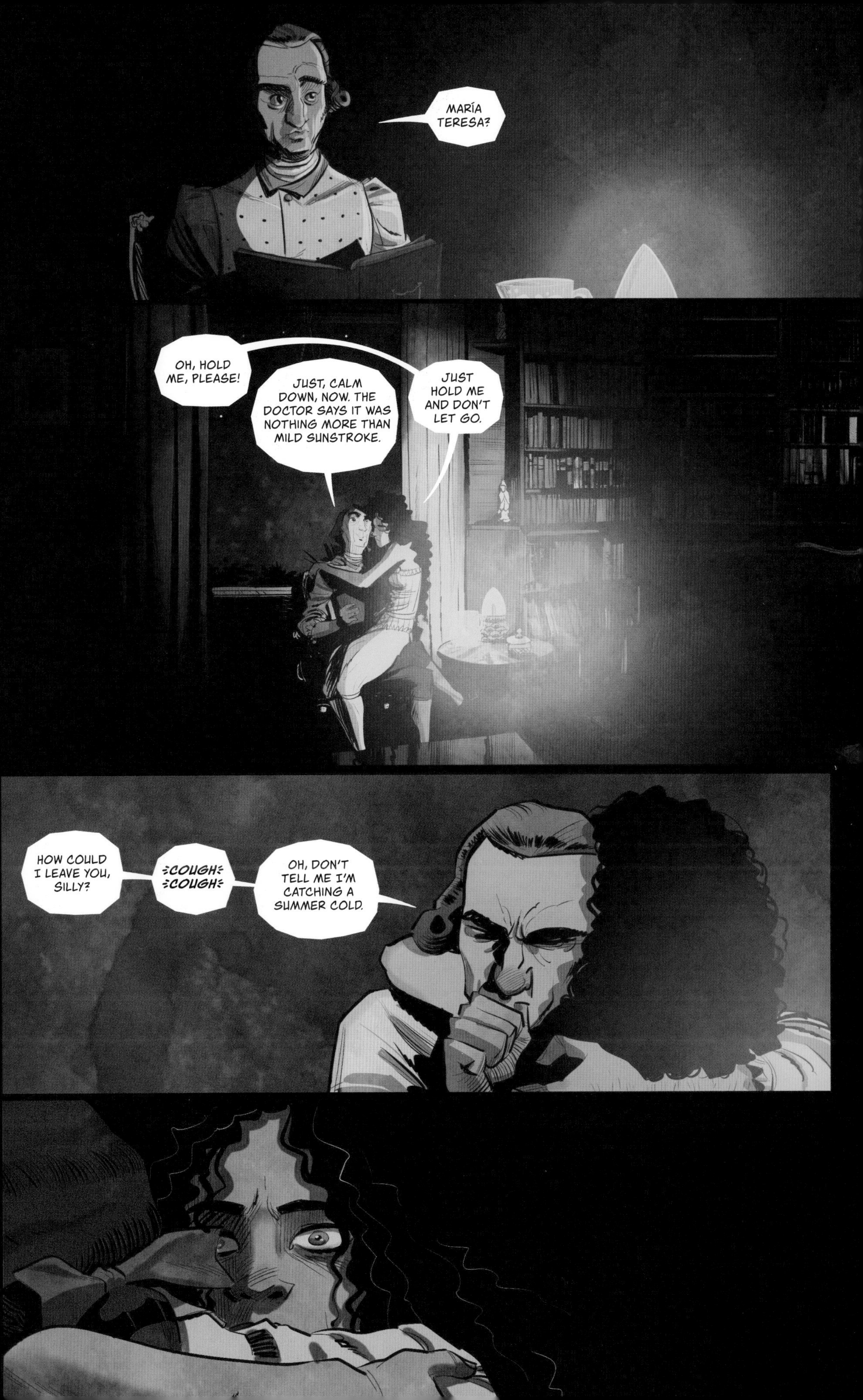
MARÍA TERESA?
OH, HOLD ME, PLEASE!
JUST, CALM DOWN, NOW. THE DOCTOR SAYS IT WAS NOTHING MORE THAN MILD SUNSTROKE.
JUST HOLD ME AND DON'T LET GO.
HOW COULD I LEAVE YOU, SILLY?
COUGH COUGH
OH, DON'T TELL ME I'M CATCHING A SUMMER COLD.

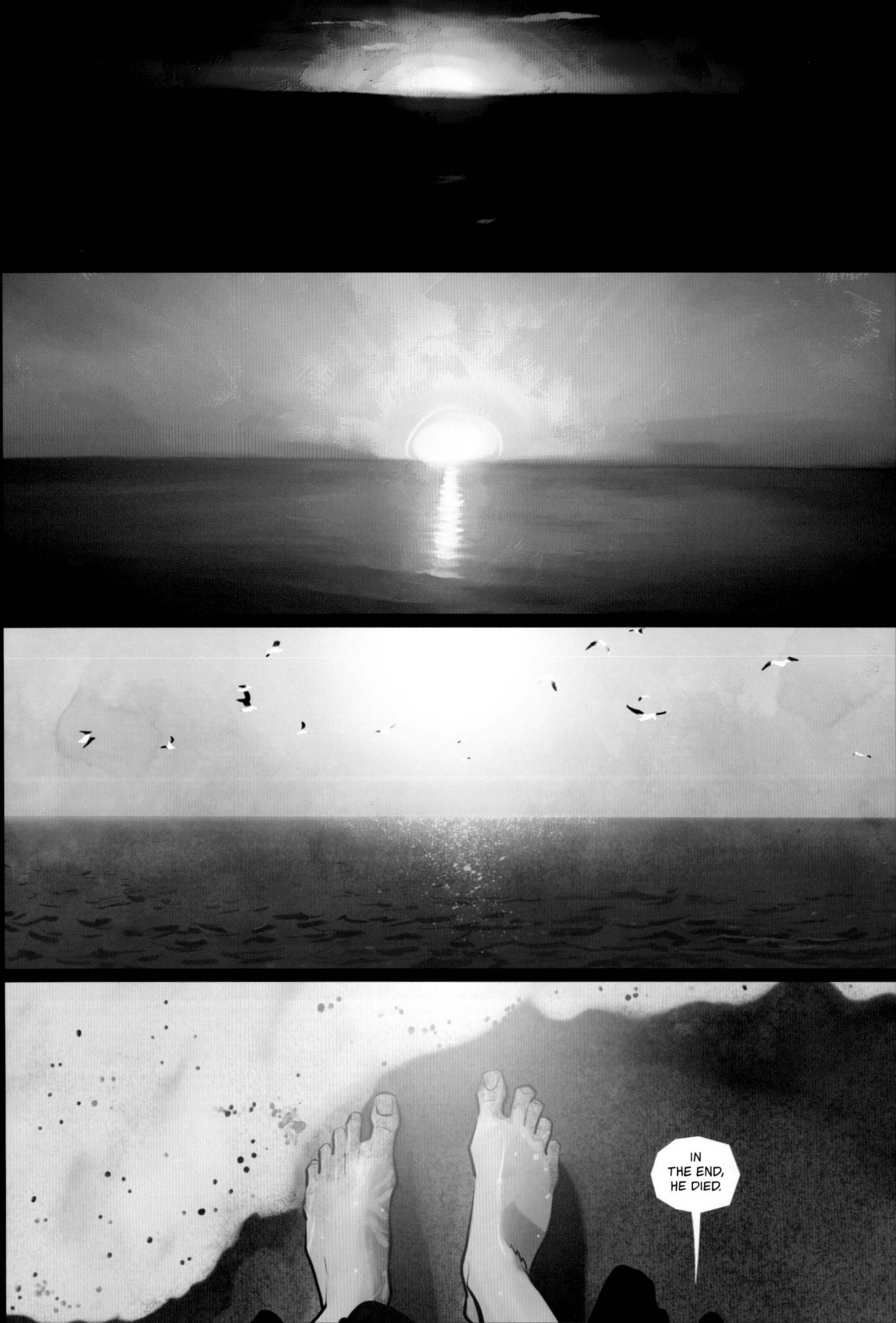
IN THE END, HE DIED.

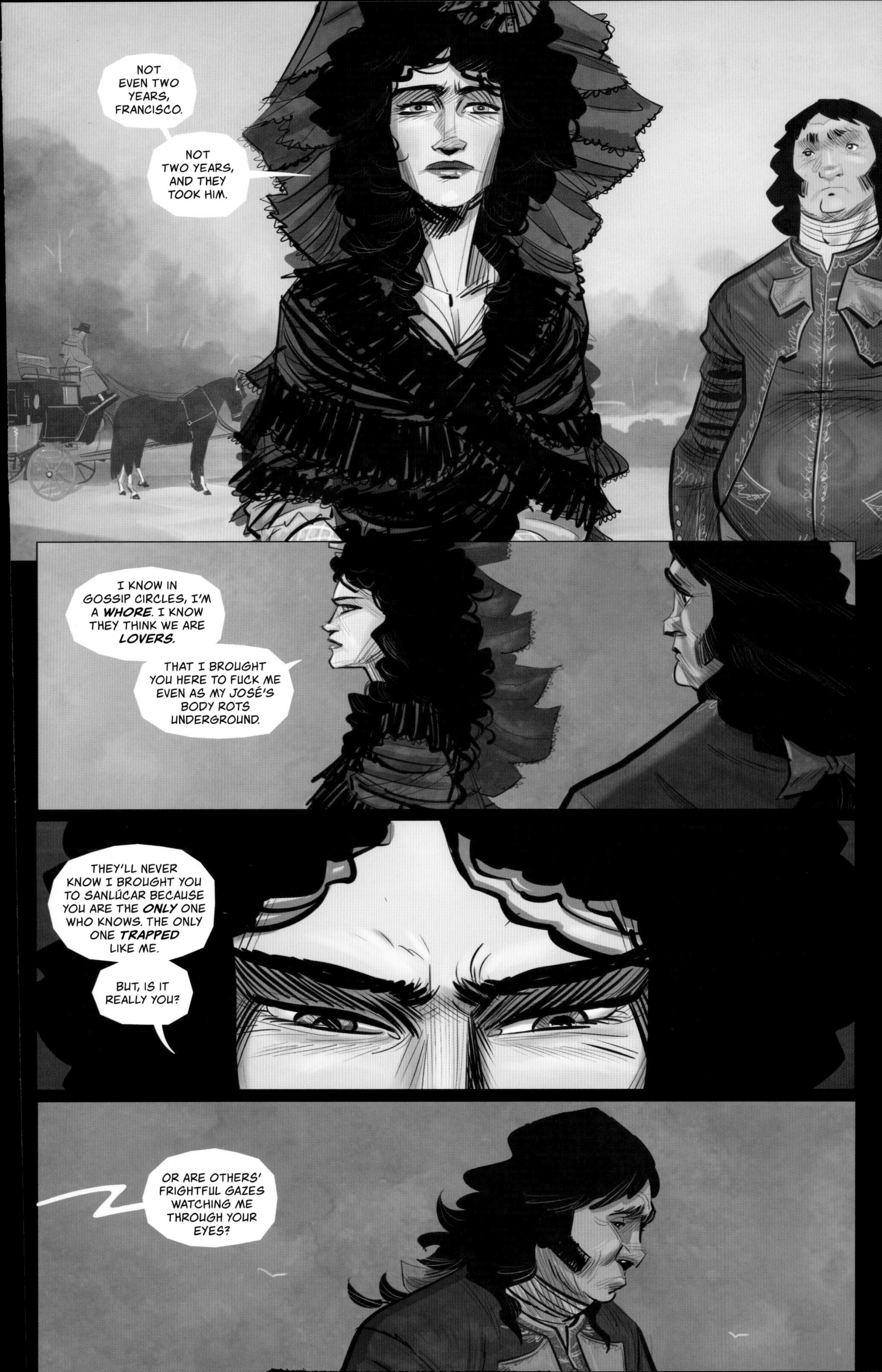
NOT EVEN TWO YEARS, FRANCISCO.
NOT TWO YEARS, AND THEY TOOK HIM.
I KNOW IN GOSSIP CIRCLES, I'M A **WHORE**. I KNOW THEY THINK WE ARE **LOVERS.**
THAT I BROUGHT YOU HERE TO FUCK ME EVEN AS MY JOSÉ'S BODY ROTS UNDERGROUND.
THEY'LL NEVER KNOW I BROUGHT YOU TO SANLÚCAR BECAUSE YOU ARE THE **ONLY** ONE WHO KNOWS. THE ONLY ONE **TRAPPED** LIKE ME.
BUT, IS IT REALLY YOU?
OR ARE OTHERS' FRIGHTFUL GAZES WATCHING ME THROUGH YOUR EYES?

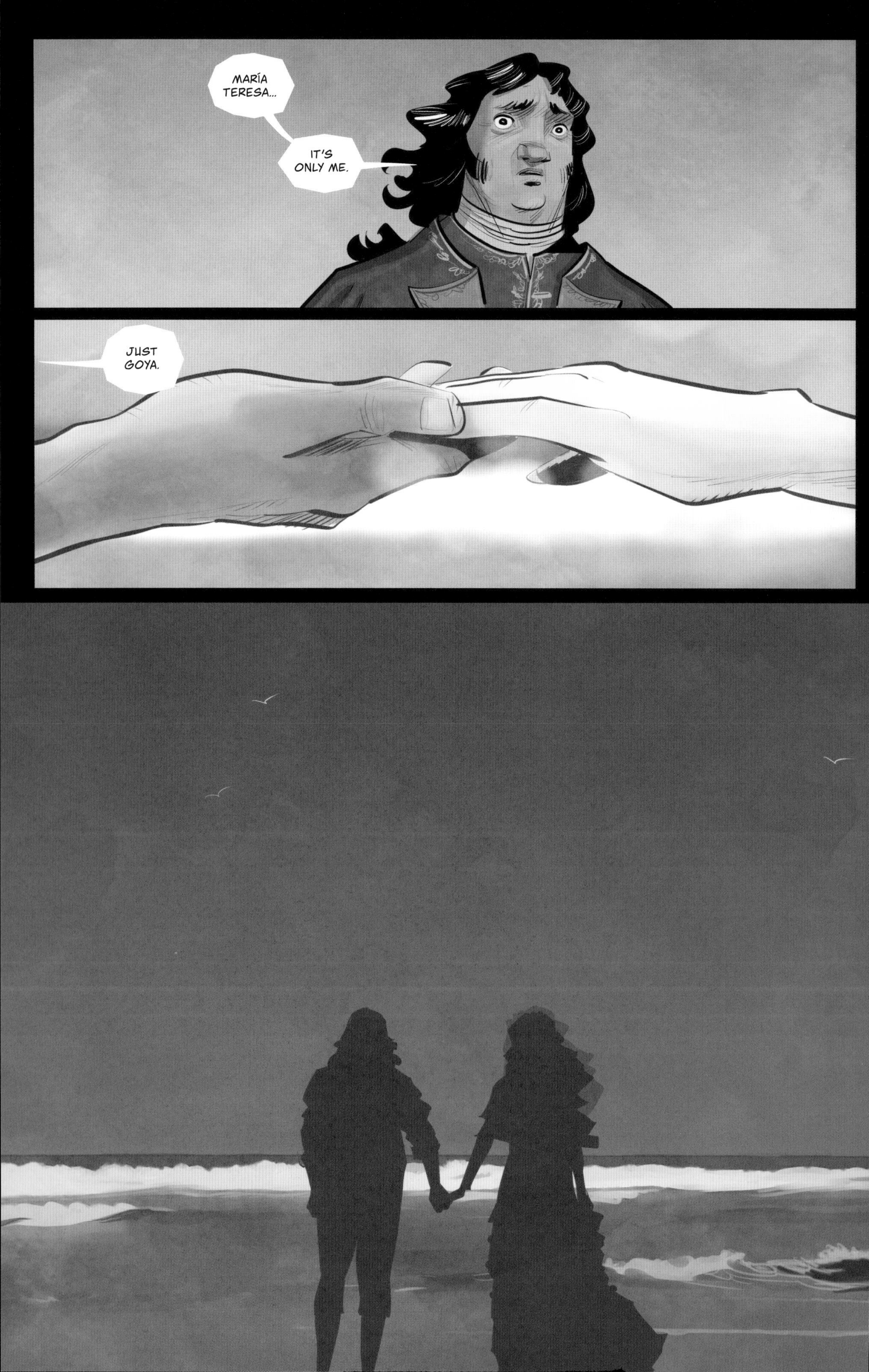
MARÍA TERESA...
IT'S ONLY ME.
JUST GOYA.

# Third act
## The Deaf Man's Villa

Madrid, 1820

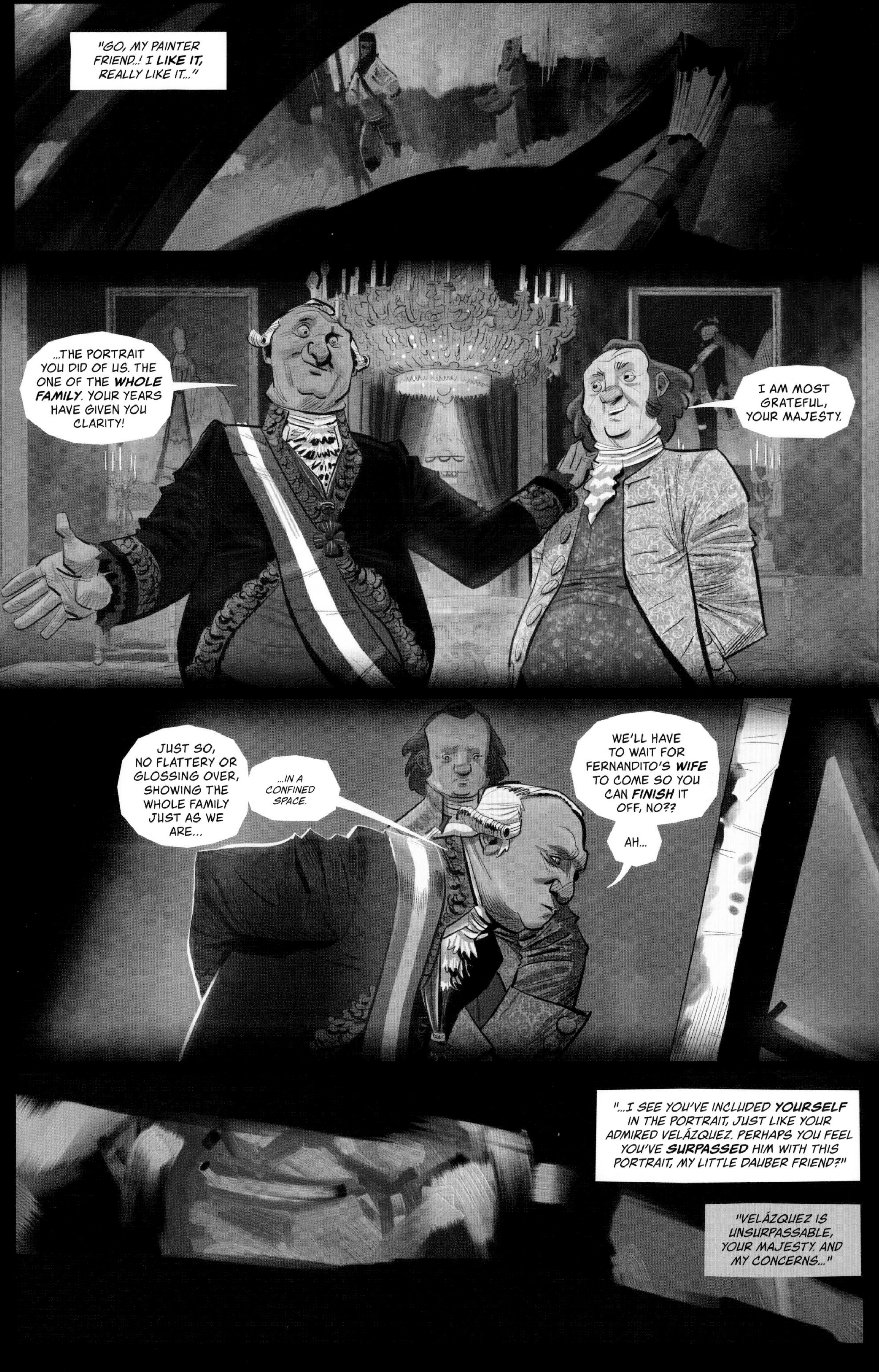
"GO, MY PAINTER FRIEND..! I **LIKE IT,** REALLY LIKE IT..."
...THE PORTRAIT YOU DID OF US. THE ONE OF THE ***WHOLE FAMILY***. YOUR YEARS HAVE GIVEN YOU CLARITY!
I AM MOST GRATEFUL, YOUR MAJESTY.
JUST SO, NO FLATTERY OR GLOSSING OVER, SHOWING THE WHOLE FAMILY JUST AS WE ARE...
...IN A CONFINED SPACE.
WE'LL HAVE TO WAIT FOR FERNANDITO'S ***WIFE*** TO COME SO YOU CAN ***FINISH*** IT OFF, NO??
AH...
"...I SEE YOU'VE INCLUDED **YOURSELF** IN THE PORTRAIT, JUST LIKE YOUR ADMIRED VELÁZQUEZ. PERHAPS YOU FEEL YOU'VE **SURPASSED** HIM WITH THIS PORTRAIT, MY LITTLE DAUBER FRIEND?"
"VELÁZQUEZ IS UNSURPASSABLE, YOUR MAJESTY. AND MY CONCERNS..."

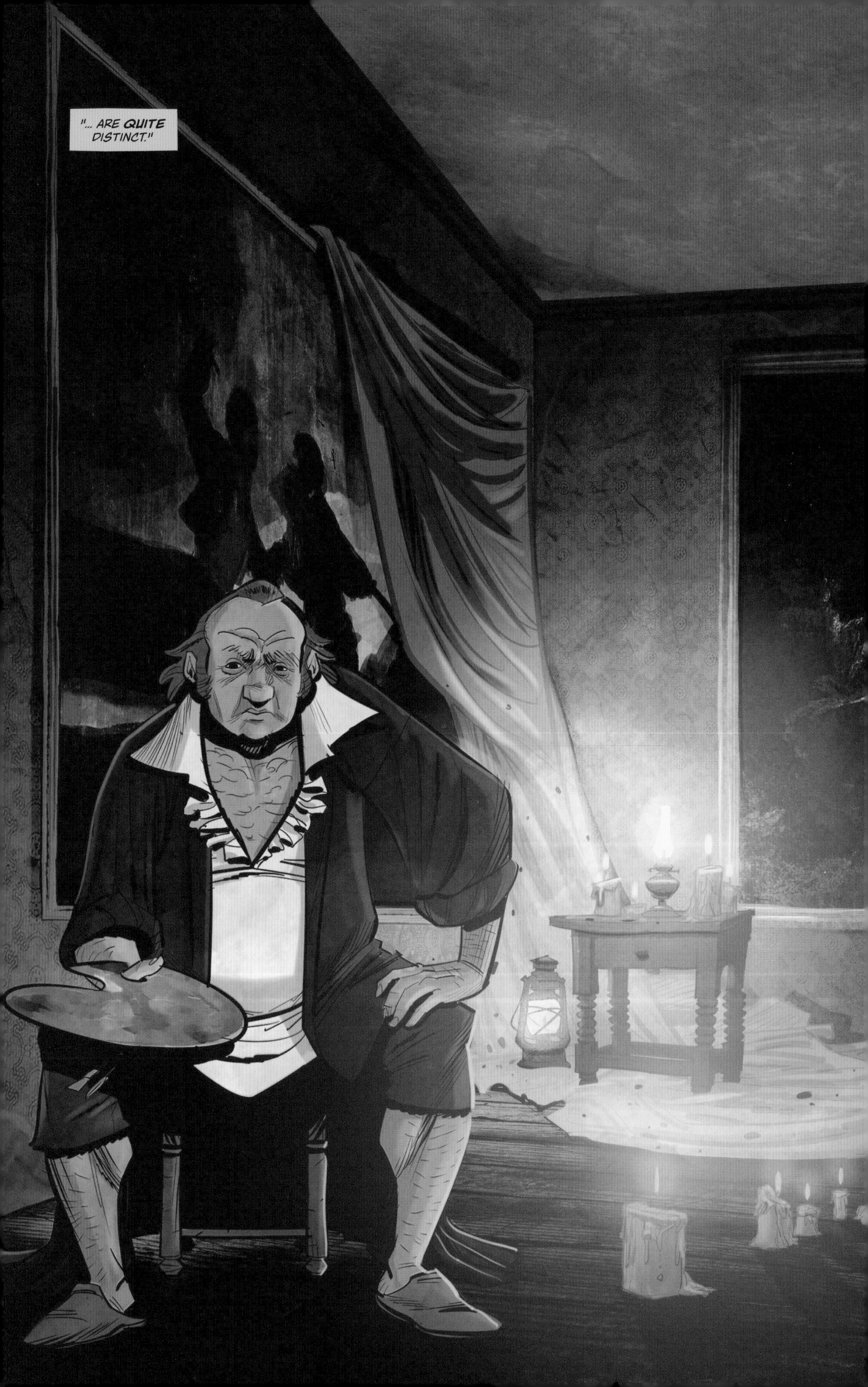
"... ARE QUITE DISTINCT."

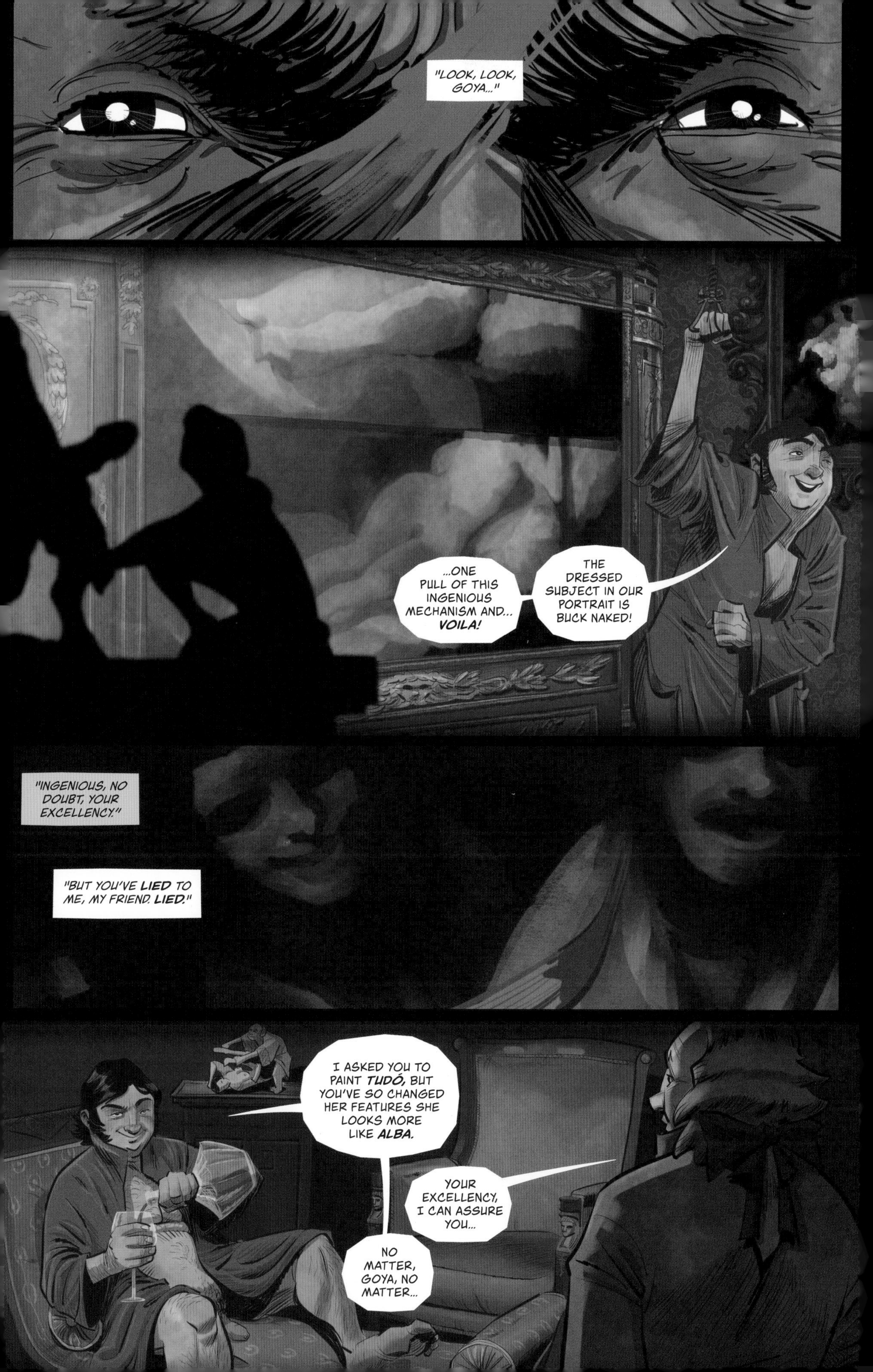
"LOOK, LOOK, GOYA..."
...ONE PULL OF THIS INGENIOUS MECHANISM AND... VOILA!
THE DRESSED SUBJECT IN OUR PORTRAIT IS BUCK NAKED!
"INGENIOUS, NO DOUBT, YOUR EXCELLENCY."
"BUT YOU'VE LIED TO ME, MY FRIEND. LIED."
I ASKED YOU TO PAINT TUDÓ, BUT YOU'VE SO CHANGED HER FEATURES SHE LOOKS MORE LIKE ALBA.
YOUR EXCELLENCY, I CAN ASSURE YOU...
NO MATTER, GOYA, NO MATTER...

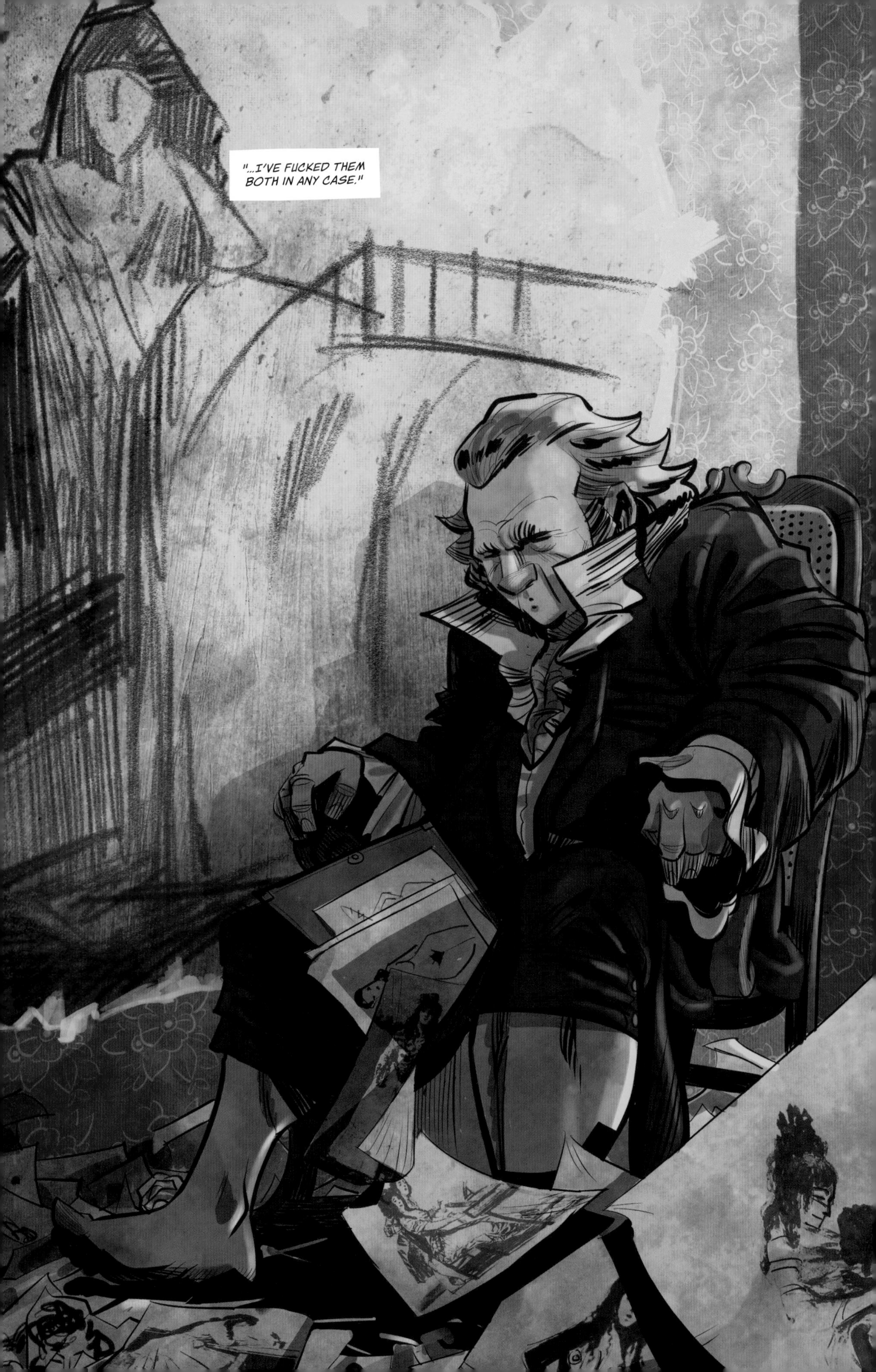
"...I'VE FUCKED THEM BOTH IN ANY CASE."

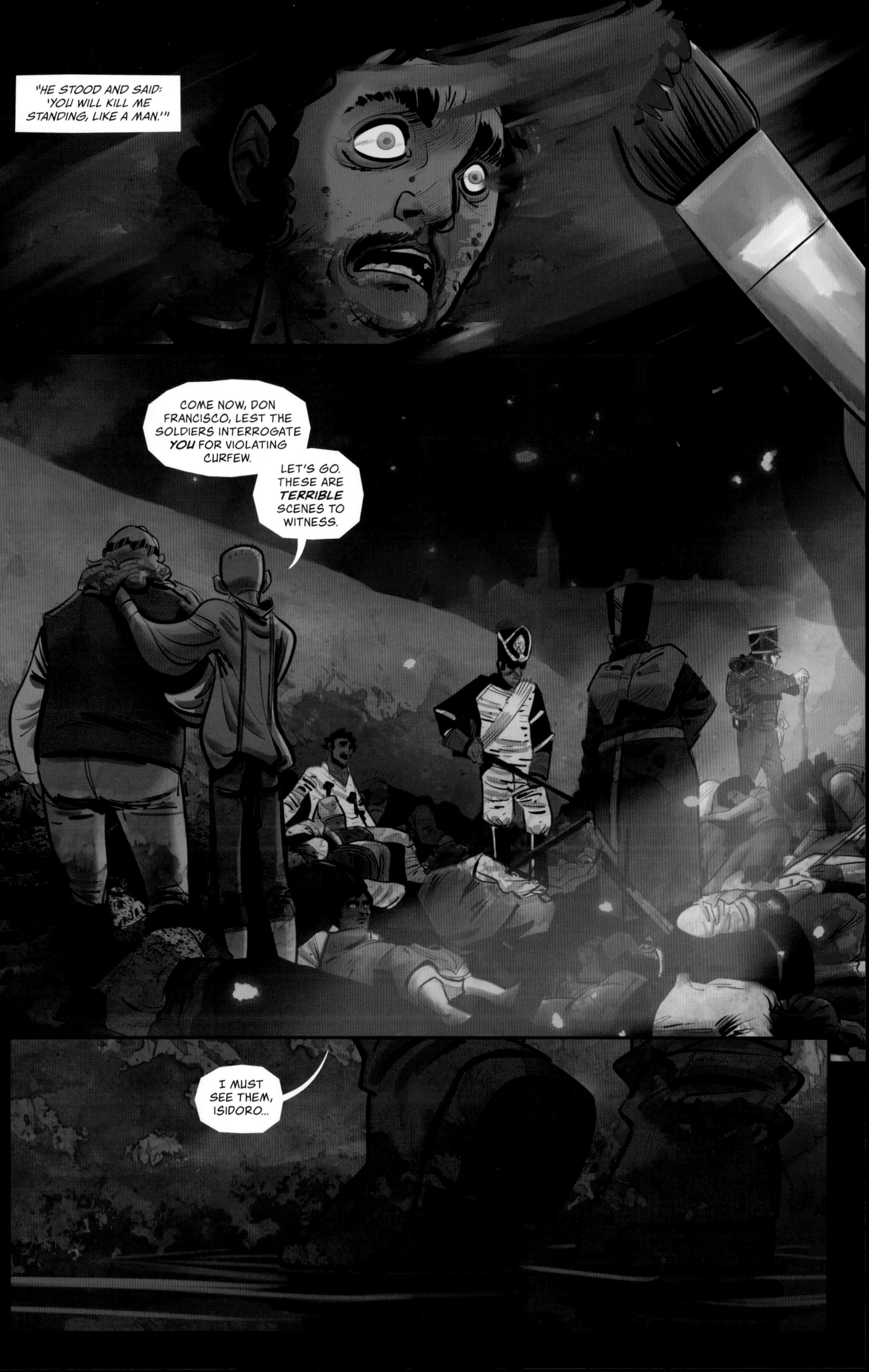
"HE STOOD AND SAID: 'YOU WILL KILL ME STANDING, LIKE A MAN.'"
COME NOW, DON FRANCISCO, LEST THE SOLDIERS INTERROGATE YOU FOR VIOLATING CURFEW.
LET'S GO. THESE ARE TERRIBLE SCENES TO WITNESS.
I MUST SEE THEM, ISIDORO...

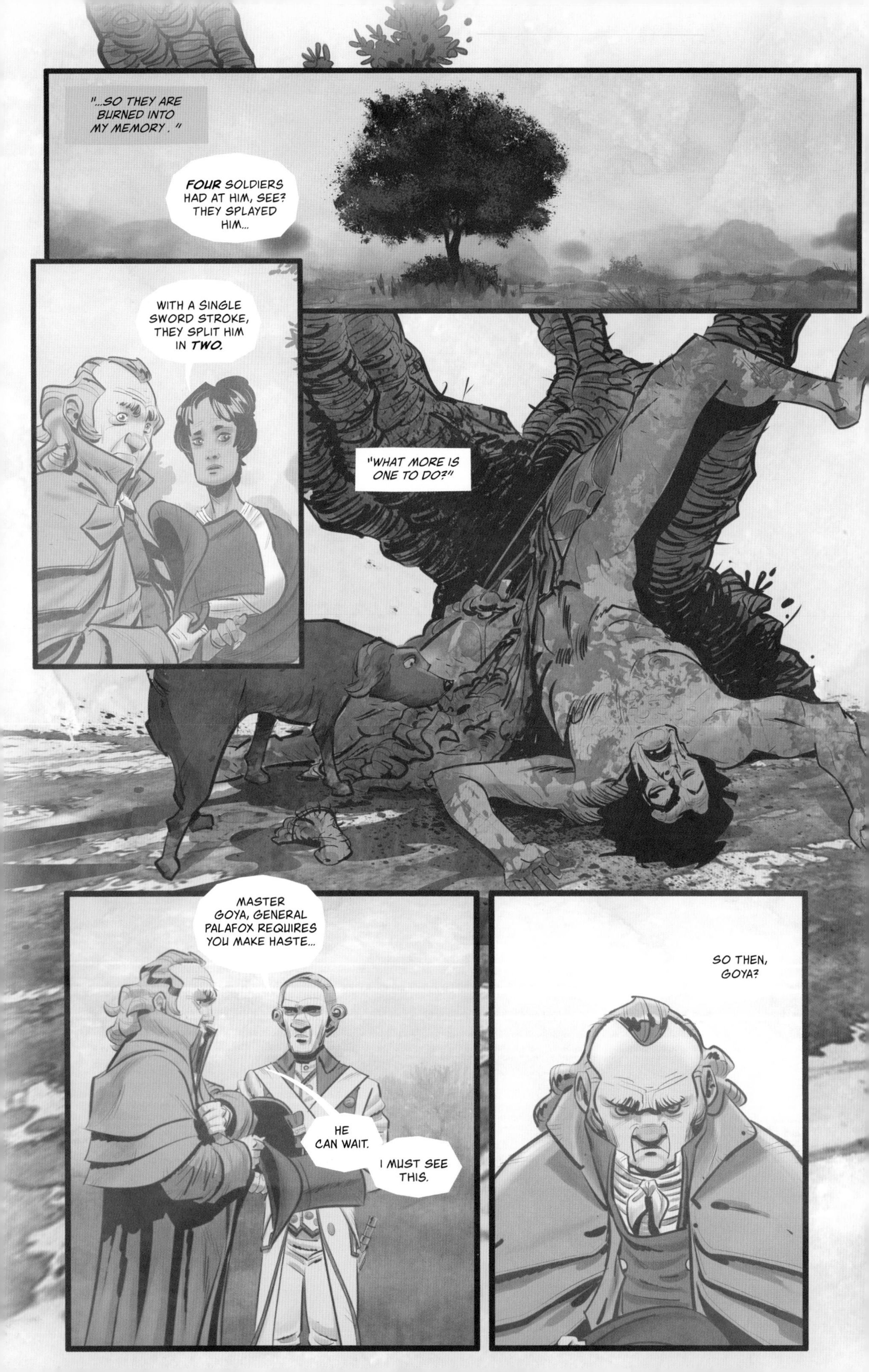
"...SO THEY ARE BURNED INTO MY MEMORY."
FOUR SOLDIERS HAD AT HIM, SEE? THEY SPLAYED HIM...
WITH A SINGLE SWORD STROKE, THEY SPLIT HIM IN TWO.
"WHAT MORE IS ONE TO DO?"
MASTER GOYA, GENERAL PALAFOX REQUIRES YOU MAKE HASTE...
HE CAN WAIT.
I MUST SEE THIS.
SO THEN, GOYA?

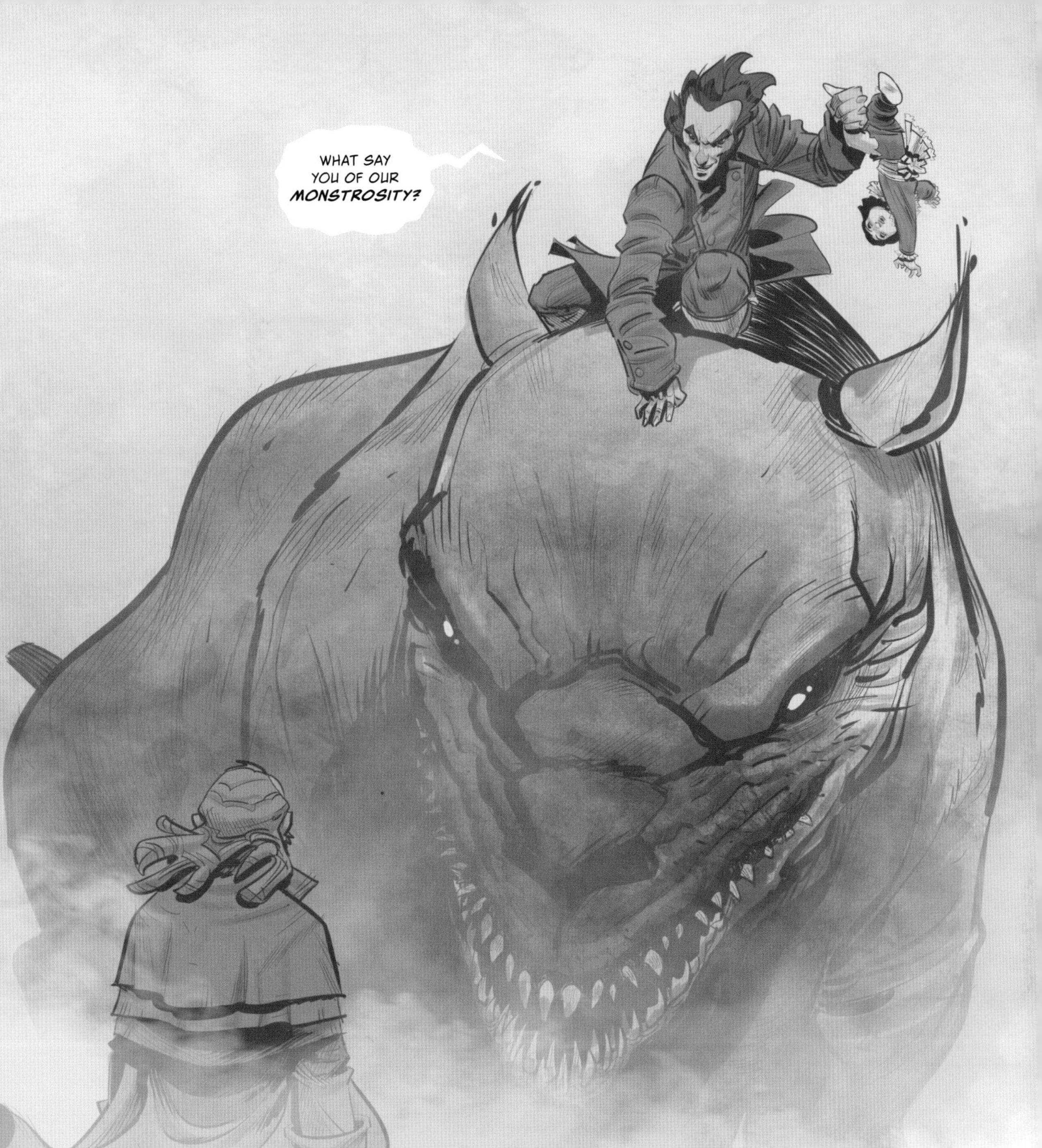
WHAT SAY YOU OF OUR MONSTROSITY?

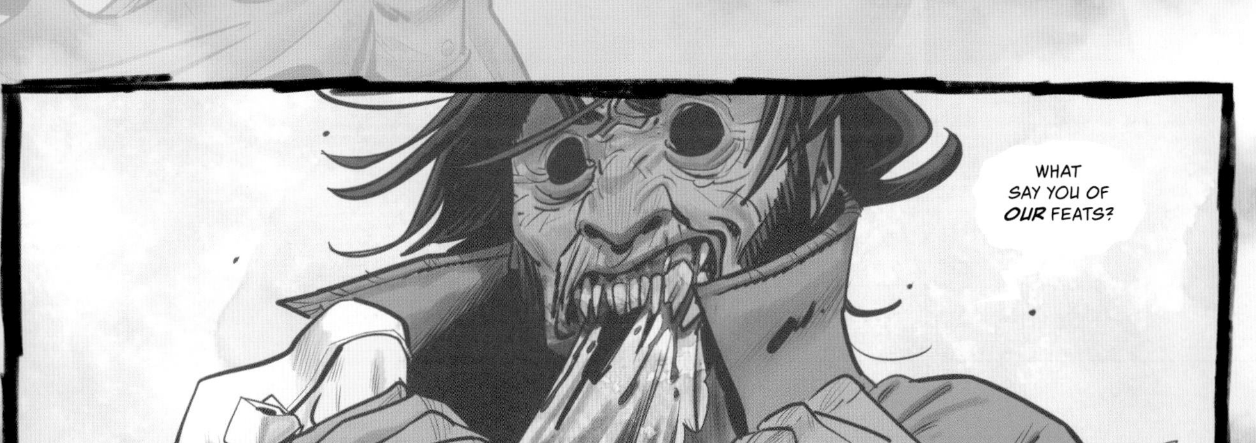
WHAT SAY YOU OF OUR FEATS?

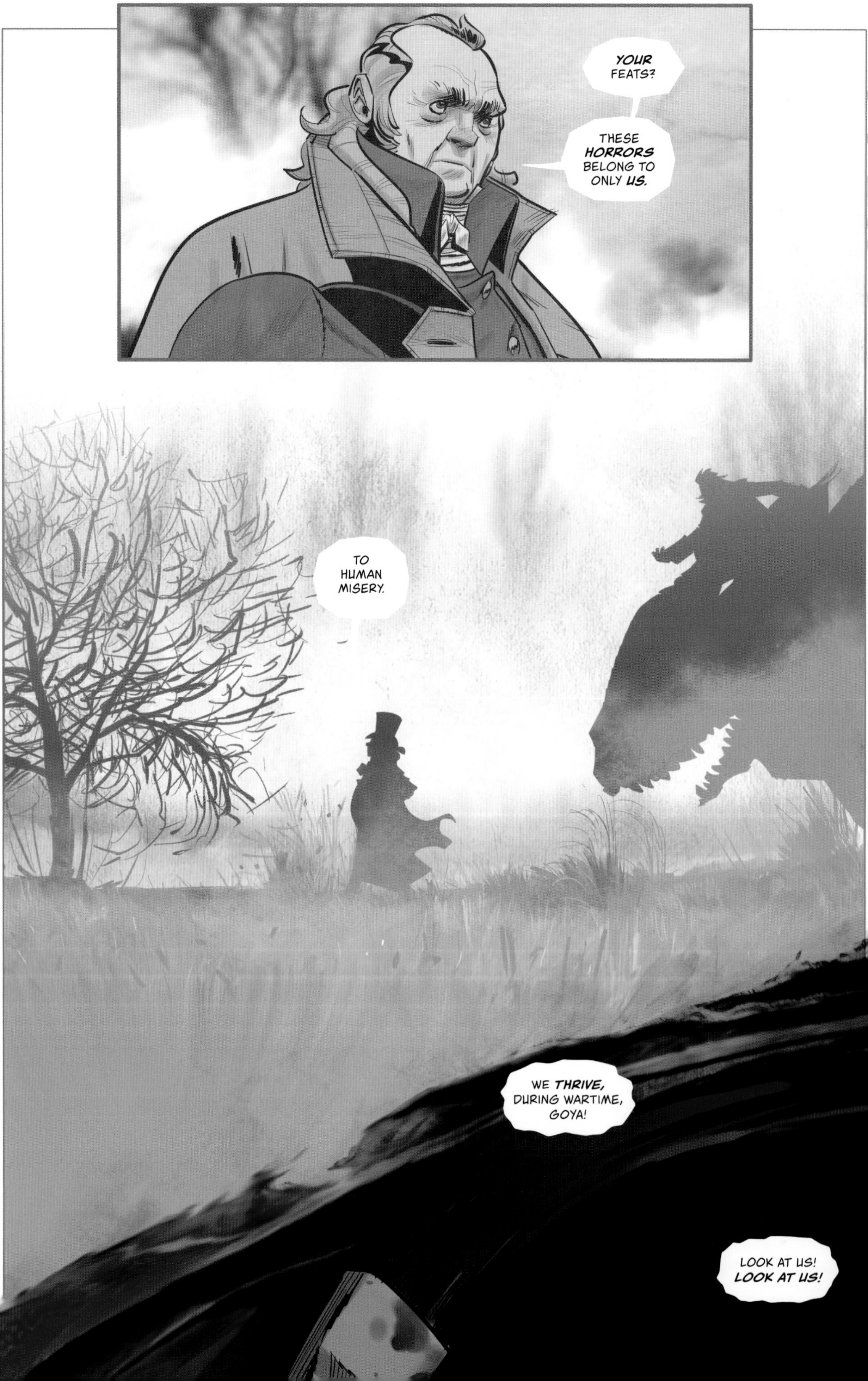
YOUR FEATS?
THESE HORRORS BELONG TO ONLY US.
TO HUMAN MISERY.
WE THRIVE, DURING WARTIME, GOYA!
LOOK AT US! LOOK AT US!

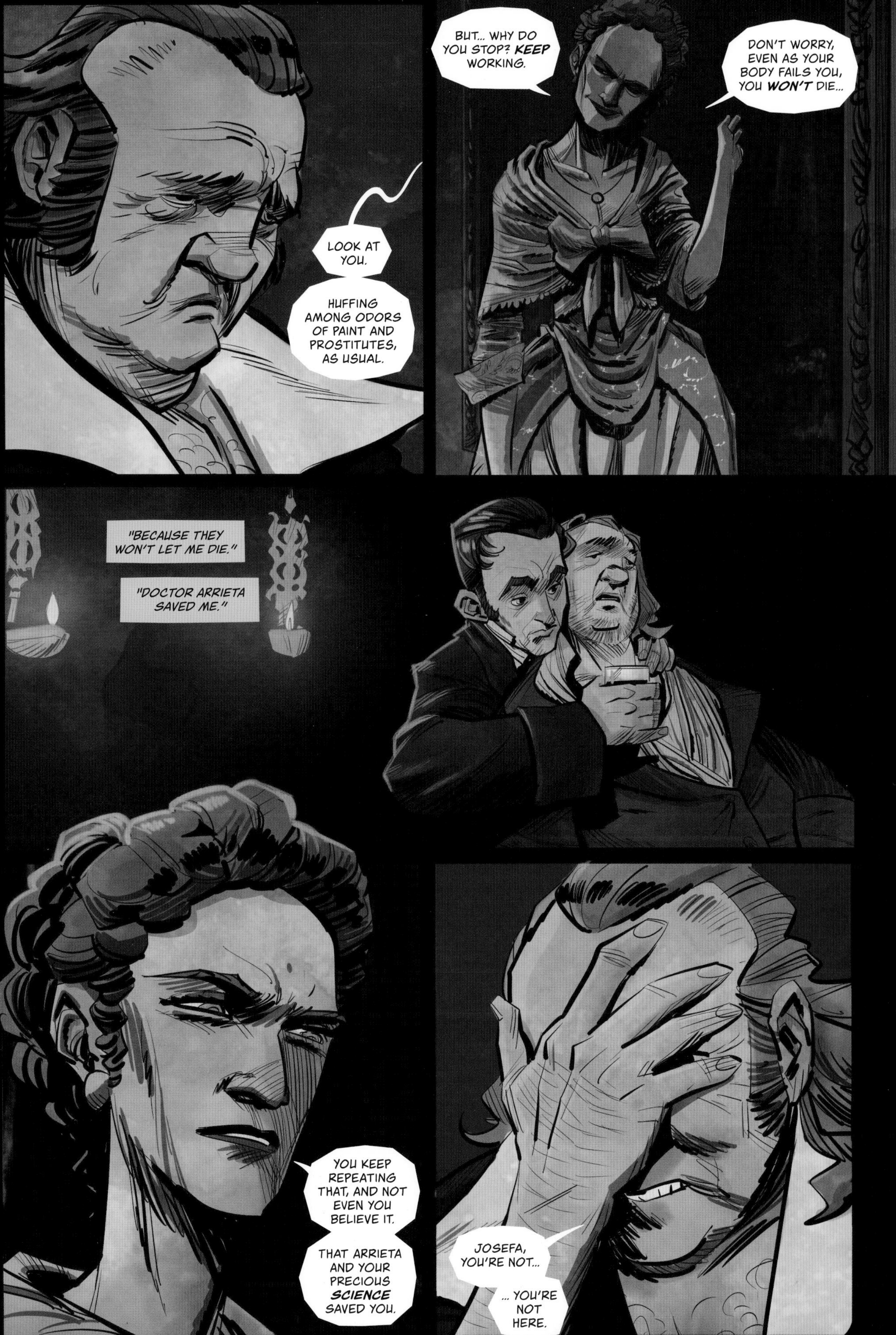
LOOK AT YOU.
HUFFING AMONG ODORS OF PAINT AND PROSTITUTES, AS USUAL.
BUT... WHY DO YOU STOP? KEEP WORKING.
DON'T WORRY, EVEN AS YOUR BODY FAILS YOU, YOU WON'T DIE...
"BECAUSE THEY WON'T LET ME DIE."
"DOCTOR ARRIETA SAVED ME."
YOU KEEP REPEATING THAT, AND NOT EVEN YOU BELIEVE IT.
THAT ARRIETA AND YOUR PRECIOUS SCIENCE SAVED YOU.
JOSEFA, YOU'RE NOT...
... YOU'RE NOT HERE.

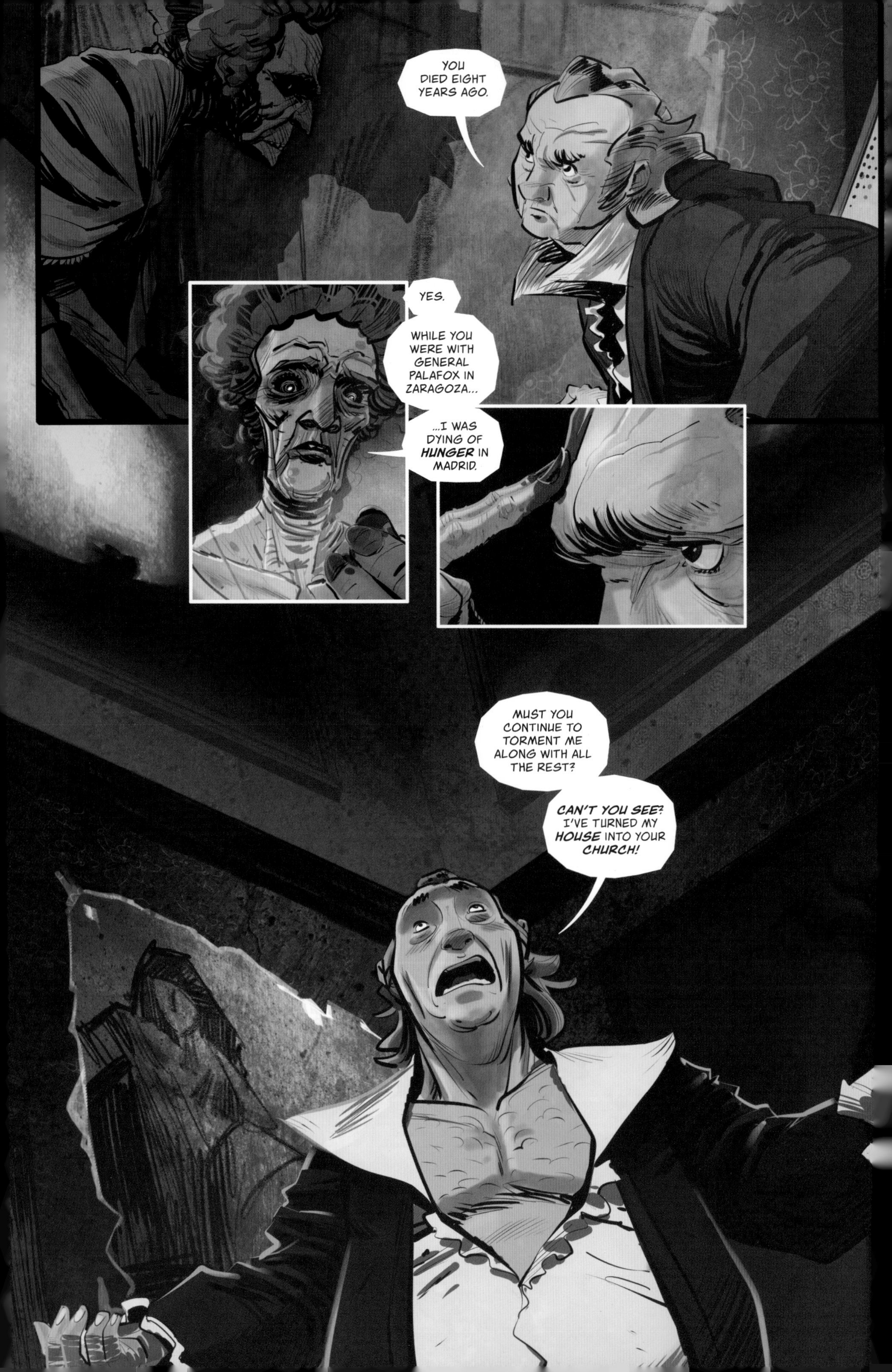
YOU DIED EIGHT YEARS AGO.
YES.
WHILE YOU WERE WITH GENERAL PALAFOX IN ZARAGOZA...
...I WAS DYING OF HUNGER IN MADRID.
MUST YOU CONTINUE TO TORMENT ME ALONG WITH ALL THE REST?
CAN'T YOU SEE? I'VE TURNED MY HOUSE INTO YOUR CHURCH!

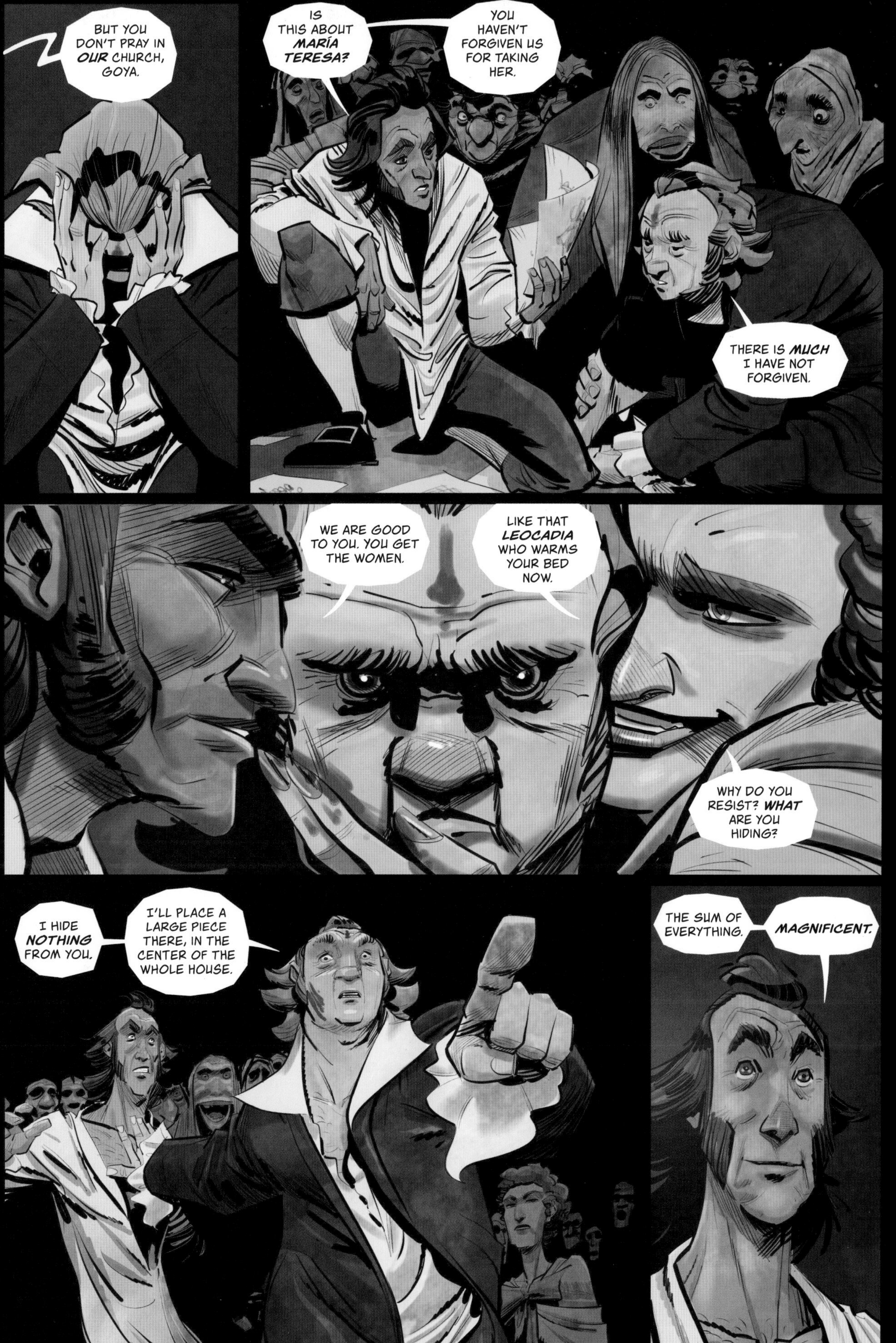
BUT YOU DON'T PRAY IN OUR CHURCH, GOYA.
IS THIS ABOUT MARÍA TERESA?
YOU HAVEN'T FORGIVEN US FOR TAKING HER.
THERE IS MUCH I HAVE NOT FORGIVEN.
WE ARE GOOD TO YOU. YOU GET THE WOMEN.
LIKE THAT LEOCADIA WHO WARMS YOUR BED NOW.
WHY DO YOU RESIST? WHAT ARE YOU HIDING?
I HIDE NOTHING FROM YOU.
I'LL PLACE A LARGE PIECE THERE, IN THE CENTER OF THE WHOLE HOUSE.
THE SUM OF EVERYTHING.
MAGNIFICENT.

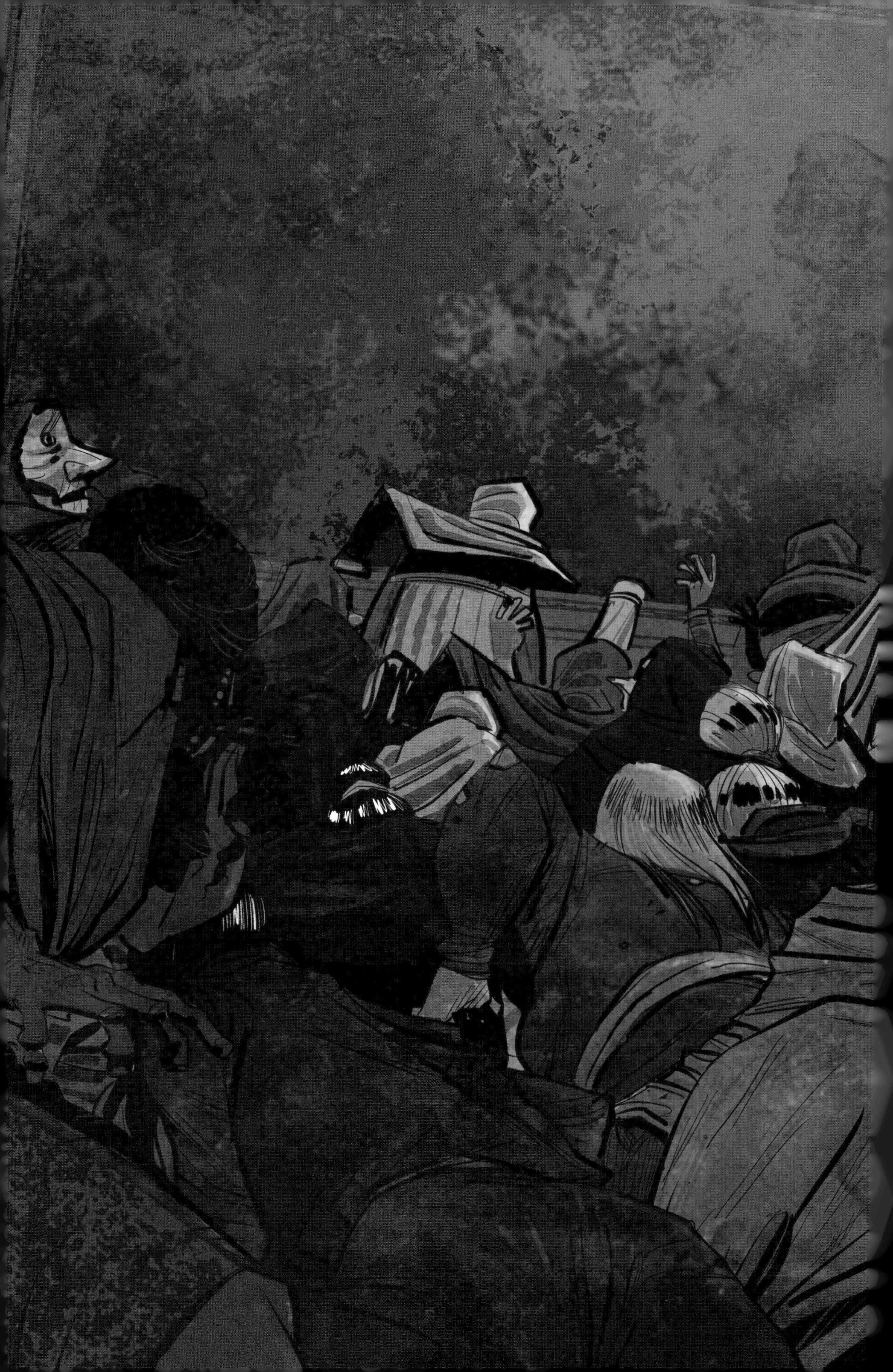

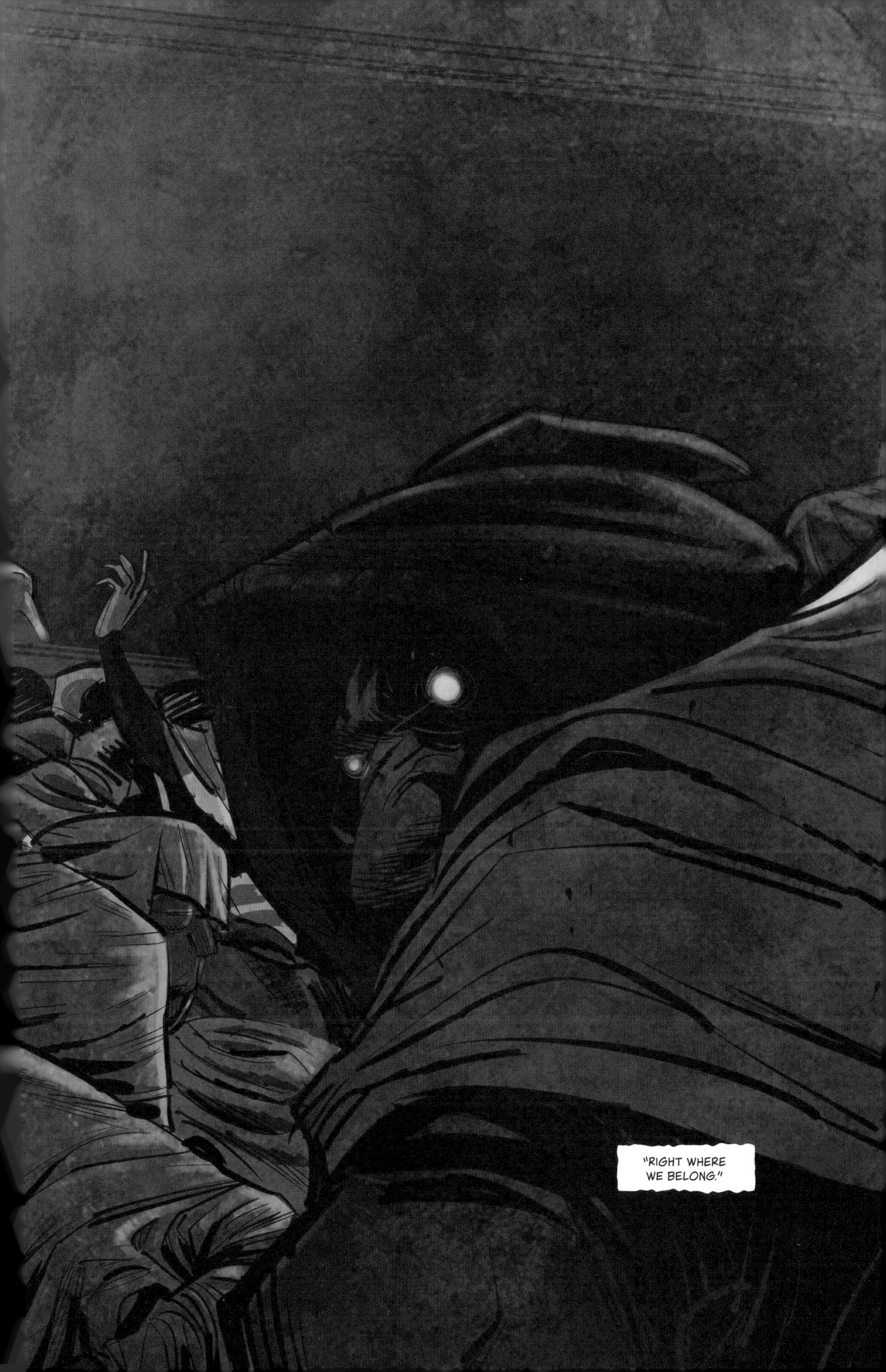
"RIGHT WHERE WE BELONG."

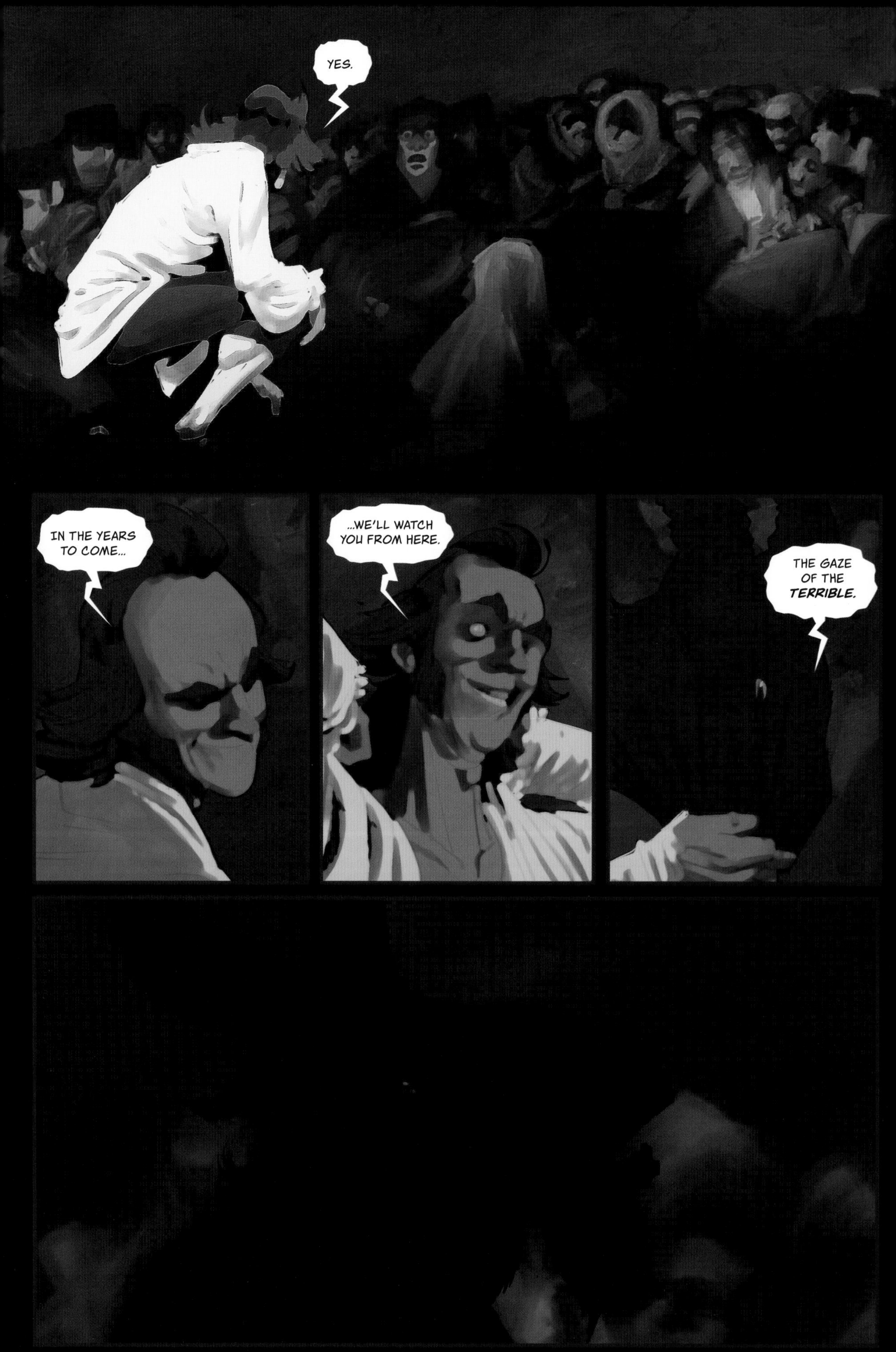
YES.
IN THE YEARS TO COME...
...WE'LL WATCH YOU FROM HERE.
THE GAZE OF THE *TERRIBLE.*

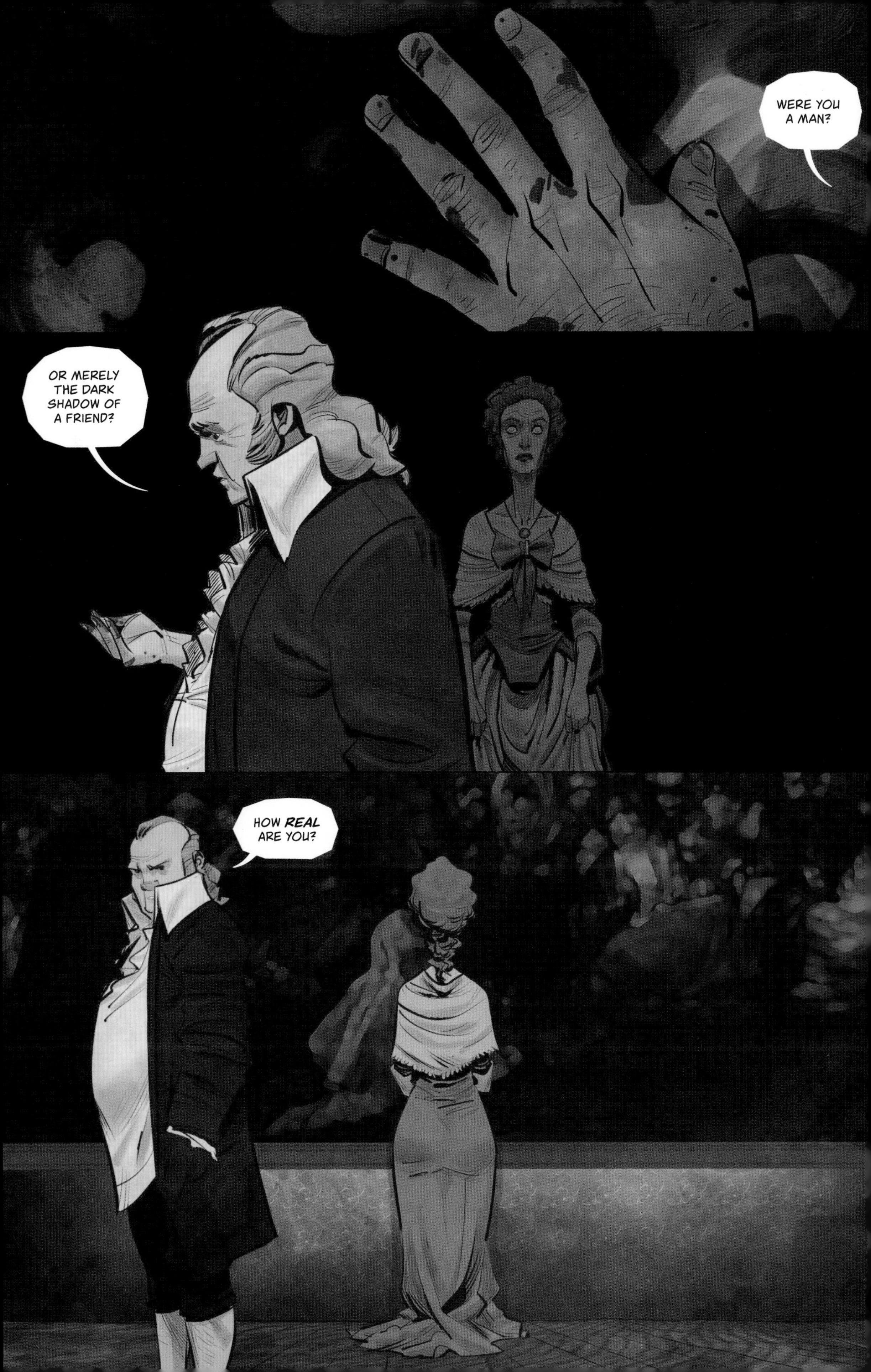
WERE YOU A MAN?
OR MERELY THE DARK SHADOW OF A FRIEND?
HOW *REAL* ARE YOU?

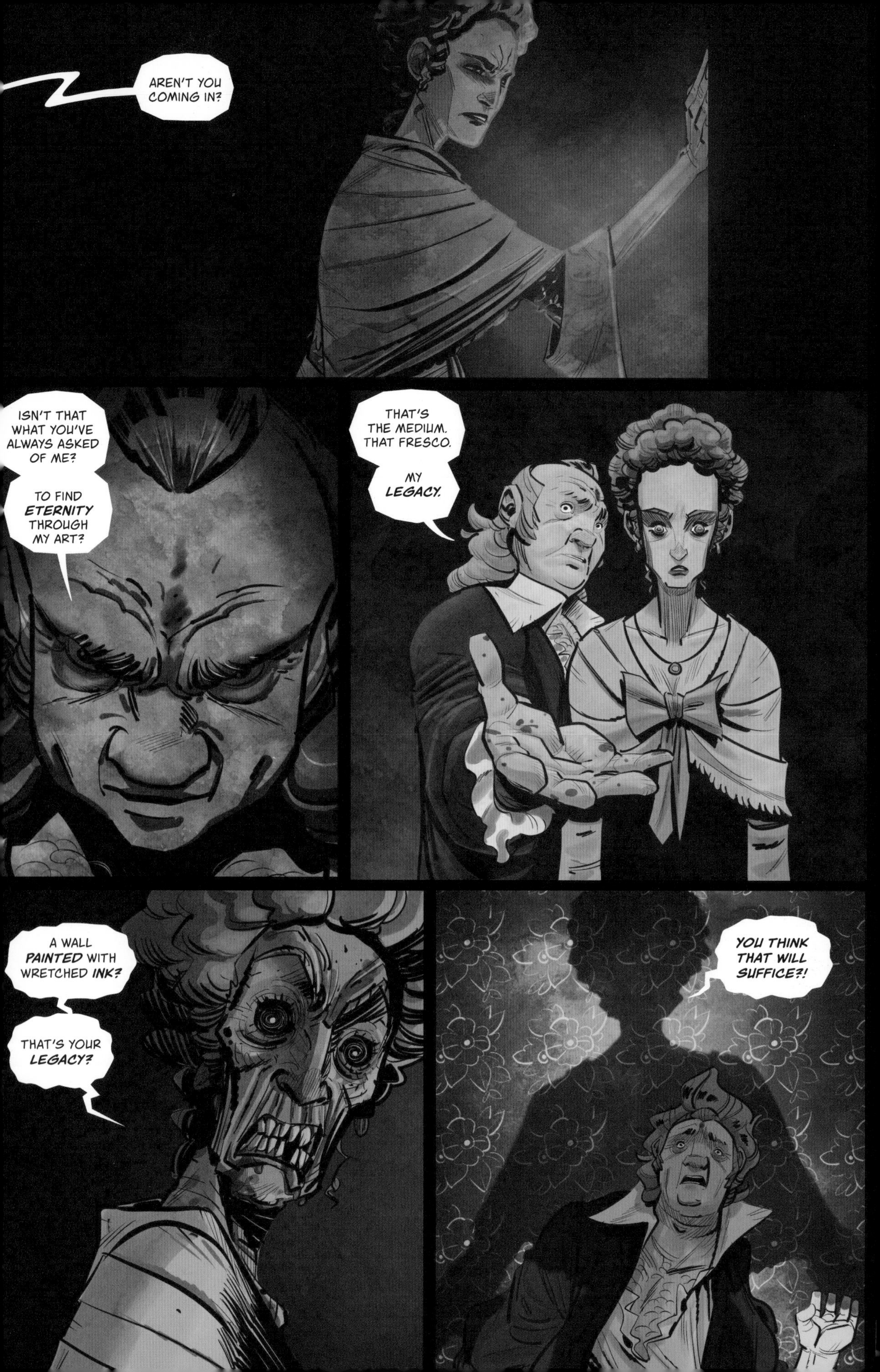
AREN'T YOU COMING IN?
ISN'T THAT WHAT YOU'VE ALWAYS ASKED OF ME?
TO FIND ETERNITY THROUGH MY ART?
THAT'S THE MEDIUM. THAT FRESCO.
MY LEGACY.
A WALL PAINTED WITH WRETCHED INK?
THAT'S YOUR LEGACY?
YOU THINK THAT WILL SUFFICE?!

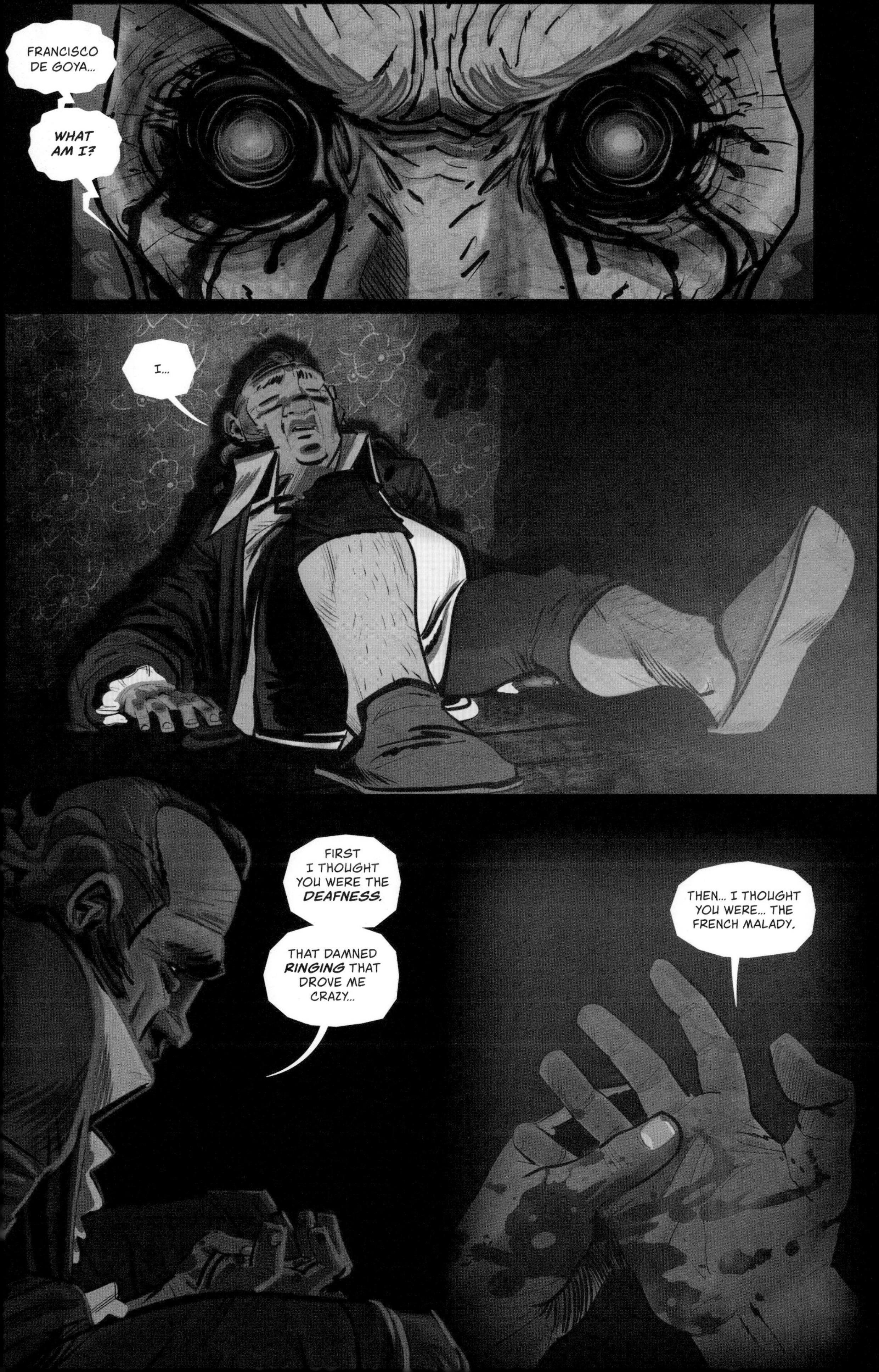
FRANCISCO DE GOYA...
WHAT AM I?
I...
FIRST I THOUGHT YOU WERE THE DEAFNESS.
THAT DAMNED RINGING THAT DROVE ME CRAZY...
THEN... I THOUGHT YOU WERE... THE FRENCH MALADY.

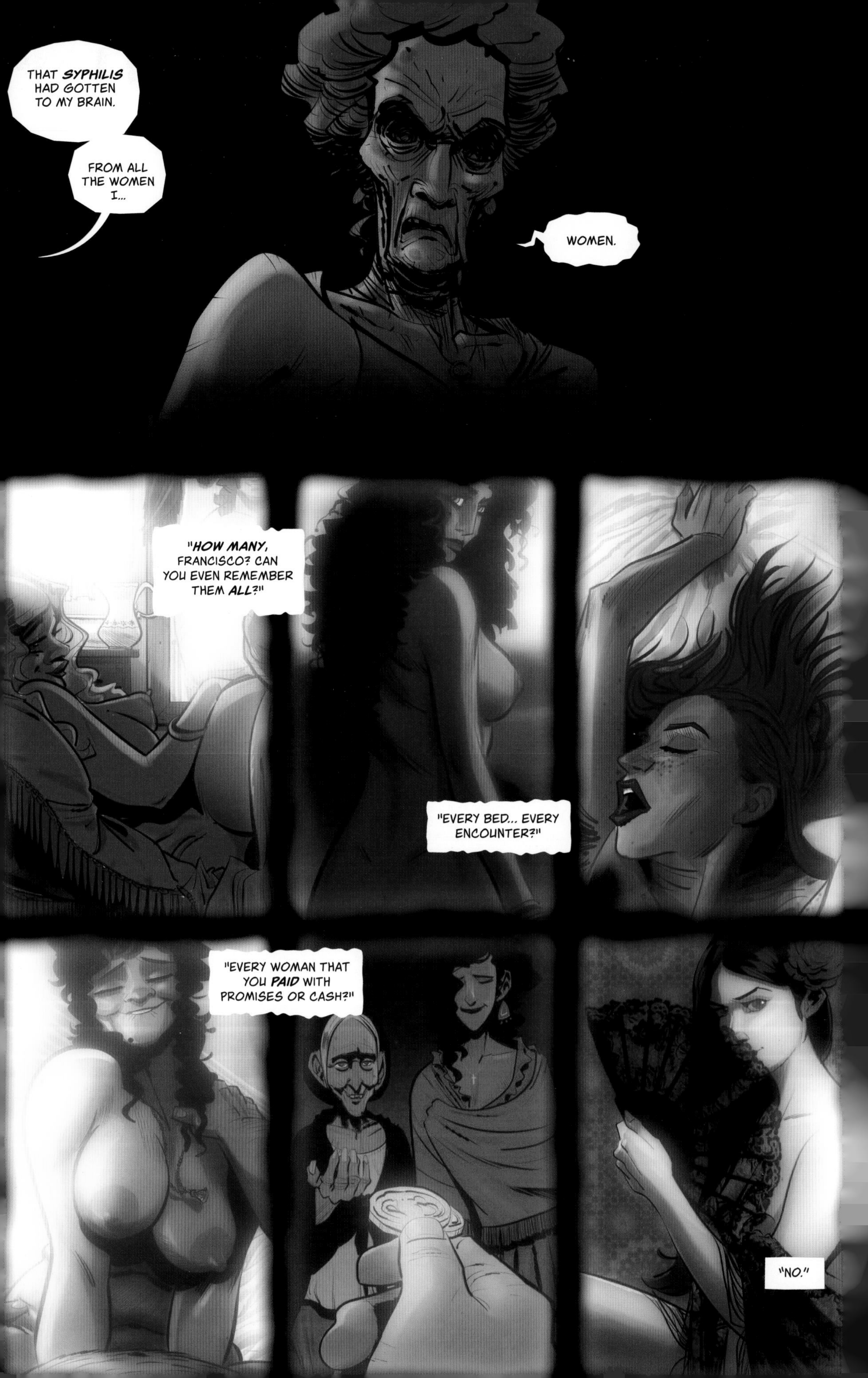

THAT *SYPHILIS* HAD GOTTEN TO MY BRAIN.
FROM ALL THE WOMEN I...
WOMEN.
"*HOW MANY*, FRANCISCO? CAN YOU EVEN REMEMBER THEM *ALL*?"
"EVERY BED... EVERY ENCOUNTER?"
"EVERY WOMAN THAT YOU *PAID* WITH PROMISES OR CASH?"
"NO."

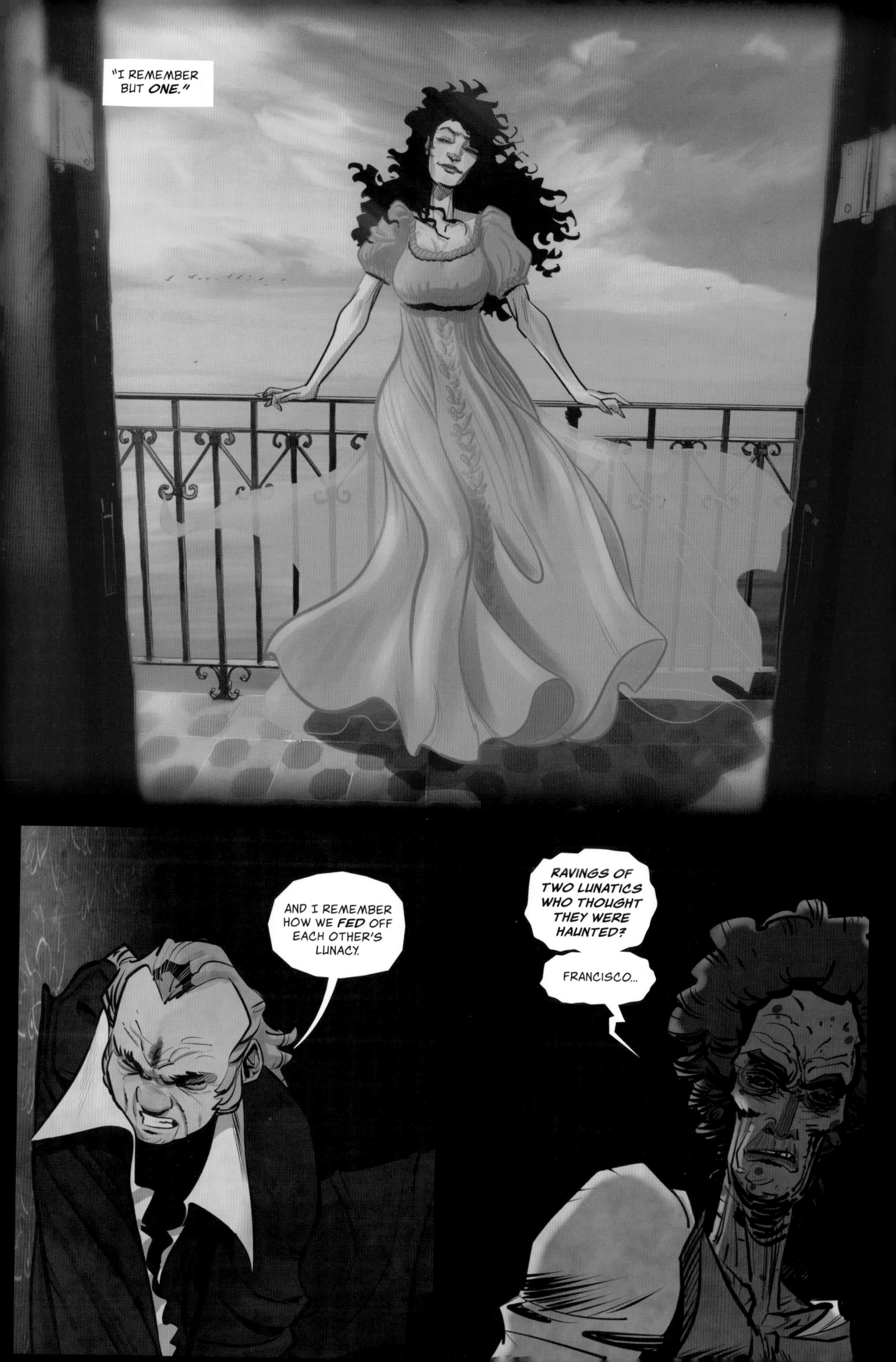
"I REMEMBER BUT ONE."
AND I REMEMBER HOW WE FED OFF EACH OTHER'S LUNACY.
RAVINGS OF TWO LUNATICS WHO THOUGHT THEY WERE HAUNTED?
FRANCISCO...

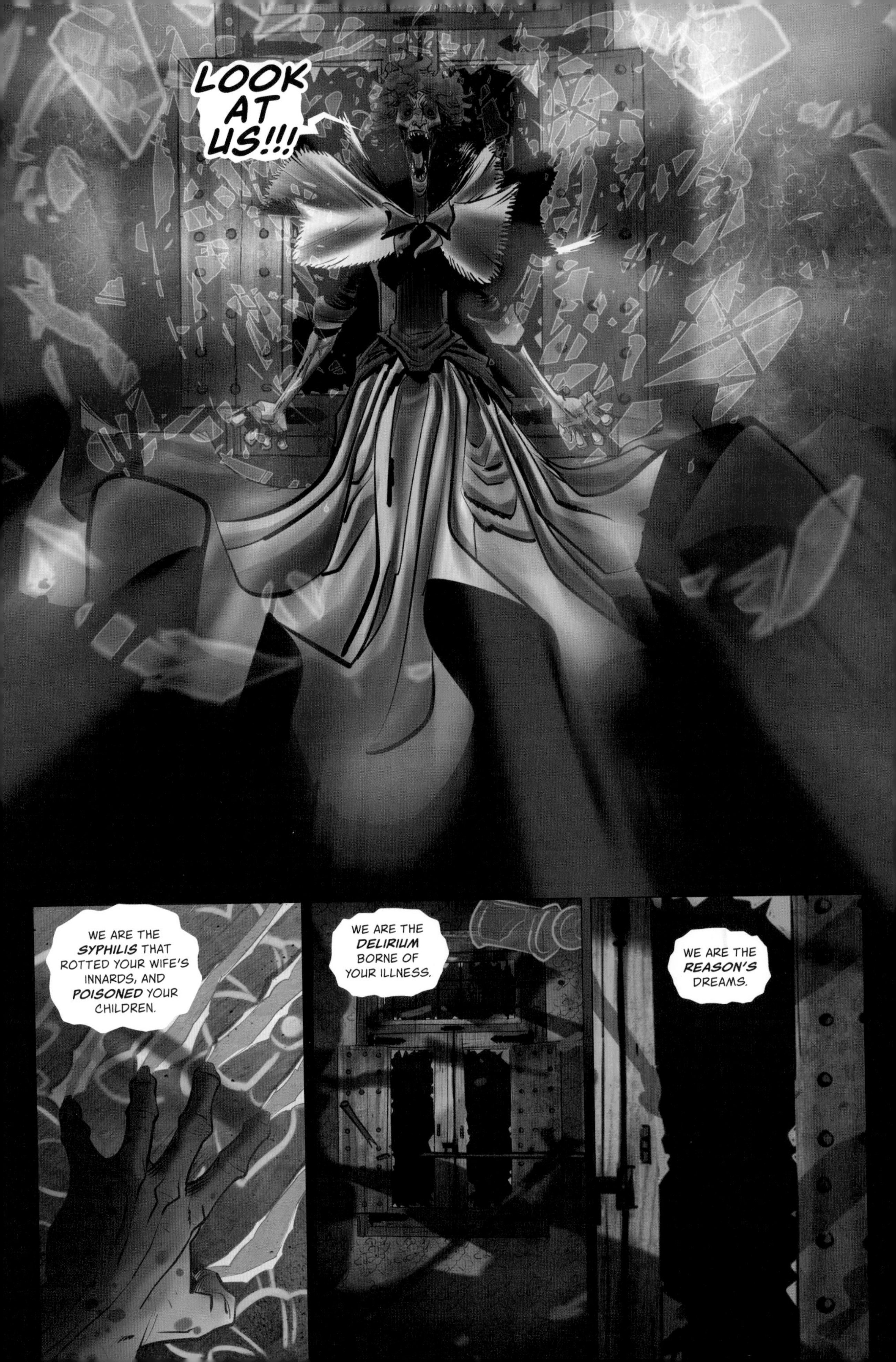
LOOK AT US!!!
WE ARE THE SYPHILIS THAT ROTTED YOUR WIFE'S INNARDS, AND POISONED YOUR CHILDREN.
WE ARE THE DELIRIUM BORNE OF YOUR ILLNESS.
WE ARE THE REASON'S DREAMS.

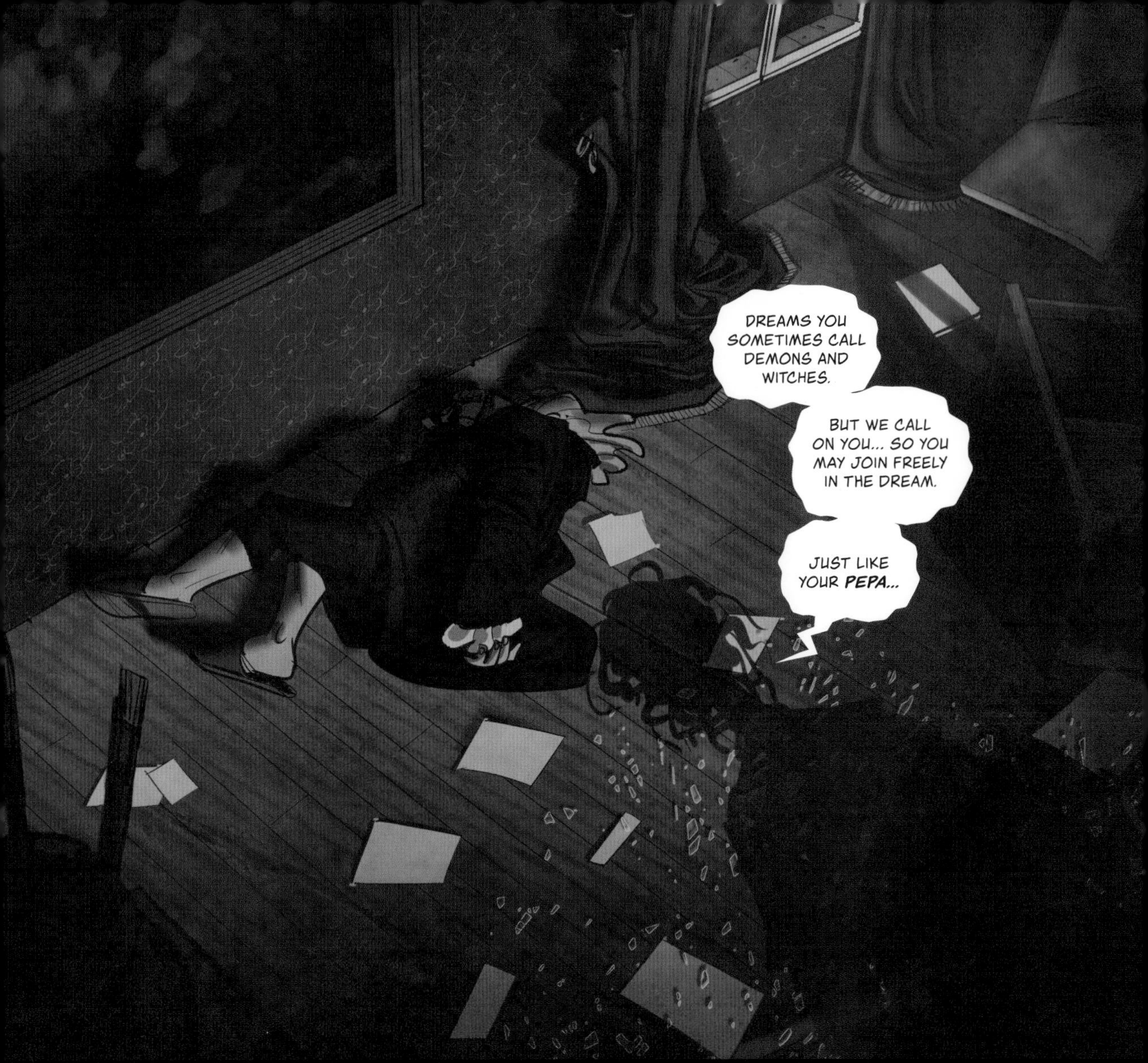
DREAMS YOU SOMETIMES CALL DEMONS AND WITCHES.
BUT WE CALL ON YOU... SO YOU MAY JOIN FREELY IN THE DREAM.
JUST LIKE YOUR **PEPA...**
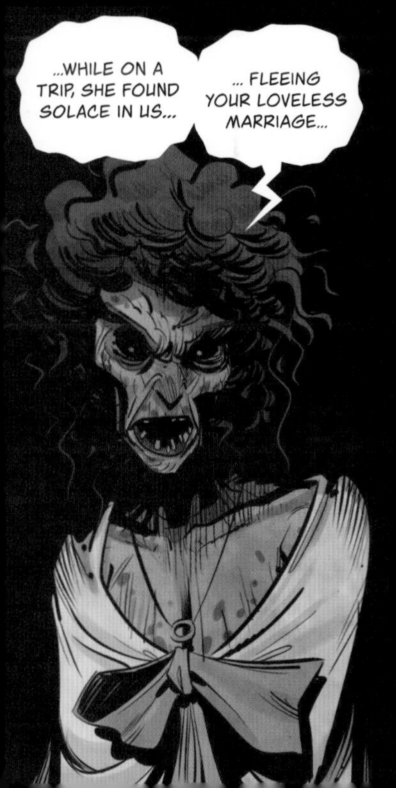
...WHILE ON A TRIP, SHE FOUND SOLACE IN US...
... FLEEING YOUR LOVELESS MARRIAGE...
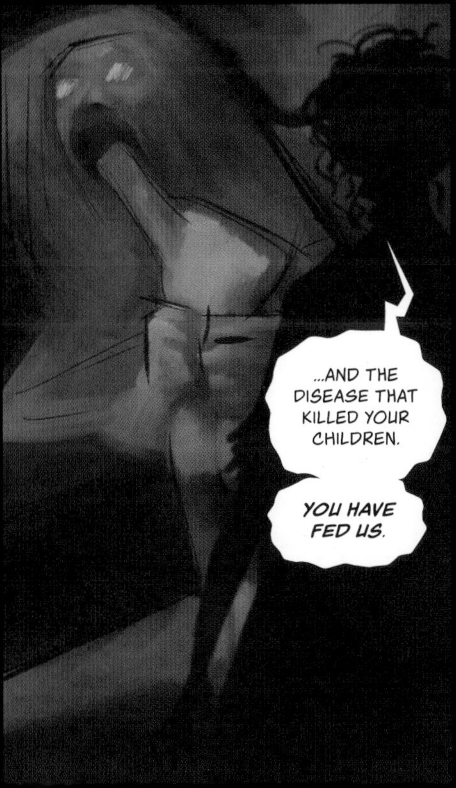
...AND THE DISEASE THAT KILLED YOUR CHILDREN.
***YOU HAVE FED US.***
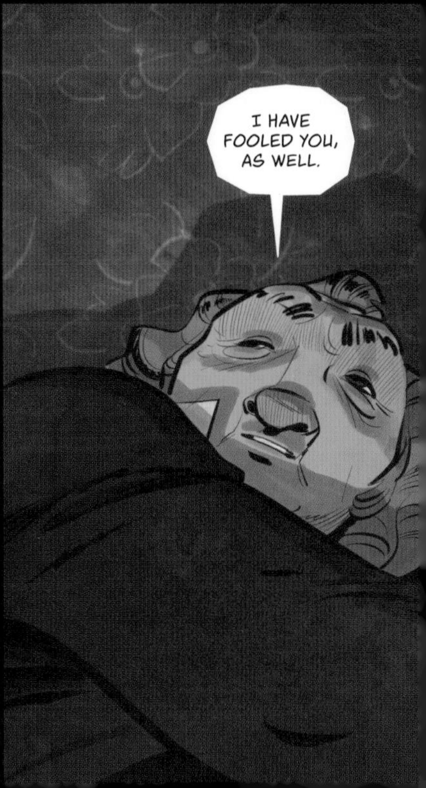
I HAVE FOOLED YOU, AS WELL.

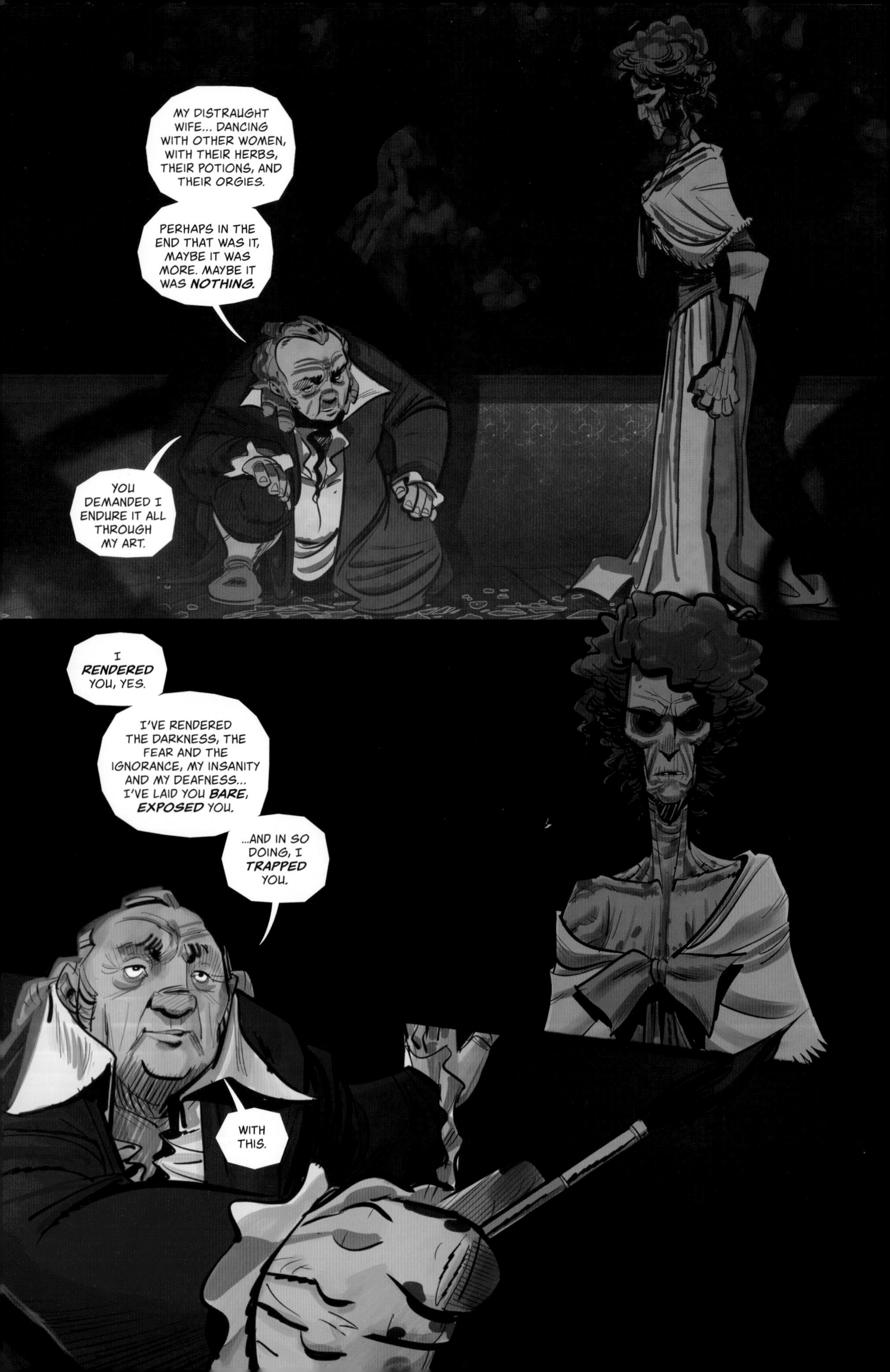
MY DISTRAUGHT WIFE... DANCING WITH OTHER WOMEN, WITH THEIR HERBS, THEIR POTIONS, AND THEIR ORGIES.
PERHAPS IN THE END THAT WAS IT, MAYBE IT WAS MORE. MAYBE IT WAS ***NOTHING.***
YOU DEMANDED I ENDURE IT ALL THROUGH MY ART.
I ***RENDERED*** YOU, YES.
I'VE RENDERED THE DARKNESS, THE FEAR AND THE IGNORANCE, MY INSANITY AND MY DEAFNESS... I'VE LAID YOU ***BARE, EXPOSED*** YOU.
...AND IN SO DOING, I ***TRAPPED*** YOU.
WITH THIS.

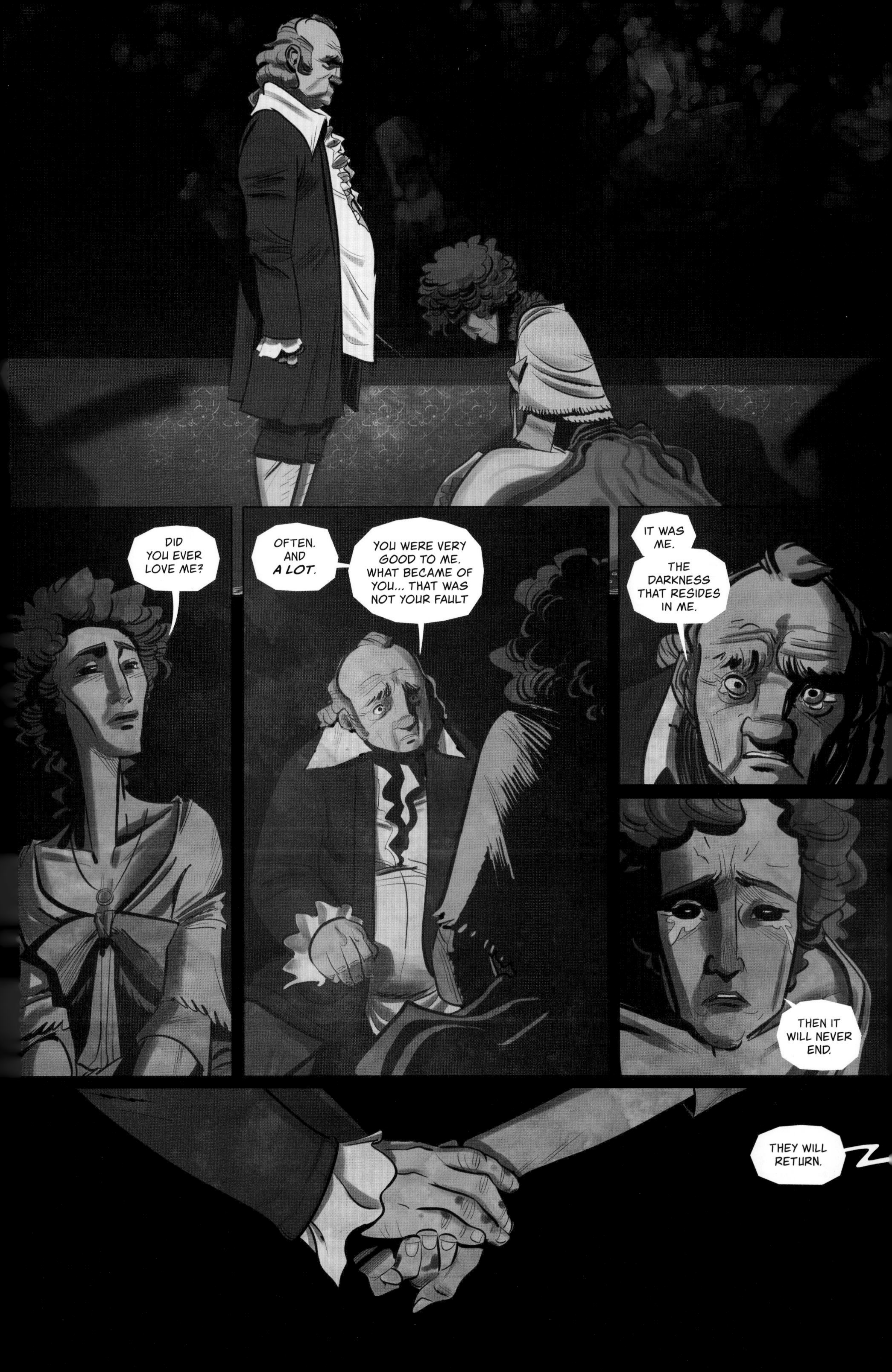
DID YOU EVER LOVE ME?
OFTEN. AND A LOT.
YOU WERE VERY GOOD TO ME. WHAT BECAME OF YOU... THAT WAS NOT YOUR FAULT
IT WAS ME.
THE DARKNESS THAT RESIDES IN ME.
THEN IT WILL NEVER END.
THEY WILL RETURN.

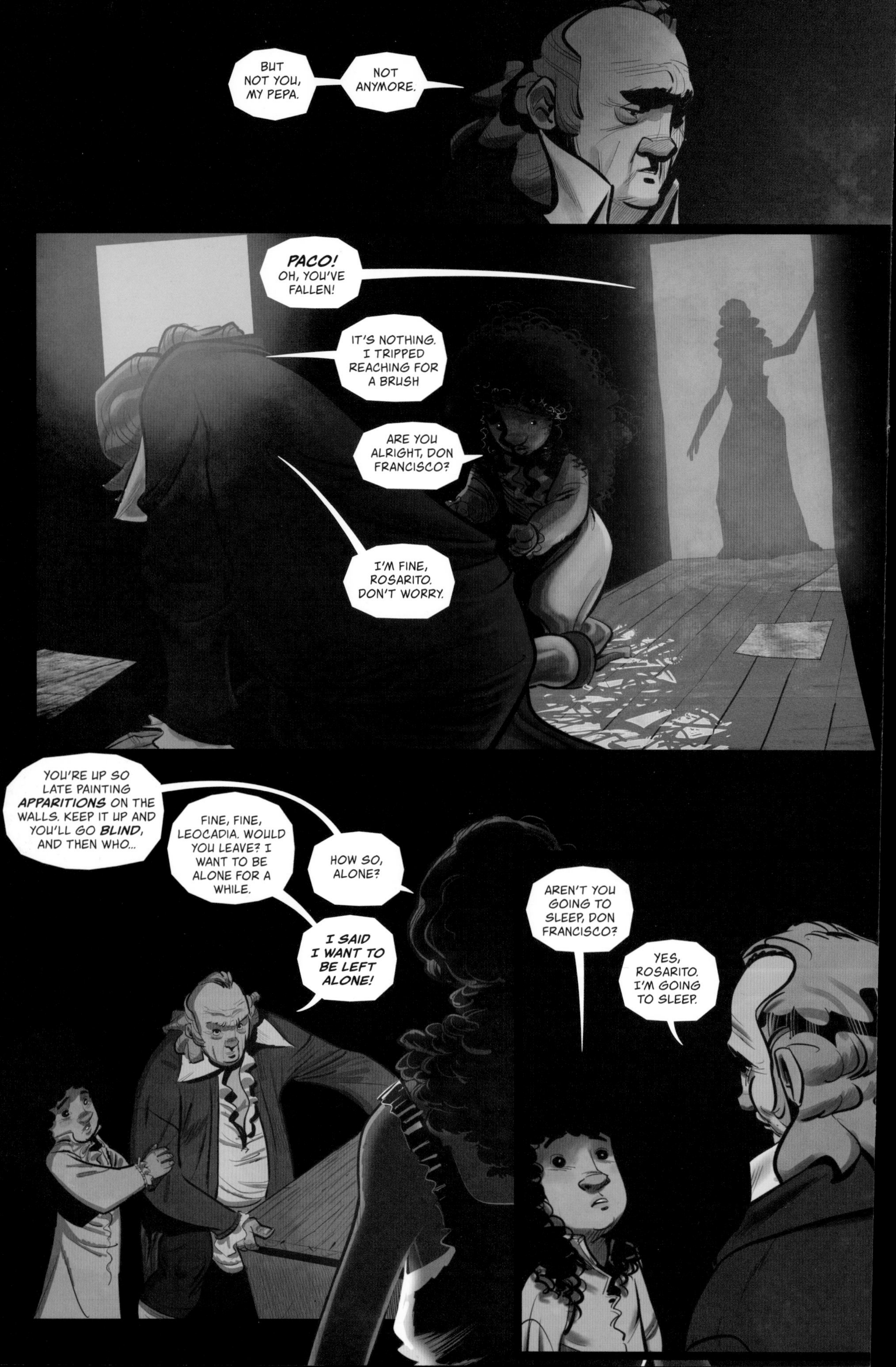
BUT NOT YOU, MY PEPA.
NOT ANYMORE.
**PACO!** OH, YOU'VE FALLEN!
IT'S NOTHING. I TRIPPED REACHING FOR A BRUSH
ARE YOU ALRIGHT, DON FRANCISCO?
I'M FINE, ROSARITO. DON'T WORRY.
YOU'RE UP SO LATE PAINTING ***APPARITIONS*** ON THE WALLS. KEEP IT UP AND YOU'LL GO ***BLIND***, AND THEN WHO...
FINE, FINE, LEOCADIA. WOULD YOU LEAVE? I WANT TO BE ALONE FOR A WHILE.
HOW SO, ALONE?
***I SAID I WANT TO BE LEFT ALONE!***
AREN'T YOU GOING TO SLEEP, DON FRANCISCO?
YES, ROSARITO. I'M GOING TO SLEEP.

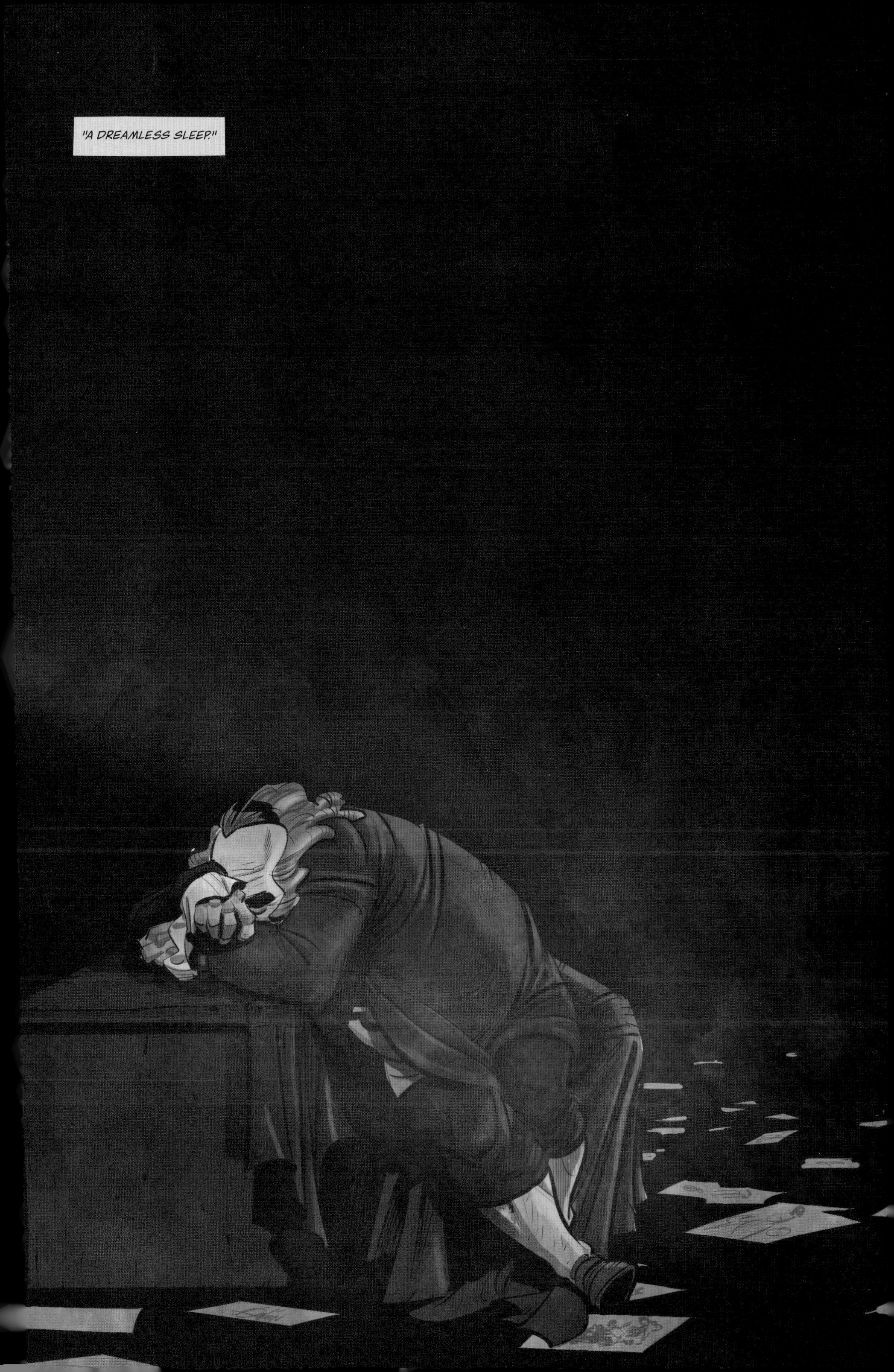
"A DREAMLESS SLEEP."

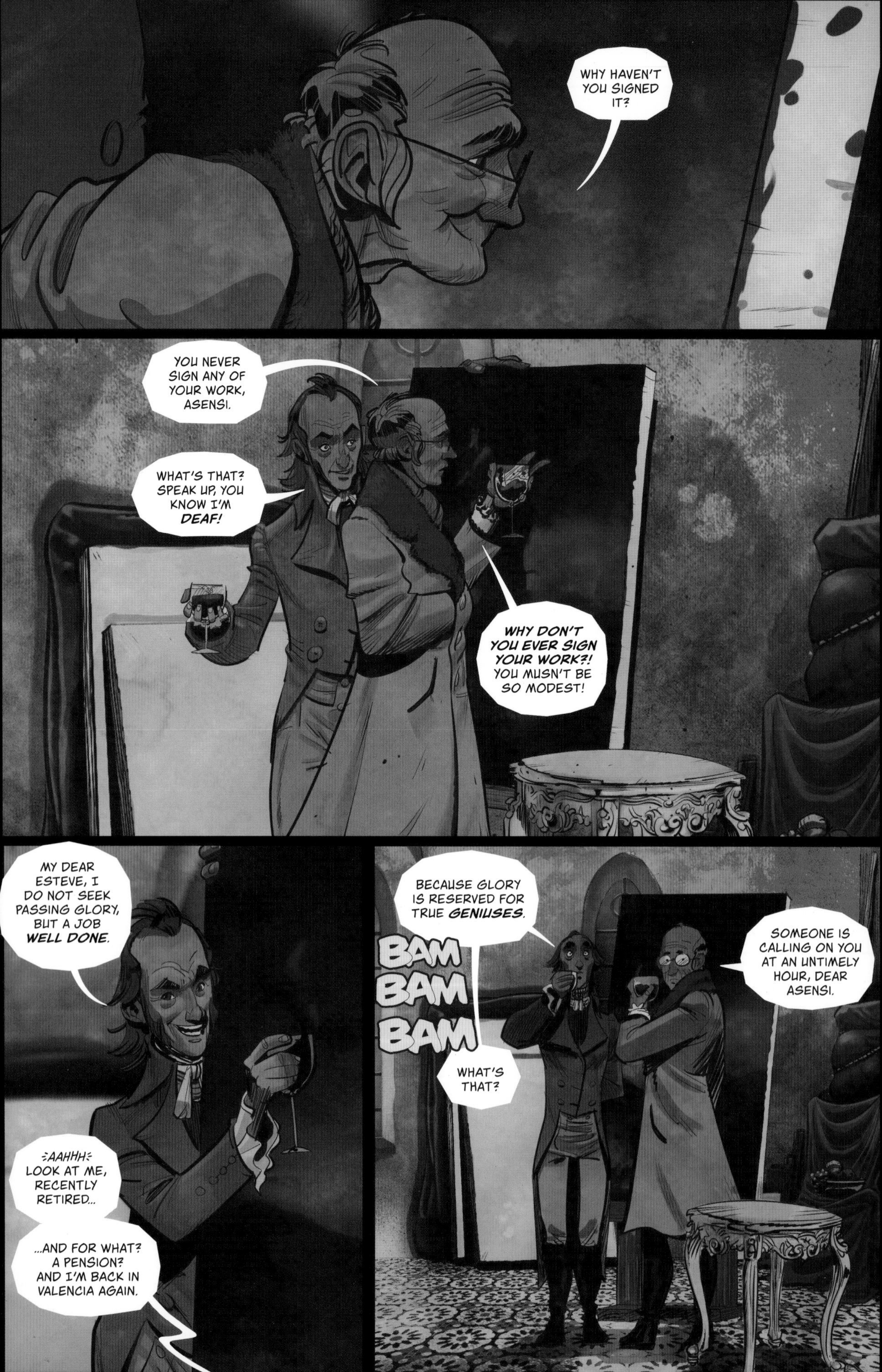
WHY HAVEN'T YOU SIGNED IT?
YOU NEVER SIGN ANY OF YOUR WORK, ASENSI.
WHAT'S THAT? SPEAK UP, YOU KNOW I'M DEAF!
WHY DON'T YOU EVER SIGN YOUR WORK?! YOU MUSN'T BE SO MODEST!
MY DEAR ESTEVE, I DO NOT SEEK PASSING GLORY, BUT A JOB WELL DONE.
*AAHHH* LOOK AT ME, RECENTLY RETIRED...
...AND FOR WHAT? A PENSION? AND I'M BACK IN VALENCIA AGAIN.
BECAUSE GLORY IS RESERVED FOR TRUE GENIUSES.
BAM BAM BAM
WHAT'S THAT?
SOMEONE IS CALLING ON YOU AT AN UNTIMELY HOUR, DEAR ASENSI.

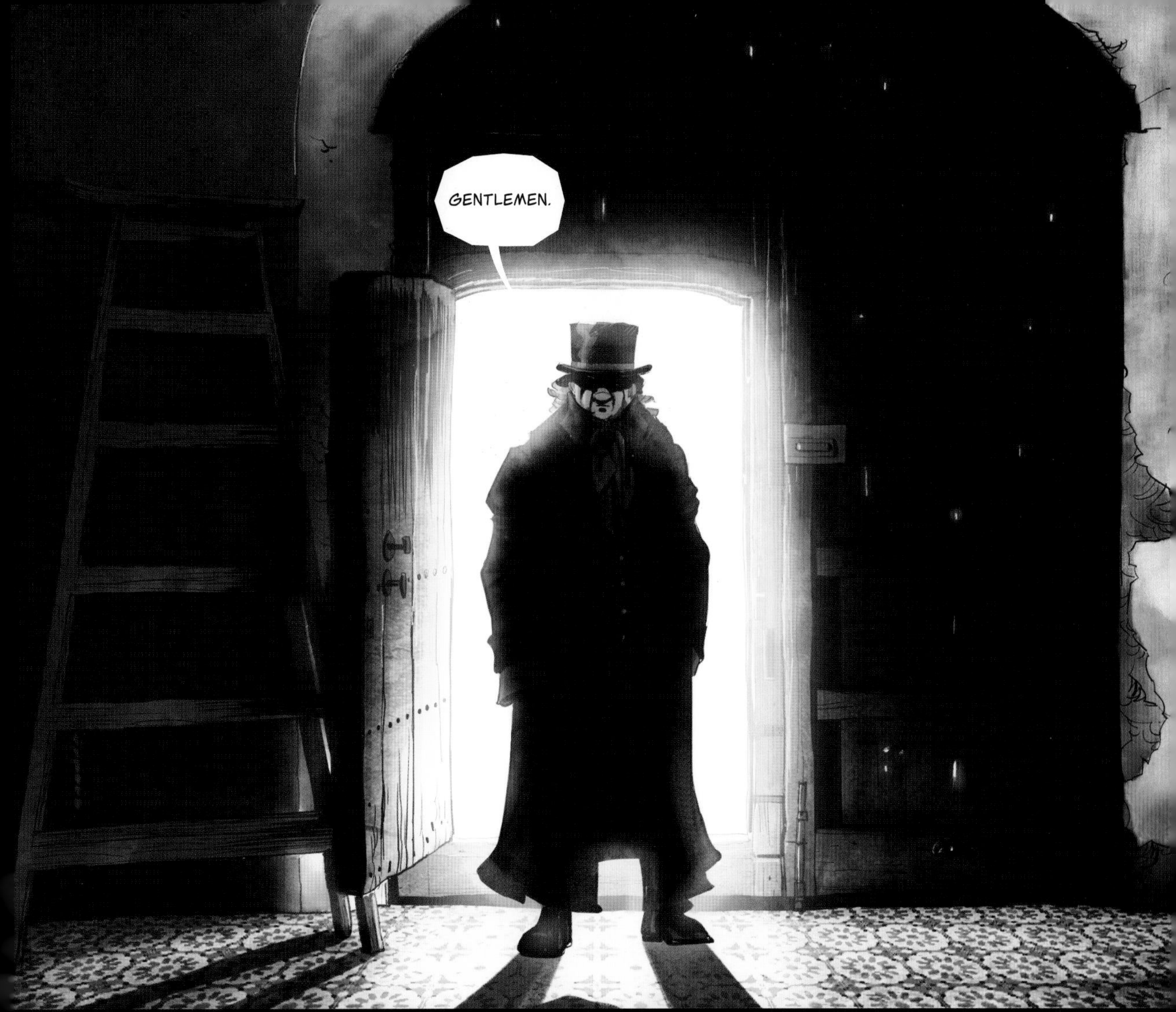
GENTLEMEN.

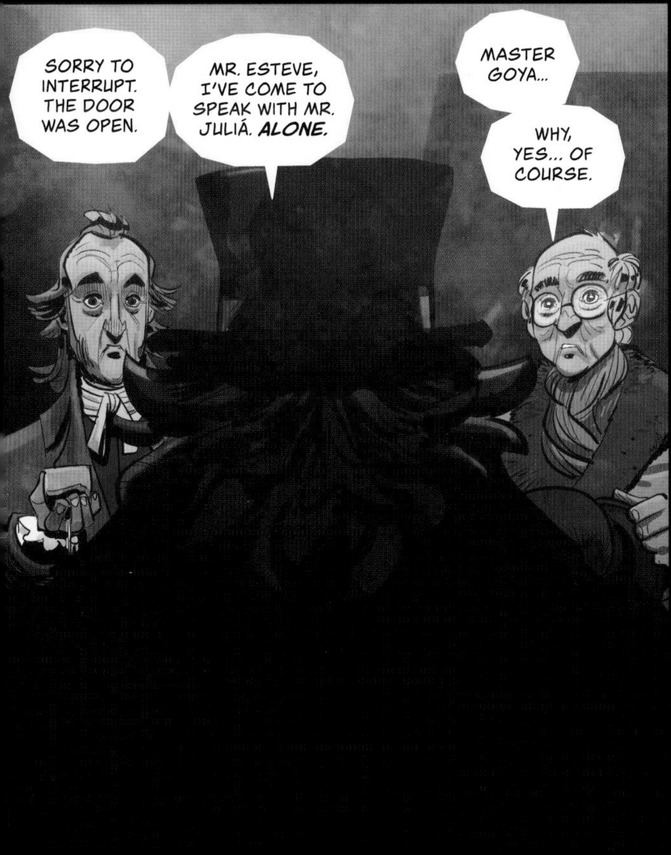
SORRY TO INTERRUPT. THE DOOR WAS OPEN.
MR. ESTEVE, I'VE COME TO SPEAK WITH MR. JULIÁ. ALONE.
MASTER GOYA...
WHY, YES... OF COURSE.

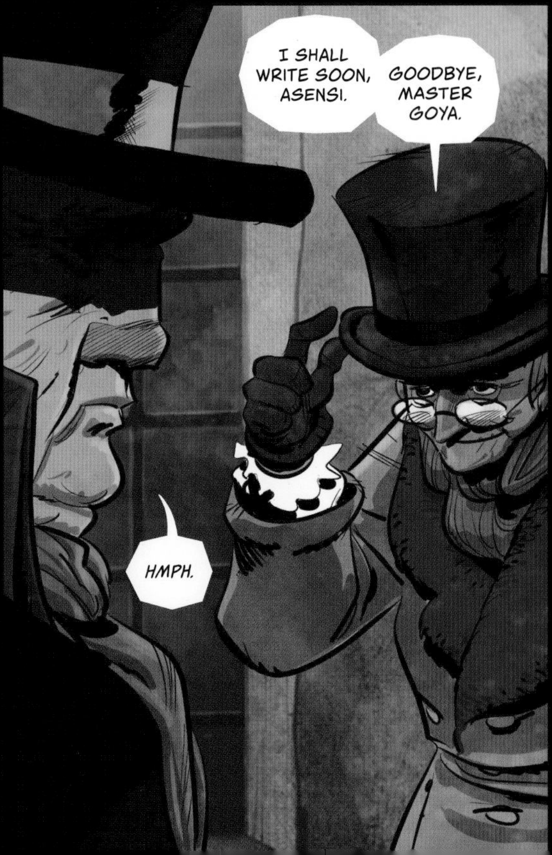
I SHALL WRITE SOON, ASENSI.
GOODBYE, MASTER GOYA.
HMPH.

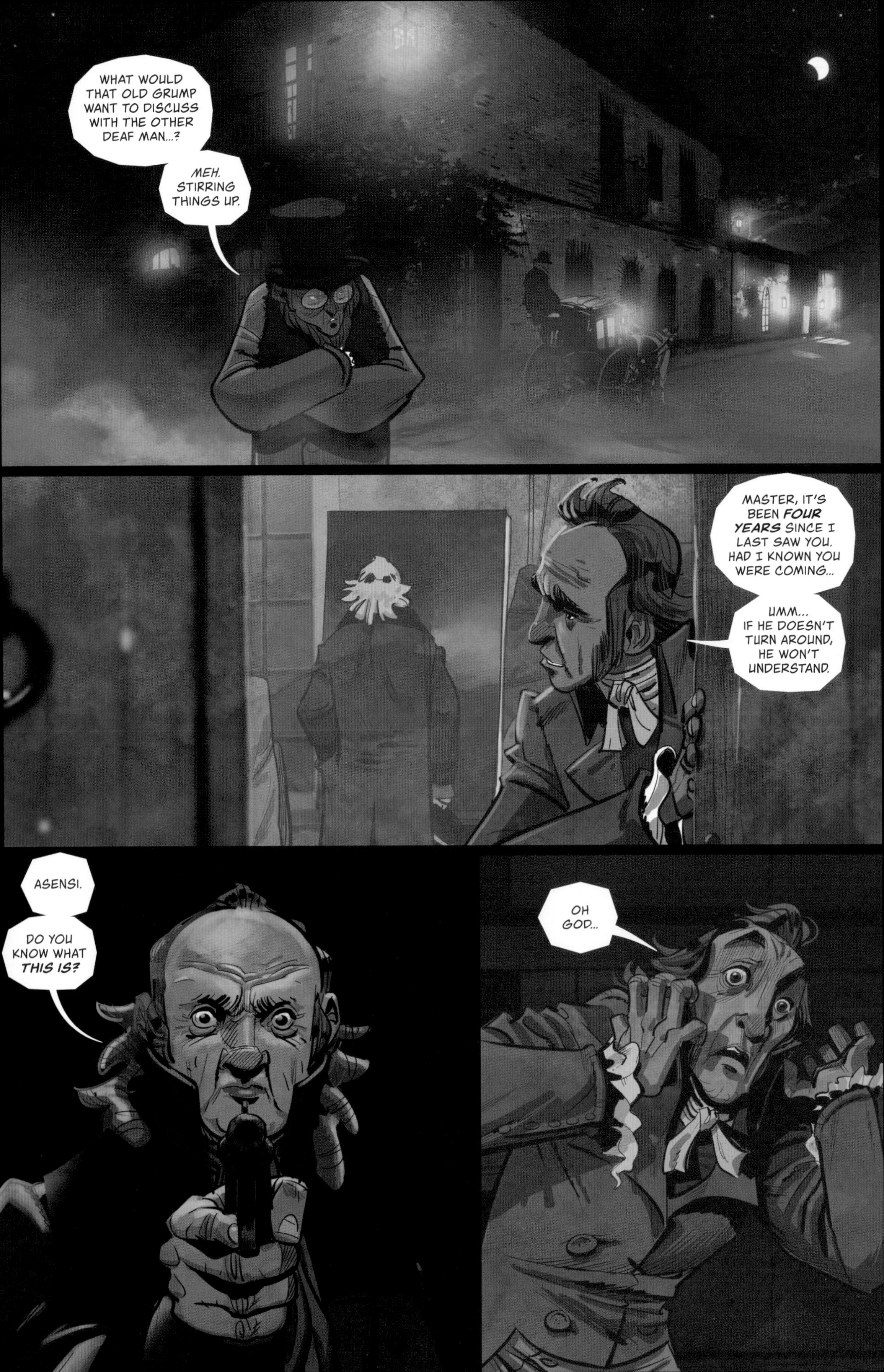
WHAT WOULD THAT OLD GRUMP WANT TO DISCUSS WITH THE OTHER DEAF MAN...?
MEH. STIRRING THINGS UP.
MASTER, IT'S BEEN **FOUR YEARS** SINCE I LAST SAW YOU. HAD I KNOWN YOU WERE COMING...
UMM... IF HE DOESN'T TURN AROUND, HE WON'T UNDERSTAND.
ASENSI.
DO YOU KNOW WHAT ***THIS IS?***
OH GOD...

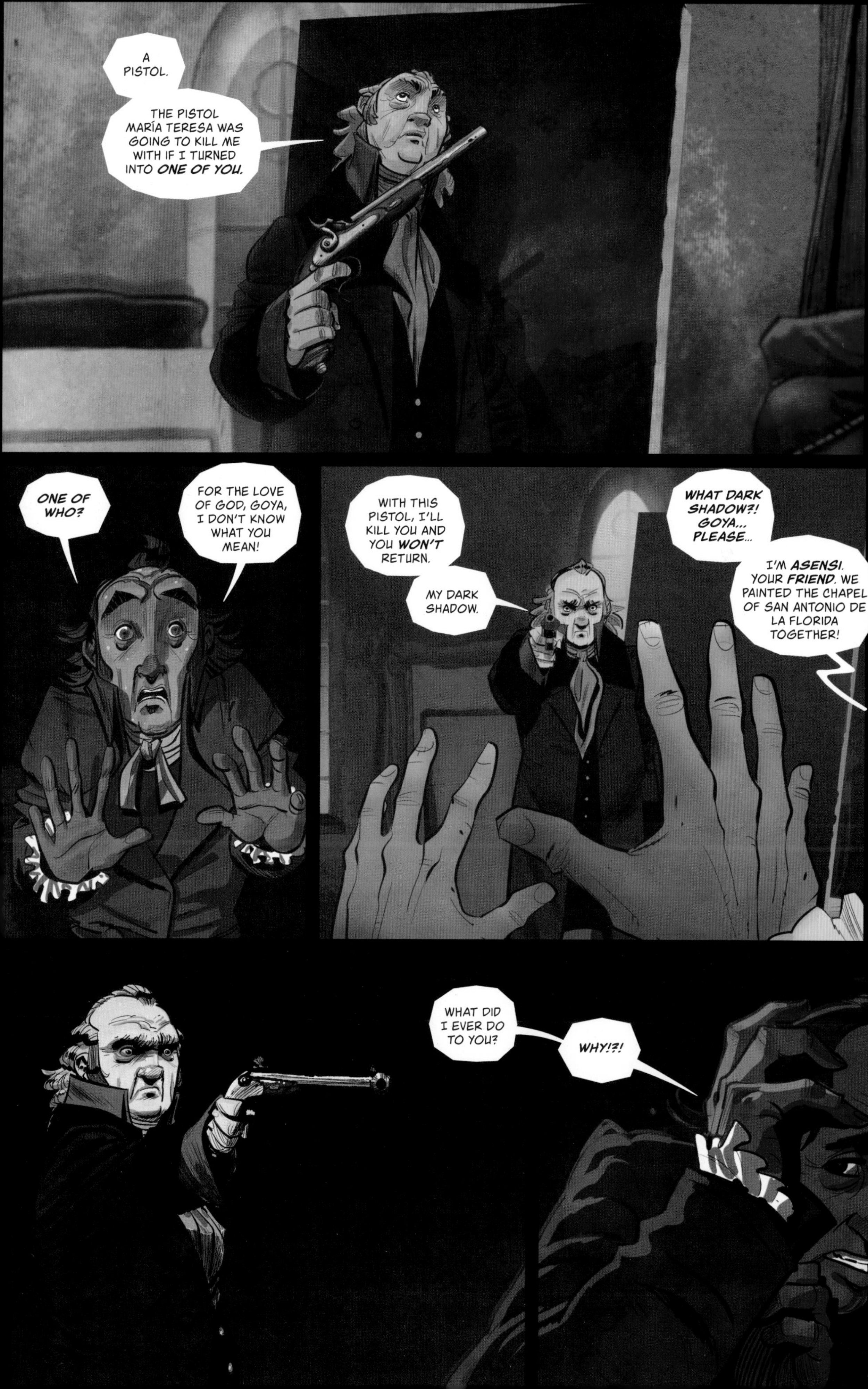
A PISTOL.
THE PISTOL MARÍA TERESA WAS GOING TO KILL ME WITH IF I TURNED INTO *ONE OF YOU.*
*ONE OF WHO?*
FOR THE LOVE OF GOD, GOYA, I DON'T KNOW WHAT YOU MEAN!
WITH THIS PISTOL, I'LL KILL YOU AND YOU *WON'T* RETURN.
MY DARK SHADOW.
*WHAT DARK SHADOW?! GOYA... PLEASE...*
I'M *ASENSI*. YOUR *FRIEND*. WE PAINTED THE CHAPEL OF SAN ANTONIO DE LA FLORIDA TOGETHER!
WHAT DID I EVER DO TO YOU?
*WHY!?!*

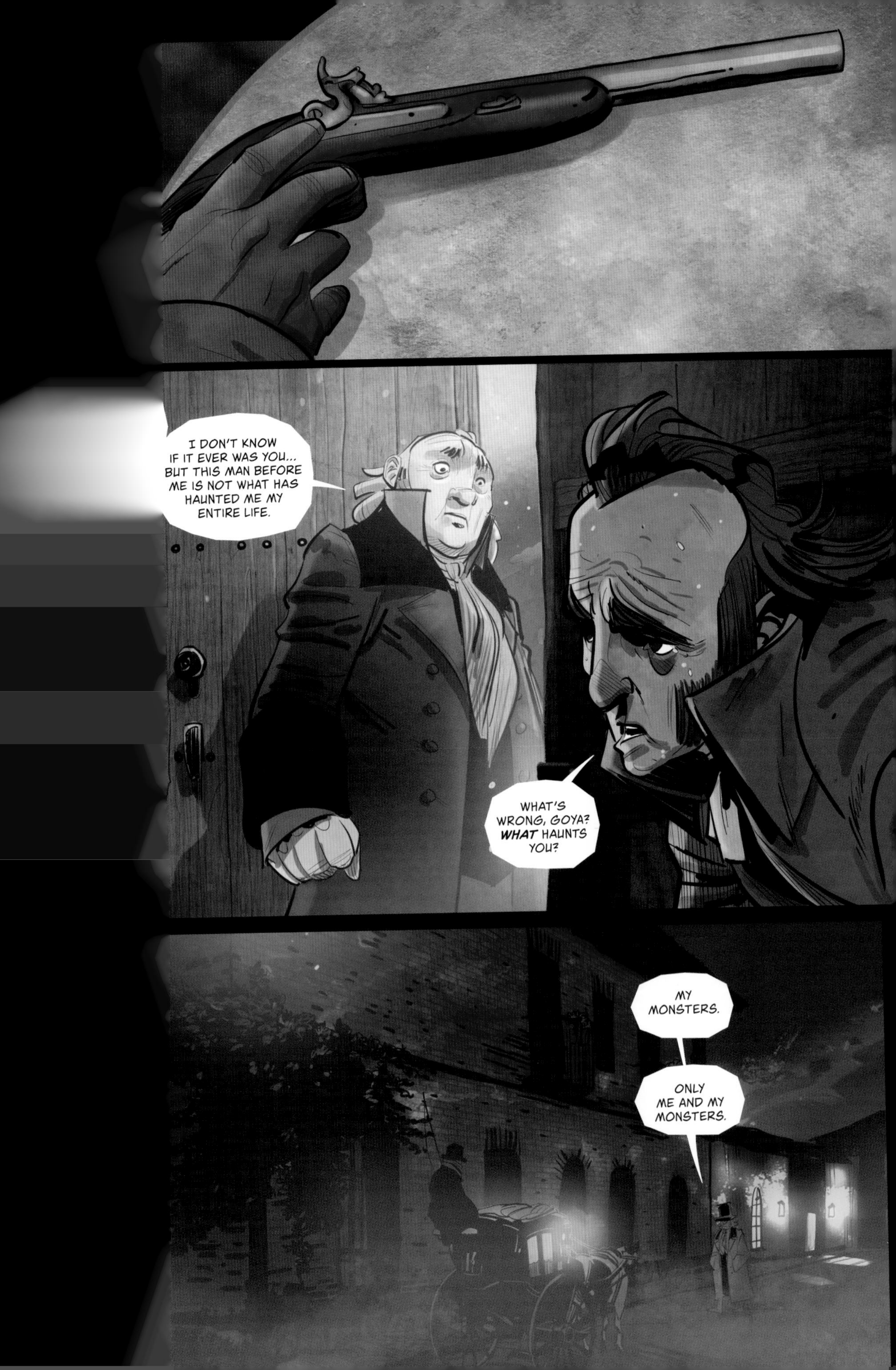
I DON'T KNOW IF IT EVER WAS YOU... BUT THIS MAN BEFORE ME IS NOT WHAT HAS HAUNTED ME MY ENTIRE LIFE.
WHAT'S WRONG, GOYA? ***WHAT*** HAUNTS YOU?
MY MONSTERS.
ONLY ME AND MY MONSTERS.

# Epilogue

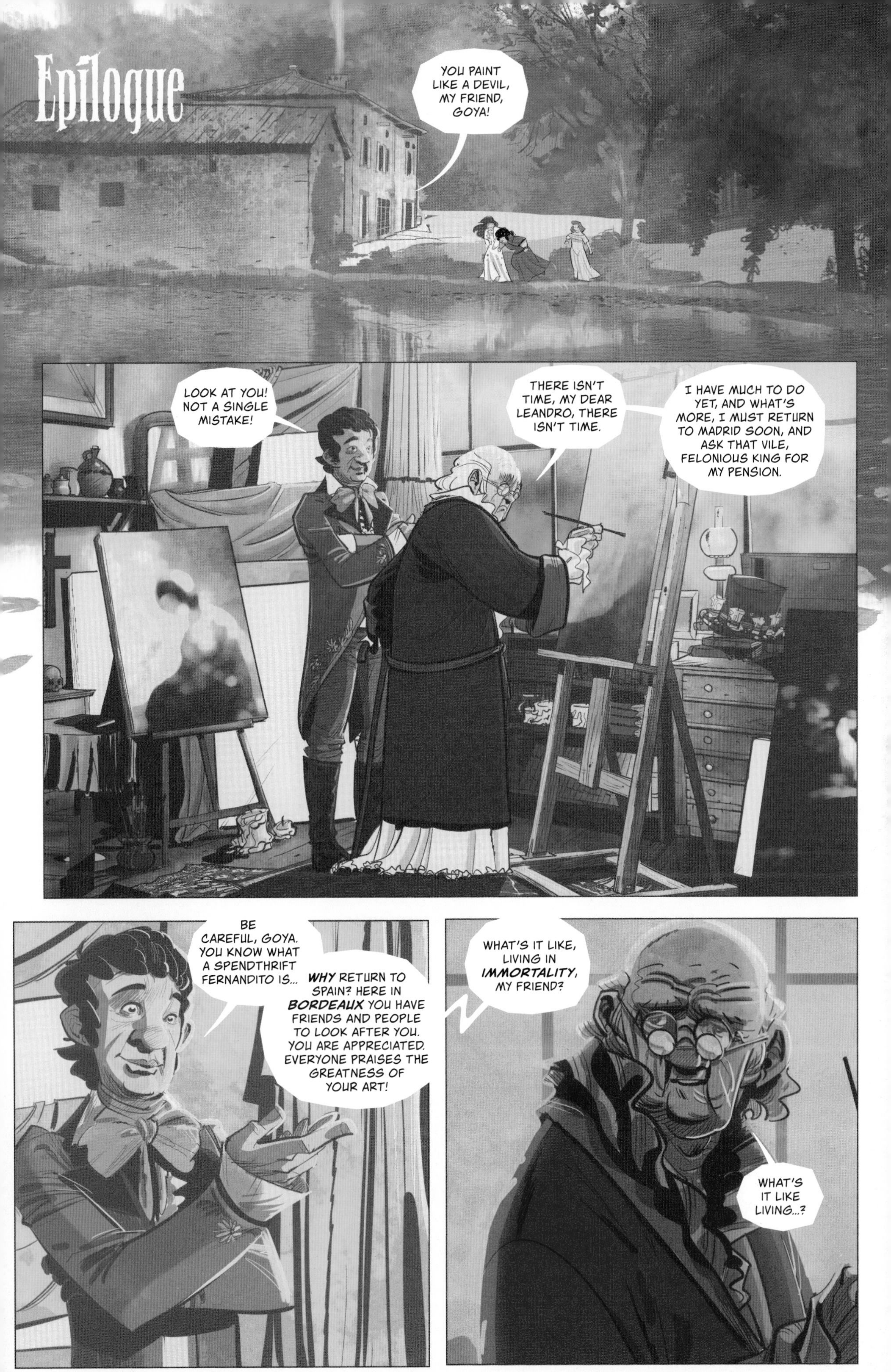
YOU PAINT LIKE A DEVIL, MY FRIEND, GOYA!
LOOK AT YOU! NOT A SINGLE MISTAKE!
THERE ISN'T TIME, MY DEAR LEANDRO, THERE ISN'T TIME.
I HAVE MUCH TO DO YET, AND WHAT'S MORE, I MUST RETURN TO MADRID SOON, AND ASK THAT VILE, FELONIOUS KING FOR MY PENSION.
BE CAREFUL, GOYA. YOU KNOW WHAT A SPENDTHRIFT FERNANDITO IS...
*WHY* RETURN TO SPAIN? HERE IN *BORDEAUX* YOU HAVE FRIENDS AND PEOPLE TO LOOK AFTER YOU. YOU ARE APPRECIATED. EVERYONE PRAISES THE GREATNESS OF YOUR ART!
WHAT'S IT LIKE, LIVING IN *IMMORTALITY*, MY FRIEND?
WHAT'S IT LIKE LIVING...?

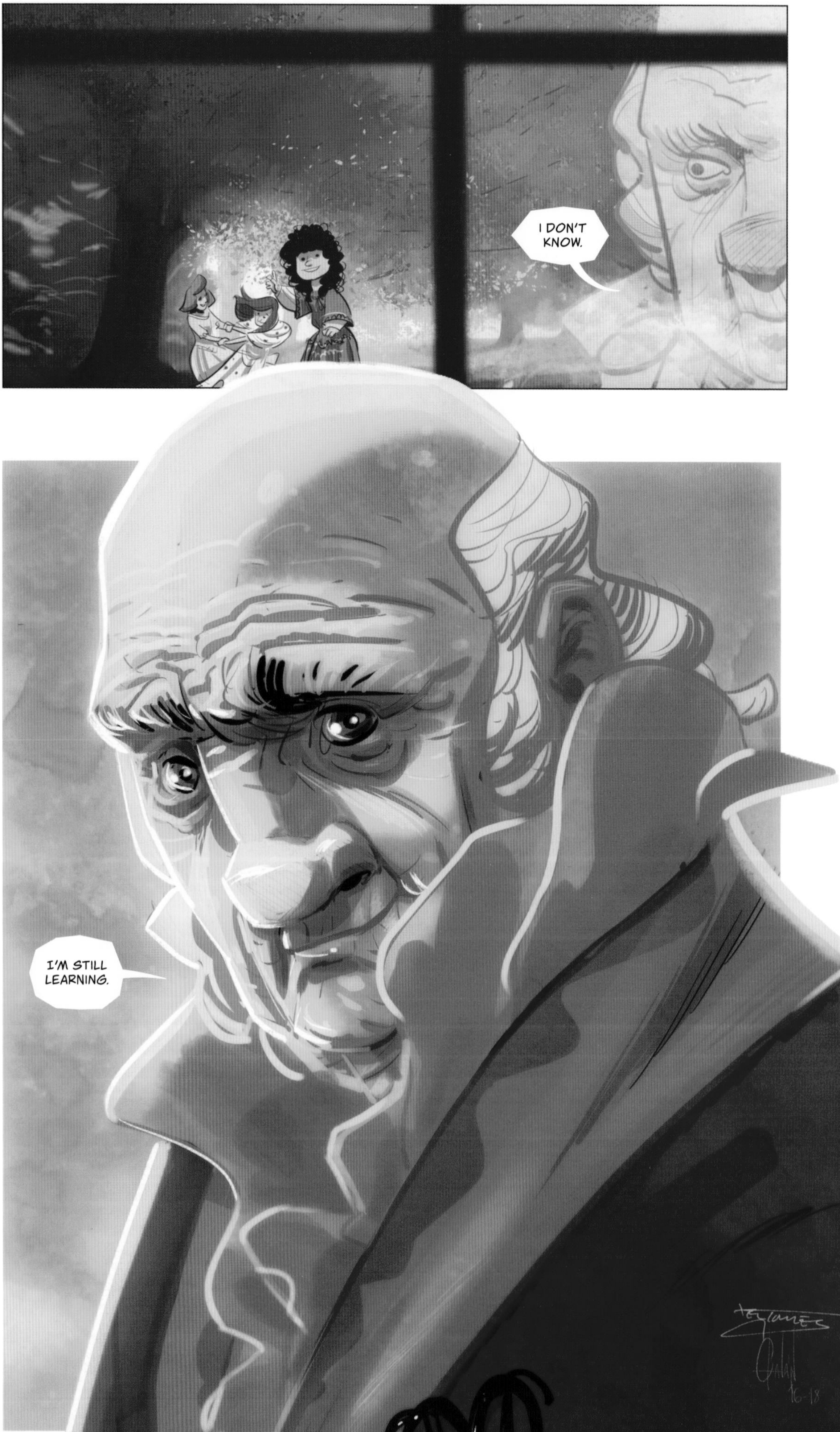
I DON'T KNOW.
I'M STILL LEARNING.

# Acknowledgments

To my most beloved daughter, Noa, my greatest motivation.

To my grandfather, who unknowingly planted the seed that would bear the fruit you hold in your hands today.

*–Fran Galán*


Everyone knows that a piece of work such as this is not created by one or two people alone. Behind it lies the constant support of those who share our lives.

Therefore, I wish to offer thanks to a lot of people.

First, to our readers; without you, none of this is possible. To my pal Fran, for embarking on this two-year journey with me. To Alejandro Romero and Rafa Marín, for your works and your keen eye for discovering cathedrals that shouldn't be there. To Ricardo Esteban, our editor, for finding Goya: The Terrible Sublime a home. To Paco Plaza, whose enthusiasm for reading this book helped us finish it. And I always wish to thank my father and mother, because well, without them, I wouldn't be here. Also to Olga, who urged me on when I fought with Goya the hardest.

And of course, to Paqui.

*–El Torres*

# Francisco De Goya y Lucientes, Master of Terror

ALEJANDRO ROMERO
with notes by El Torres

*"No other romantic artist opened instinct and subconscious impulse so completely to public view."*
—*The Penguin Encyclopedia of Horror and the Supernatural*
**Entry on Goya, written by CARL WOODRING**

*"Other men have to fill their mouths all day, I have to cram my eyes. Looking's a vice with me. I have to devour everything I so much as glance at, what the angels and the fallen angels made, it's the same to me. And when I've got the sights in here I want to make them all over again, in paint, and sign them, yes sign the world and say: 'Goya saw this!'"*
—*Colossus, CLIVE BARKER*

It was high time Goya found his rightful place, no?

In other countries, others have already done so. For Noël Carroll, Goya's place was the very same cover of his *Philosophy of Horror or Paradoxes of the Heart* (1990), the contemporary classic indispensable for philosophical musings on the genre of terror.

After appropriating Saturn and the half-eaten corpse of a child, Carroll ostensibly defines terror, citing superlative examples across multiple mediums and artistic formats. His cornucopia of horrors overflows with Mary Shelley's *Frankenstein*, Lovecraft's *The Dunwich Horror*, Scott's *Alien*, Romero's *Night of the Living Dead*, H.R. Giger's airbrush paintings, and the paintings and engravings of Francisco de Goya.

All from one family. All in good company.

A few years earlier, Clive Barker had found another worthy spot for Goya: the backdrop to his last theatrical piece, *Colossus* (1984), based on *The Disasters of War* and *The Colossus* (which at the time was attributed without doubt to Goya, but today is believed to have been painted by Asensi Juliá, copying the style of Goya's *The Giant*).

After that final, horrific tragicomedy with Goya as protagonist and a cast of drawn and quartered corpses, Barker exited the stage and leapt to international fame with his *Books of Blood* (1984-1985).

But Goya stuck with him. As he recognizes in Douglas E. Winter's authorized biography, (*The Dark Fantastic*), *The Colossus* is behind *In the Hills, the Cities*, perhaps the most visionary first

volume's stories. In his prologue to the first edition, Ramsey Campbell praises it for offering irrefutable proof that completely new ideas can emerge within the terror genre.

But of course they can: by returning to Goya, just like Juliá did.

In Spain, apart from the occasional cover on anthologies or collections of horror stories, we still hadn't done justice to Goya in good measure.

Universal genius? Without doubt. Incorruptible —or corruptible only to a point—chronicler of his time? Of course. Pioneer in romanticism, herald of vanguards to come and, accordingly, vanguard of vanguards? It all falls short!

What's more, and above all else, master of terror.

Just like Poe. No need to look any further—another universal genius and pioneer of pioneers, trapped between the lucidity of reason and violent undercurrents of romantic passion. Think of "The Black Cat," "A Tell Tale Heart," and "William Wilson," all tormented, diminished souls in the likeness of Vincent Price, toys in the hands of perverse demons who, like their author, are slaves to destructive, irrational impulses they cannot control.

However, Poe is more than just an obstinate loser that finds his own death in the bottom of the bottle. He is also the cold, analytical mind that disects "Maelzel's Chess Player," that disembowels the hidden order of the universe in Eureka, that invents Monsieur Dupin's deductive reasoning and puts it to work solving the murder of young Mary

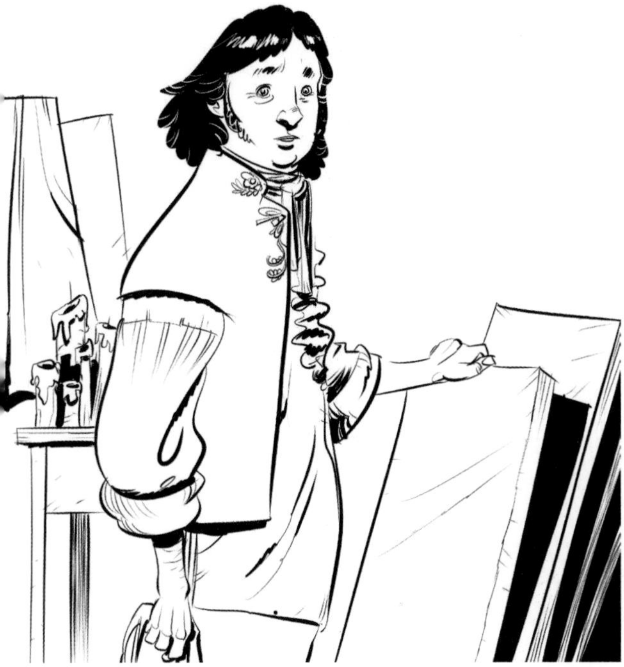

PROMOTIONAL BLACK AND WHITE DRAWING SHOWING GOYA IN HIS STUDIO.

Rogers before the police can. (Required reading: *The Beautiful Cigar Girl: Mary Rogers, Edgar Allan Poe, and the Invention of Murder*, by Daniel Stashower. You're welcome.)

So rich were his life and his work that we have been unable to resist the urge, time and again, to conflate the two in storytelling. Everyone has their favorite among the ever-growing and evolving Poe interpretations. I have a particular weakness for two small screen versions, one produced by Chicho Ibáñez Serrador for the last episode of of the 1967 season of *Stories to Stay Awake* ("The Raven"), the other by Stuart Gordon for the second season of *Masters of Horror* ("The Black Cat," 2007). Where cameos are concerned, there is *Castle of Blood* by Sergio Corbucci and Antonio Margheriti. But there are many, many more, and he deserves them all.

As was Goya, the master of terror, deserving of his interpretation—the one you just read.

Of course, there have been others, more focussed on Goya as war correspondent or Goya as witness to a tapestry of infernal processions. See, for example, Mario Camus' miniseries *Los Desastres de la Guerra* (1983).

That was not the only Spanish public television production dedicated to Goya. A couple of years later, in *Goya* (1985), viewers could journey through the entire life of the painter and, as a perverse parting gift, spend a whole episode as a guest at the Deaf Man's Villa. If you didn't know the director, José Ramón Larraz, you'd be forgiven for thinking such an immersion into the *Black Paintings* inspired his subsequent horror films (*Rest in Pieces*, 1987; *Edge of the Axe*, 1988; *Sevilla Connection*, with Los Morancos, 1992). You would be mistaken. Larraz had arrived at Goya on the backs of his own baggage of grotesque visions (see his earlier filmography, or read his memoirs, *Del tebeo al cine, con mujeres de película*).

To be sure, outside of his own eloquent work, we have only ever glimpsed at Goya, master of terror, for brief moments, in certain sequences by Luis Buñuel or Orson Welles (*Confidential Report*, 1955). It is worth noting that Buñel was never allowed to film *Goya*, a movie commissioned to commemorate the first centenary of the genius'

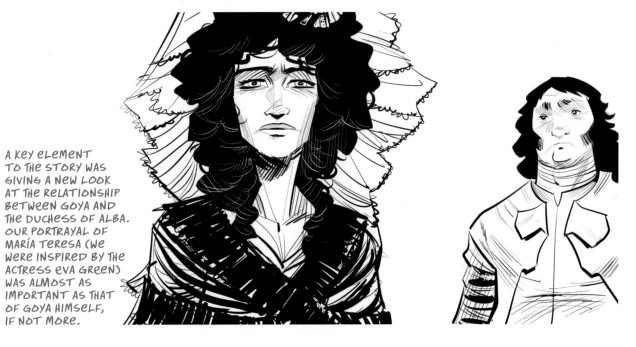

A KEY ELEMENT TO THE STORY WAS GIVING A NEW LOOK AT THE RELATIONSHIP BETWEEN GOYA AND THE DUCHESS OF ALBA. OUR PORTRAYAL OF MARÍA TERESA (WE WERE INSPIRED BY THE ACTRESS EVA GREEN) WAS ALMOST AS IMPORTANT AS THAT OF GOYA HIMSELF, IF NOT MORE.

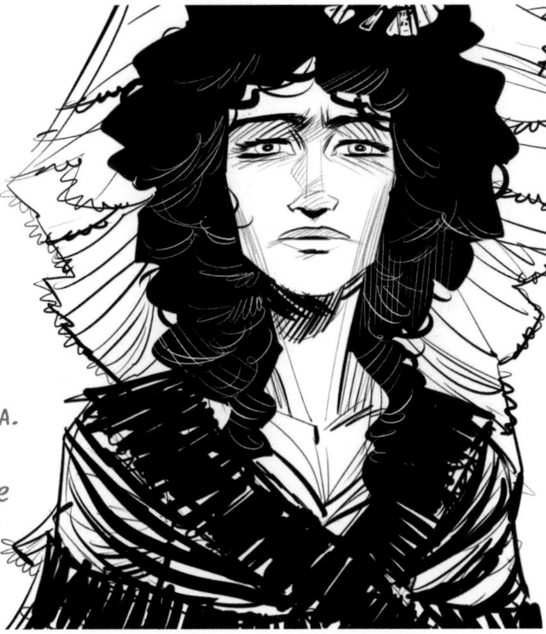

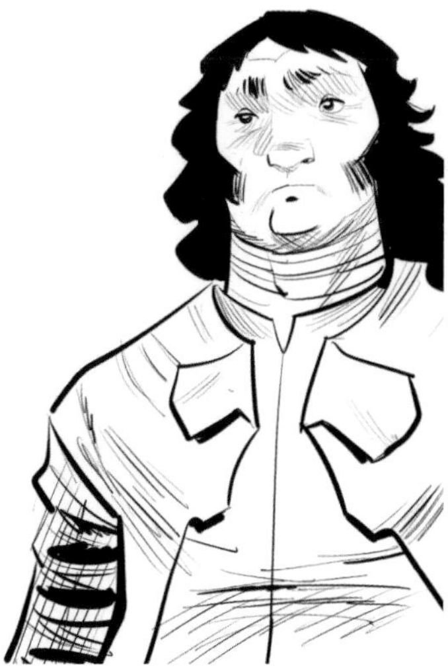

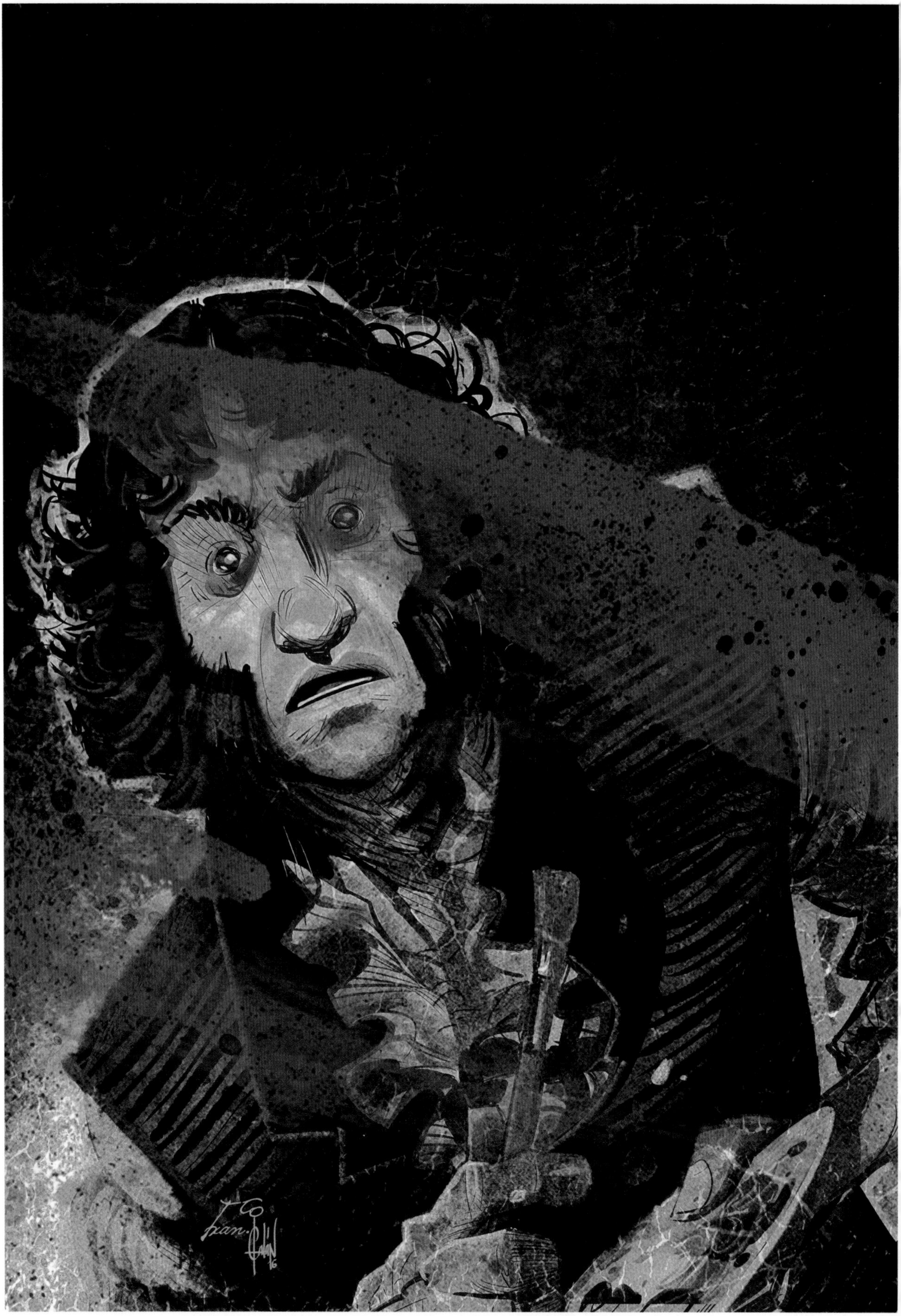

WE BEGAN CONSTRUCTION FROM THE ROOF DOWN. FIRST, WE NEEDED AN ILLUSTRATION, A COVER PAGE TO ORIENT OURSELVES AS TO WHICH WAY WE WERE HEADING. THE BASIC IDEA WAS THERE--WE GOT IT ON THE FIRST GO--BUT LATER WE SIGNIFICANTLY CHANGED GOYA'S CHARACTER, WHICH IN THIS ATTEMPT SEEMED TO US A LITTLE TOO... MUTANT.

death: the script survives, that we may pine over what could have been.

This may be owing to the fact that, for far too long, we have "out-Menéndez Pidaled" Menéndez Pidal himself, as it were. If he characterized Spanish literature as essentially realist, we have taken pains to self-impose this principle on any form of artistic interpretation to arise within our borders, however capricious.

To gain importance, we believed, a piece must be realist. To be great, we must be truthful.

Just as Goya who, in the sketches he made public and the sketchbooks that remained unpublished throughout his life, insisted on a recurrent theme: "I saw it."

So, once we've been shown the customary prints... once he's snuck us into the Bourbon's Court... once we've seen portraits so scrupulously faithful they verge on insulting... once he's appalled us with the horrors of the War of Independence... once we've witnessed all of these realities... what to do with the Goya of fantasy?

Commentators, especially after the verdict delivered by the inexorable Ortega in his *Writings on Velázquez and Goya*, have insisted on the exceptionally "symptomatic" nature of Goya: his work is always a response to the sociohistorical circumstances that determine it. (Does Ortega believe anyone isn't conditioned by their circumstances? Ortega aside, is there anyone who isn't?)

One can dig deeper: In his fascinating book, *El enigma Goya*, Doctor Francisco Alonso-Fernández has ventured a posthumous psychiatric diagnosis, attributing the master's keen awareness of his surroundings to his cyclothymic personality, which would explain the major contrasts between his life and his work.

*The Follies* and the *Black Paintings* remain as a testimony of nineteenth-century Spain, told in a metaphoric language corresponding to the emotional state of an author residing in that Spain. As underscored by Gaspar Gómez de la Serna in his book *Goya y su España*, their correct interpretation should be anchored more "in the here and now than in the great beyond." Seen thusly, the *Black Paintings* are "the final step in the process of Spanish disillusion; the bitter affirmation of the bleak hopelessness of its people's destiny. Goya seems to shout that there is nothing more to do in this society that bargains away the peaceful and progressive Enlightenment; senselessly ruining the freedoms won through the blood of war;

energetically resigning itself to be bound by the chains of absolutism."

All true, but it shouldn't make us forget that witches—beautiful teachers!—fly.

They are not chained to the earth, like us pathetic little humans. They can emerge from any corner of the world, even in realist, ordinary Spain, and, riding their sticks, bathed in babies' innards, conquer the globe from the heavens.

And, having captured our imagination, they can strike us like lightning and meet in their covens wherever they please. For there is not one centimeter of reality in which the knotted trees in the dark forest of imagination cannot take root.

Just like the adventurers of yore, risking life and lucidity, the masters of terror, Poe and Goya, searched inward to explore uncharted territories that others would later map systemically. The maps drawn by Freud and his followers seem more precise and rigorous than Goya's field sketches or Poe's fever-ridden reports, but that is precisely what makes them less accurate, given the cloudy and elusive nature of the territory.

When we experience a Poe or a Goya nightmare, we feel the words or brushstrokes have trapped something much bigger than the nightmare itself. When we contemplate the sad dispossession of dreams on Freud's operating table, we know he has missed the most important point--he has measured and catalogued absolutely everything except the selfsame dream. Thus, we believe Chicho Ibáñez Serrador's origin story of "The Raven" more than Poe's own, "The Philosophy of Composition," in which he tries to convince us each verse came to him by following a sterile set of self-evident poetic axioms.

Goya doesn't tell the truth just because he documented Spanish history from the second half of the 17th century to the first quarter of the nineteenth century. He tells the truth because he is faithful to his imagination. Duly informed after reading a report from the frontline, we can declare, "It is true!" With Goya, the master of terror, when we see his images we need not say anything, for even before our intellect can react, *we know they are true*. We know, because every night, when we turn off the light, we all sleep in the Deaf Man's Villa.

This is why Goya belongs to everyone. Even the Spanish.

We have carried the cross of Menéndez Pidal long enough. For years we considered Bécquer a lucky, capricious folklorist, or we invoked

**ABOVE:** WE'LL NEVER KNOW EXACTLY WHAT MADRID'S CALLE DEL DESENGAÑO LOOKED LIKE IN 1794, BUT THERE IS ENOUGH DOCUMENTATION FOR US TO CONJURE UP AN IMAGE.

**FOLLOWING PAGE:** A SAMPLE OF THE PROCESS FRAN GALÁN EMPLOYED IN THESE PAGES. HERE, THE RECREATION OF THE WITCHES' SABBATH PAINTING. GETTING THE RIGHT COLORS AND TONES ON PAR WITH THE ORIGINAL PIECE WAS A TITANIC ENDEAVOR ON HIS PART.

comedic license and *animus iocandi* to justify the fantastical excursions of Ramón and Fernández Flórez. We have been compelled to calling ourselves Ralph Barby or Paul Naschy, despite being easily identifiable as Jacinto Molina—fully surrendering to the platonic ideal of an American family in a horror movie.

AFortunately, we now know that a mysterious force can make the children in Almanzora murder all the grownups, that the Antichrist can be born in Madrid, that the apocalypse can start in house 34 on the Rambla de Catalunya, that evil can be invoked in Vallecas, and exorcised with the song from the Centella ad.

SYes, it was time to reclaim Goya, the master of terror, in his own country. If Clive Barker can, why not Goya's own compatriots?

We are lucky cartoonists exist. In his 2011 *Goya*, Diego Olmos took the Devil himself to the Deaf Man's Villa in a powerful, black-and-white nightmare. And now—I'm not telling you anything you don't know, nor trying to sell you a book you've already bought—Goya: *The Terrible Sublime* creates another life for Goya, the master of terror, with all the best comics have to offer: the irresistible drawings of Fran Galán, in which live, in perfect harmony, his classic comic foundation, contemporary graphic resources and a talent for caricature that puts him on the same level as satirical Goya; and the masterful script by El Torres, among the few in Spain who truly understand the horror genre, demonstrating once

again truly scary stories say only what they need to, without forcing metaphors to extract morals, or worse, pleading that Menéndez Pidal might spare them their lives.

In a perfect world, Chicho Ibáñez Serrador would already be working to adapt *Goya: The Terrible Sublime*, as the first installment in reboot of *Stories to Stay Awake*. In our much less-than-perfect world, Chicho has retired. But how immensely fortunate that El Torres and Fran Galán have brought us this perfect graphic novel.

Remember the perfect ending when you re-read Ortega. Ortega is Ortega and his circumstances. Goya is Goya and his monsters, which are ours.

*"I think maybe the worst monsters are almost invisible, just seen out of the corner of the eye. And I think the future will be full of them."*
—Colossus, CLIVE BARKER

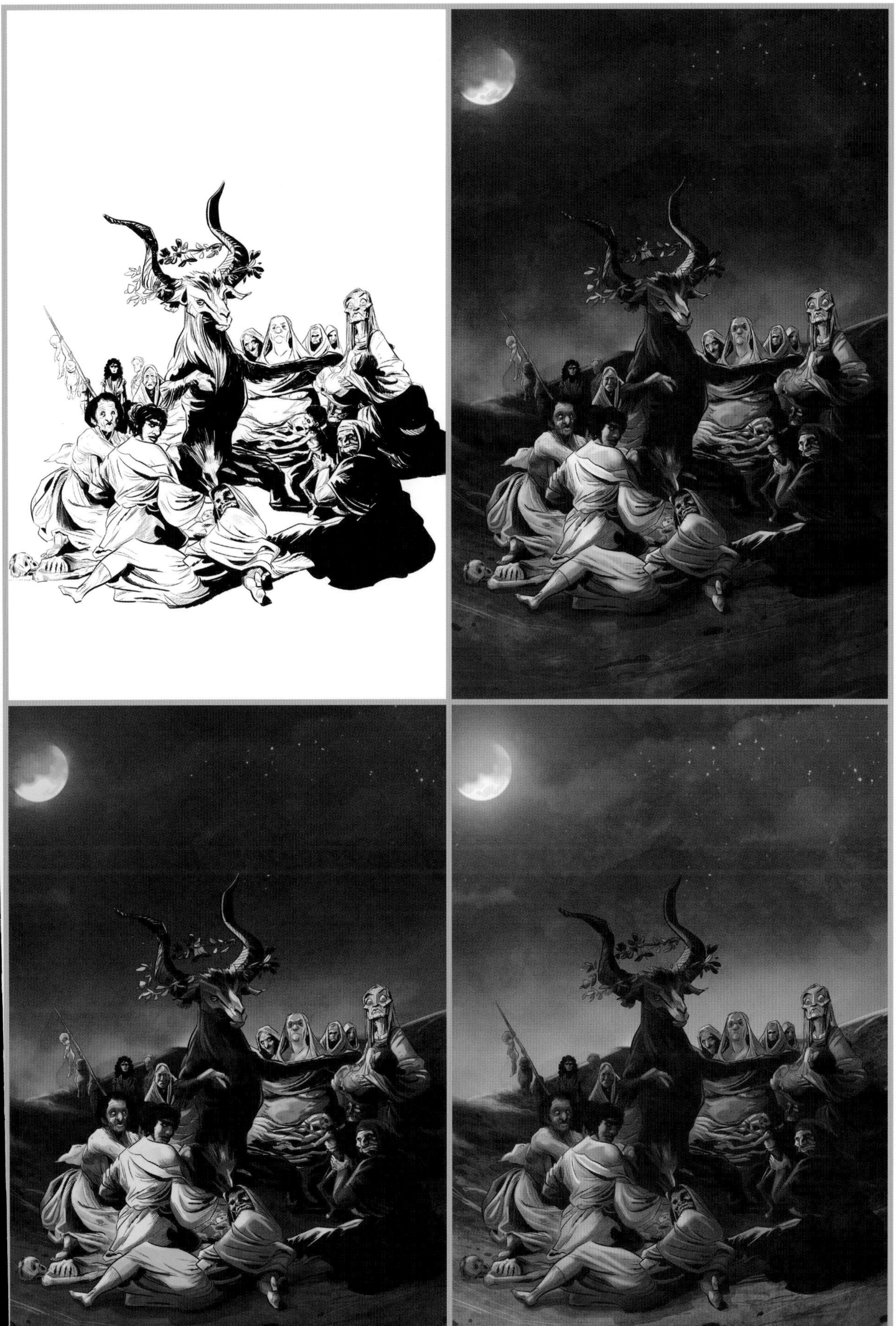

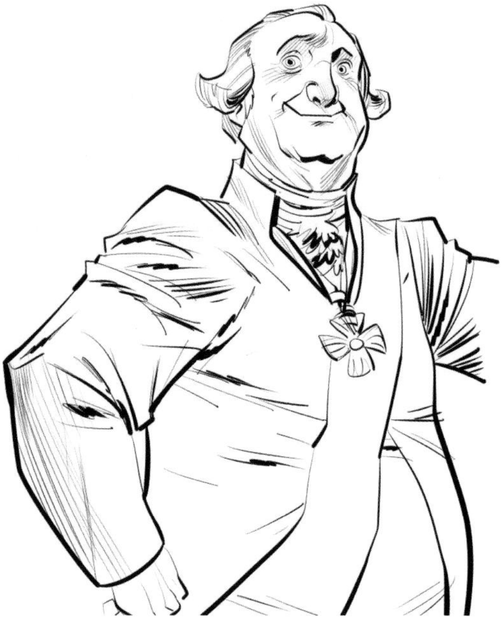
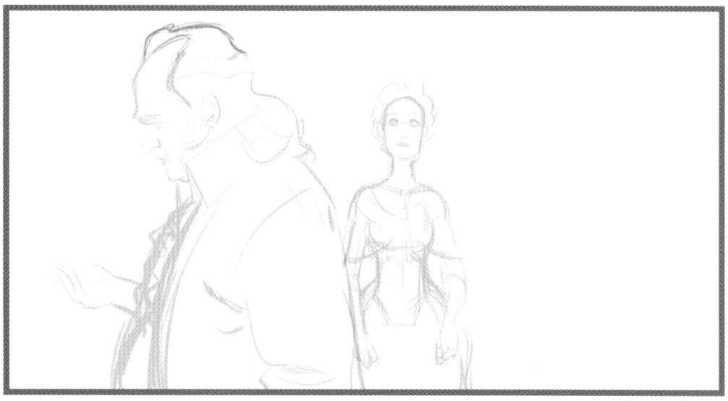
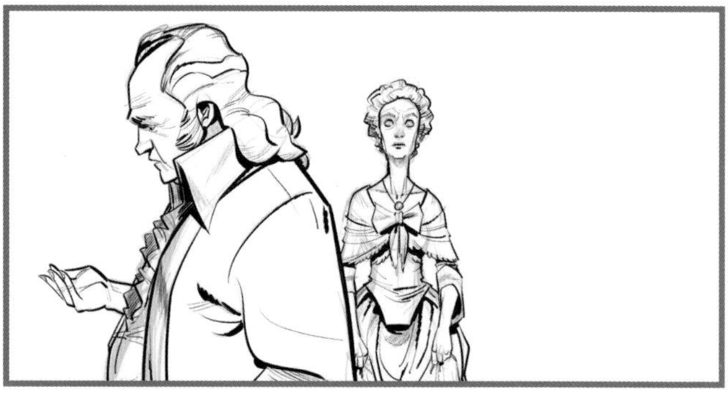
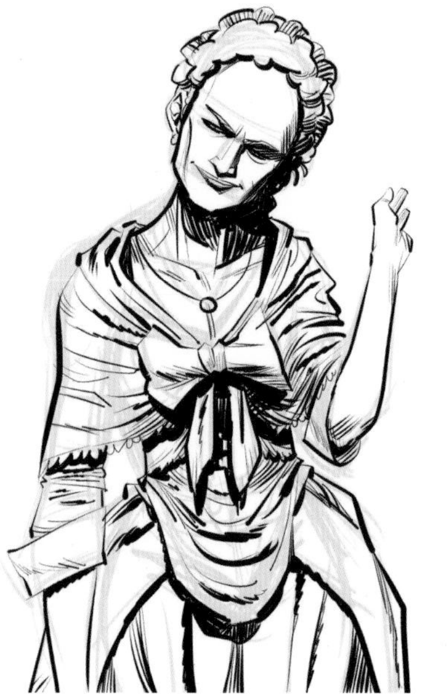
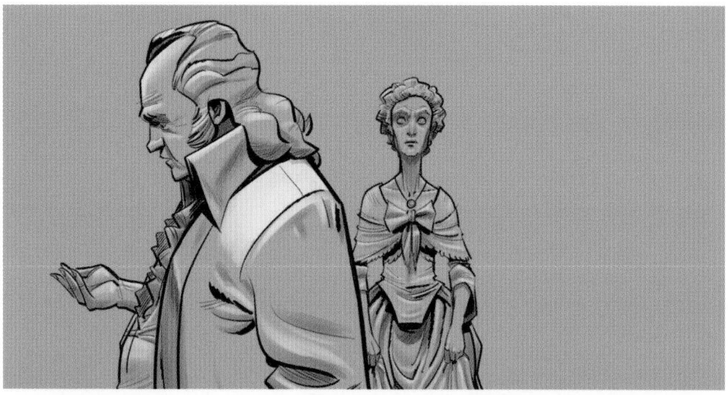
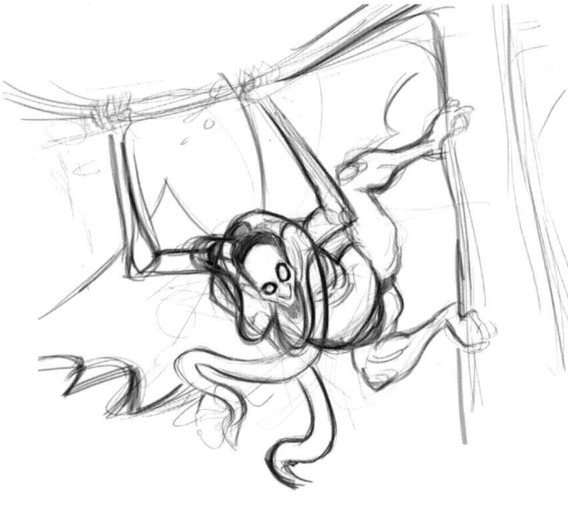
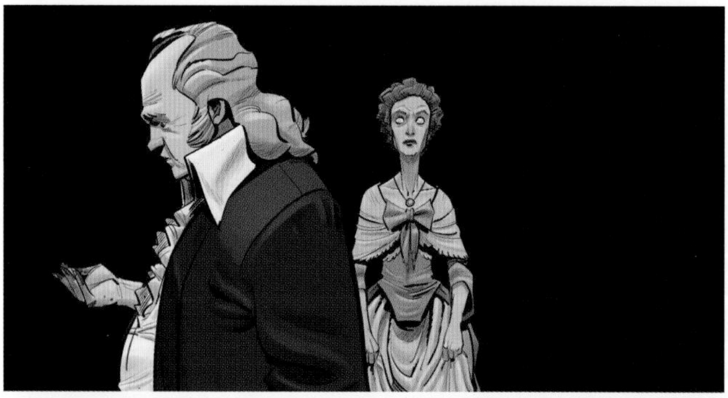
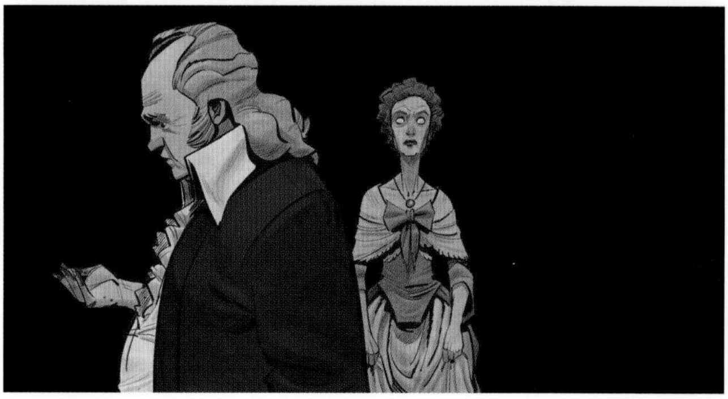

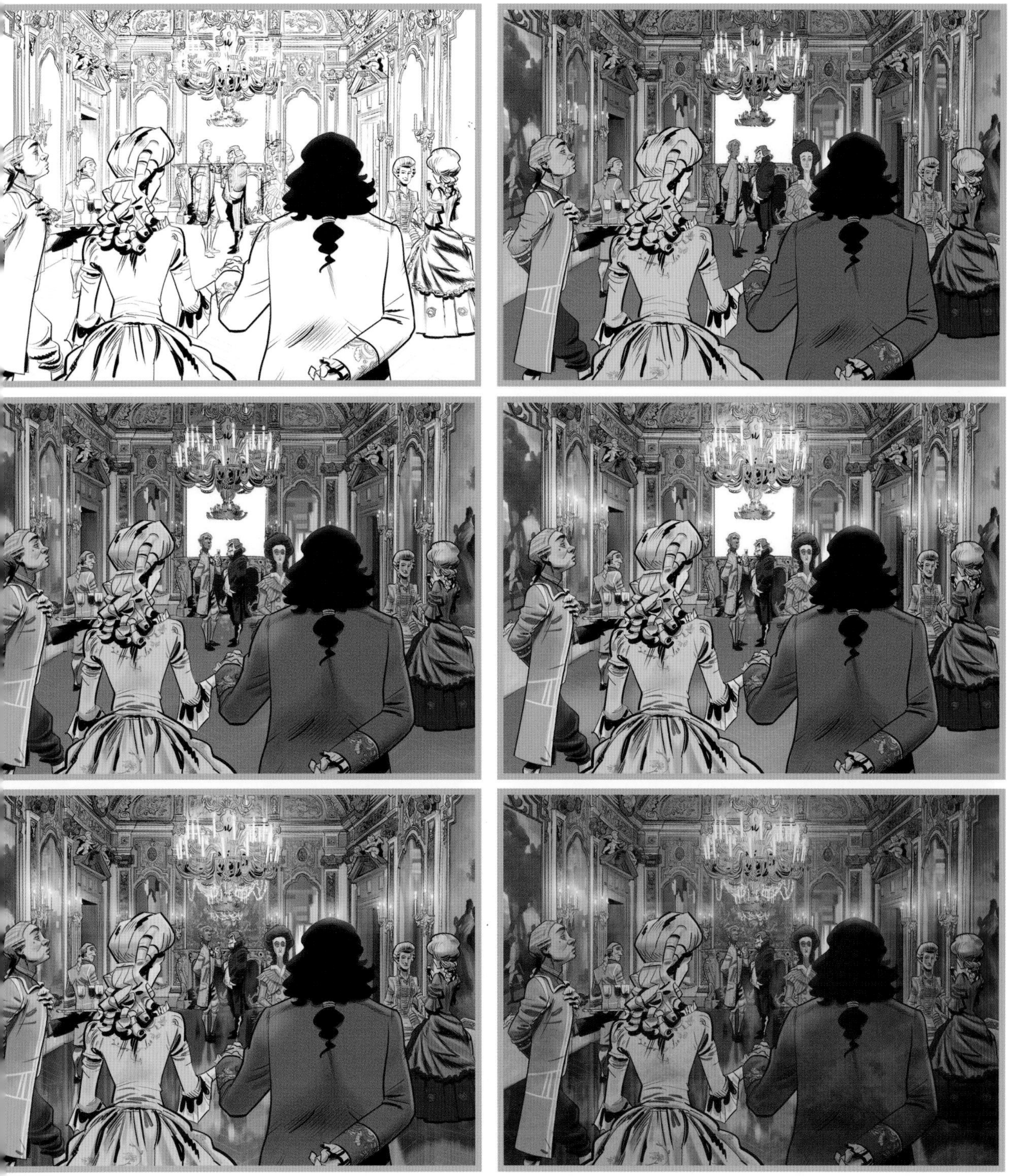

**PREVIOUS PAGE:** SEVERAL DIGITAL SKETCHES, SOME REJECTED, OF VARIOUS CHARACTERS: KING CHARLES IV PRIOR TO THE "PORTRAIT OF THE WHOLE FAMILY," ONE OF THE MAIN CHARACTERS, JOSEFA BAYEU, GOYA'S WIFE (IN HER WITCHING MODE), AND A PHANTOM, BASED PRECISELY ON GOYA'S WHIMSY.

WE CAN ALSO SEE THE PROCESS FRAN GALÁN USED ON EVERY SINGLE PAGE, IN THE VIGNETTE WHERE GOYA FINALLY CONFRONTS HIS DEMONS.

**ABOVE:** ONE OF THE MOST COMPLICATED VIGNETTES TO RECONSTRUCT, INASMUCH AS THIS HALL IN MONCLOA PALACE NO LONGER EXISTS, AND WHERE WE CAN SEE THE THOROUGHNESS OF FRAN'S WORK. FROM DIGITAL SKETCH, MOVING THROUGH FLAT COLORS, LIGHT PHASES AND SHADOWS TO ARRIVE AT THE FINAL LIGHTING AND FEEL. TO SAY THE LEAST, BETWEEN RECONSTRUCTING THE FRAMES AND THE FEEL OF THE ERA, FRAN SUFFERED A LOT!

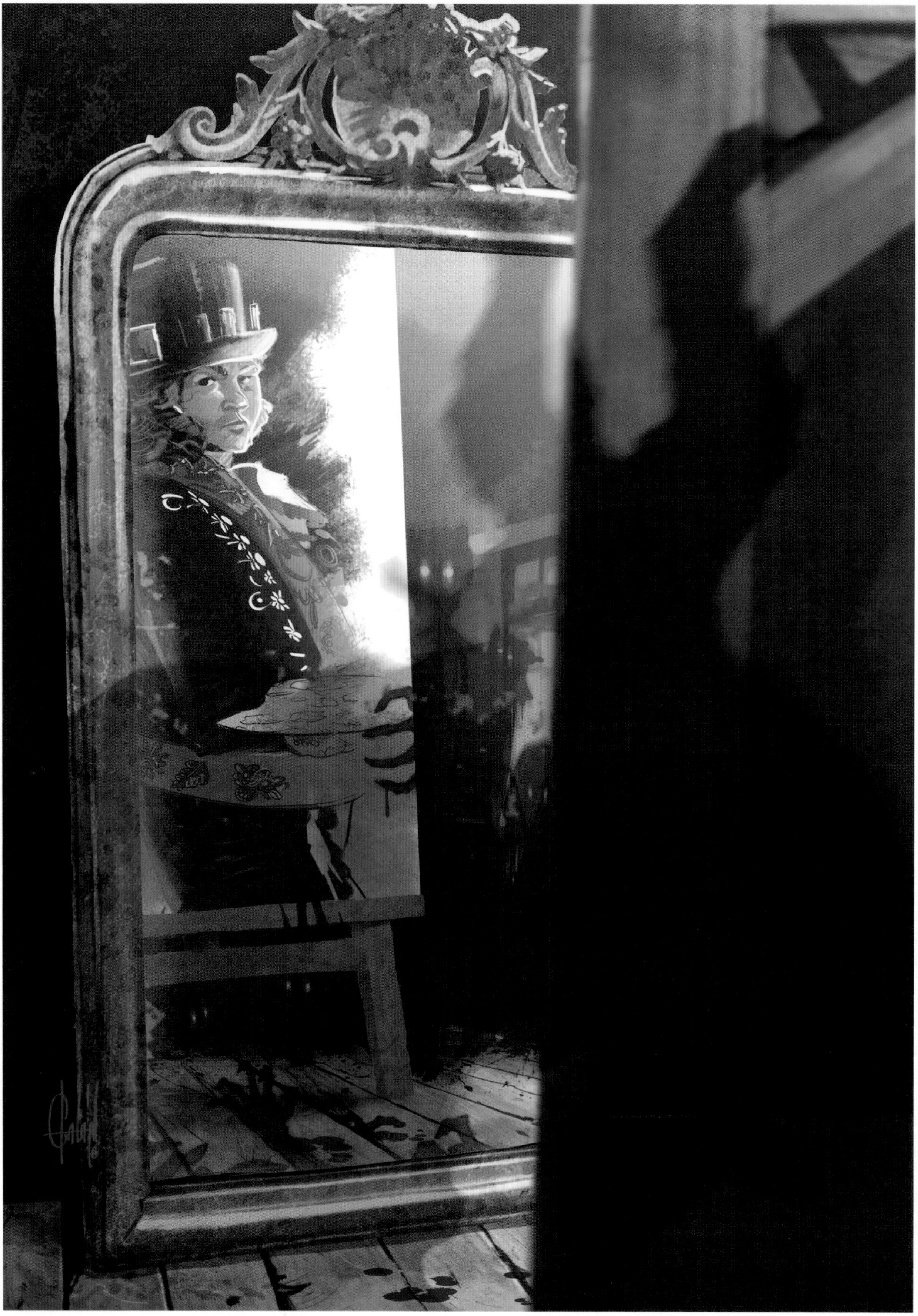

ANOTHER PROMOTIONAL SKETCH WHICH WE REJECTED BECAUSE IT DID NO REFLECT THE OVERALL STYLE USED TO DRAW THE STORY. I LOVED THE IMAGE OF THE CANDLES ON THE TOP HAT USED AS LIGHTING TO PAINT... I NOW REGRET NOT HAVING USED IT IN THE SCRIPT.

GOYA: THE TERRIBLE SUBLIME HAS BEEN A JOURNEY FOR US, ARDUOUS AT TIMES, BUT ALWAYS EXCITING... WE HOPE YOU ENJOYED IT!

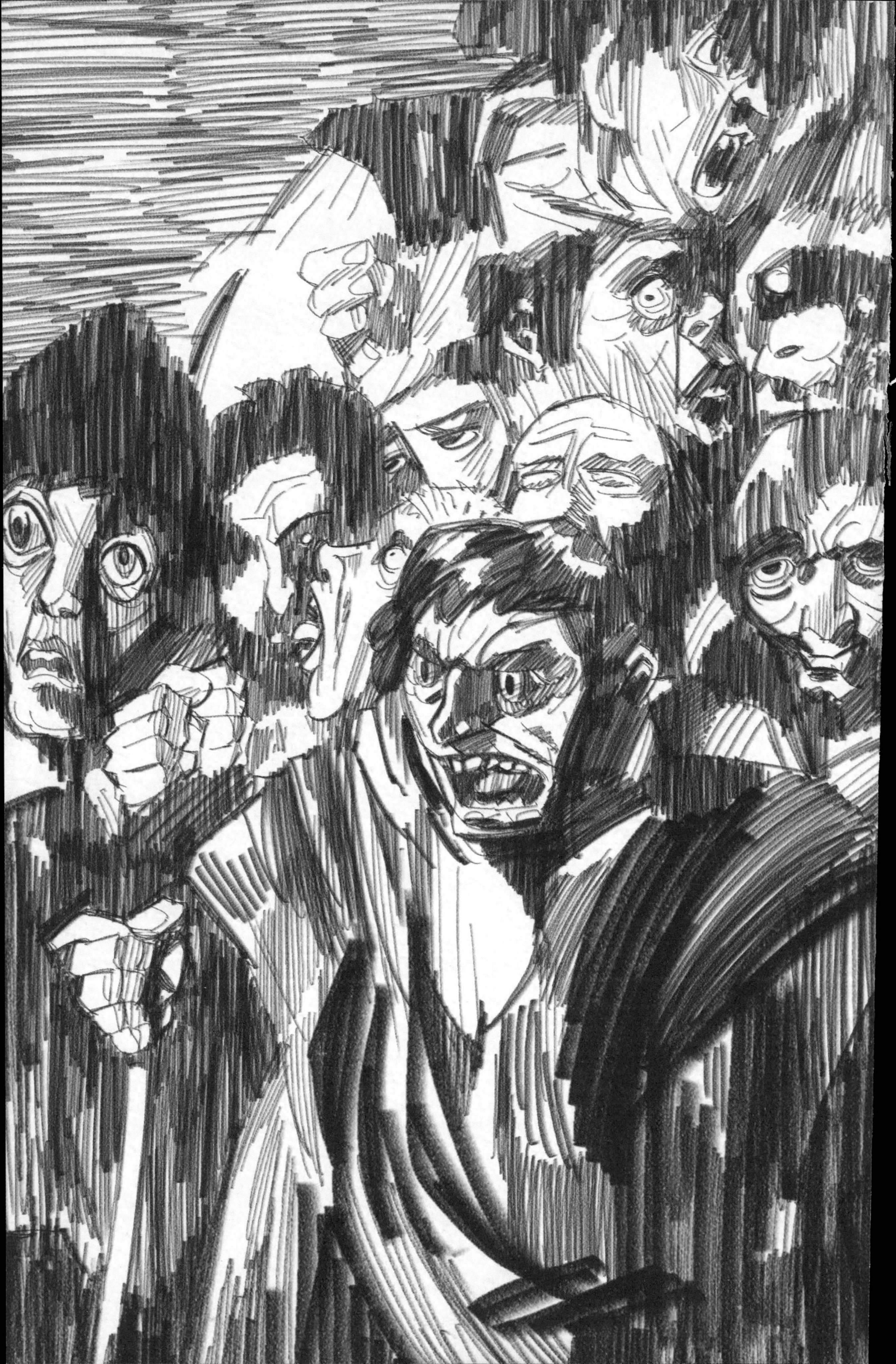